THE POWER OF A Creed

How a "Company Conscience" Can Contribute to Bottom-line Success

THE POWER OF A *Creed*

How a "Company Conscience" Can Contribute to Bottom-line Success

PUBLISHED BY

Wetterau Associates, LLC
St. Louis, Missouri

AUTHOR

SHELLIE M. FREY

Vice President and Chief Branding and Communications Officer
Golden State Foods

MANAGING EDITOR

Suzanne Kimball Rekow
Kimball Communications

COPY EDITOR

Kate Starr
Group Vice President, Communications
Golden State Foods

DESIGN

Ron Scheibel
Synergy, Inc.

Jason B. Van Dorn
Manager, Global Branding and Multimedia Production
Golden State Foods

Wetterau Associates, LLC

Copyright © 2023 by Wetterau Associates, LLC

All rights reserved under the Pan-American and International Copyright Conventions. This book may not be reproduced or distributed, in whole or in part, in any form or by any means without written permission of the publisher.

ISBN: 979-8-9894256-0-0
LIBRARY OF CONGRESS CONTROL NUMBER: 2023921453
Printed in South Korea

DEDICATION

This book is dedicated to Mark Wetterau — who left this life too soon — passing away just before this book went to print. Mark embodied the power of The Creed *in word and deed. His fidelity to the ideals and principles therein positively influenced thousands of people worldwide to make caring, ethical decisions every day for the benefit of all involved. A true bearer of* The Creed, *Mark's example illuminated and inspired the hearts and minds of all he touched. His light will never dim.*

AUTHOR'S NOTE

When Mark Wetterau asked me to write a book about *The Creed* back in 2008, I was more than honored. After all, *The Creed*, he said, was one of the most cherished gifts that his father, Ted Wetterau, had passed down to him and his brother, Conrad. For more than half a century, it has been the heart of the Wetteraus' business success in an array of companies. So naturally, it was important to them to continue this values-based tradition and pass on the history, evolution, and power of *The Creed* to the associates of all the Wetterau companies, so they could fully understand and appreciate its unique value in their own business environments.

Additionally, Mark, Conrad, and business partner Mike Waitukaitis — along with many other leaders and associates of the Wetterau companies — have often been asked by other business colleagues about *The Creed* and what it means in business today. Some have spoken publicly about it, which is why this book was also written for business leaders, who may be interested in incorporating a creed of their own into their organizations.

And so, my journey began. It has been an experience nothing short of a labor of love for many years. What a privilege it's been to be favored with this special glimpse into the minds and hearts of so many hard-working associates, who have sought to conduct business ethically and morally in their respective companies over the last 150 years. I have enjoyed learning how it has positively affected not only their businesses, but how it's enhanced their own lives as individuals as well.

Fifteen years later, after hundreds of interviews, discussions, and testimonials, years of in-depth research, and more than two decades of working at a creed-based organization myself, I've learned many things about *The Creed* and its applications:

THE POWER OF A CREED

First, *The Creed* is an ideal, not a proclamation of one's perfect state. In fact, most subscribers readily admit their imperfections. But looking to a creed as an ideal inherently aligns people insofar as it's defined. A creed, therefore, serves as a North Star of sorts, which provides a moral and ethical direction that constantly shines in the distance — despite the missteps of those who are striving to follow it. When one gets off track, by listening to their own conscience — and perhaps contemplating their "company conscience" (which is what a creed essentially becomes to an organization that upholds it) — they can reconnect, realign, and recharge their course through its power.

Next, the premise of *The Creed*, which is based on the Golden Rule, is not new. But its applications within a business setting might be to some. In fact, in today's politically correct society, even mentioning the idea of God in business is either highly offensive and extremely radical to some, or puzzlingly incongruent to others. Most can't comprehend the "disconnect" between the two. But what's fascinating is how in actuality, the power of *The Creed* and its correlating principles resonate with associates of all walks of life — spanning political persuasions, religious beliefs, ethnic backgrounds, geographic locations, genders, and ages.

Finally, as one who constantly strives to follow *The Creed* and all too often falls short, I can personally attest to its power — despite occasional mistakes. I know first-hand that when lived — albeit imperfectly — *The Creed* brings power, peace, and clarity into the lives of its followers. It fosters humility, empathy, equity, and deeper, more thoughtful decisions. And it unites people together in a unique way, with a common bond of shared goals and mutual success for all stakeholders.

I'm deeply grateful to Mark for the special invitation to write this book. I'm thankful to Conrad for his support throughout the process and for inviting me to share my perspectives of this rich experience. And I'm sincerely appreciative of the entire Wetterau family — past, present, and future — for their exemplary ethics and standards. They have and

AUTHOR'S NOTE

will continue to positively influence countless associates worldwide for generations. I'm thankful for every associate of all the Wetterau companies for keeping *The Creed* alive year after year, decade after decade, generation after generation. I'm truly appreciative of the dedicated team that helped bring this book to fruition: Suzanne Kimball Rekow, Ron Scheibel, Jason Van Dorn, and Kate Starr. And I'm grateful to you for being a part of this experience. I hope you enjoy exploring *The Power of a Creed*.

–Shellie M. Frey

ACKNOWLEDGEMENTS

A sincere thanks to all those individuals who participated in the development of this book — from the many first-hand experiences, insights, and perspectives, to the special heart-felt memories from associates, suppliers, and customers — it's truly the people who "bring *The Creed* to life," as Ted Wetterau would say. Because it's the associates within all the Wetterau companies who embody *The Creed* and shape the rich cultures within which it flourishes, enabling "the success of all partners to be assured."

Wetterau Inc./Wetterau Associates

Brent Baxter
Andie Blassie
Cathy Heimberger Cortright
Bob Crutsinger
Duane Daniels
Jim Duban
Dick Federer
Fred Heimberger
Lucille Heimberger
Lois Laverty
Andy Levy
Jack Ryan
Merwyn Sher
Stanley Simon
Debbie Thompson
Paul Vogel
Mike Waitukaitis
Conrad Wetterau
Helen Wetterau
Mark Wetterau
Ted Wetterau

Quality Beverage/Consolidated Beverages

Ted Audet
Tom Clark
Steve Doherty
David Fields
Ronnie Fields
Tim Moran
Tom Nicholson
George Wetterau

Golden State Foods

Jose Armario
Steve Becker
Ron Burkle
Lourdes Cerpa-Smith
Sharon Davis
Brian Dick
Nabil El-Hage
Carol Fawcett

Golden State Foods *(continued)*

Dick Gochnauer
Lisa Gottlieb
Lee Gragnano
Tom Haggai
Ryan Hammer
Joe Heffington
Sherrie Homer
Chad Hopkins
Carolina Jaramillo
Guilda Javaheri
Hugues Labrecque
Frank Listi
Donnie Little
Saeed Mahmoud
John Marin
Tess McAnena
Rene McNary
Mary Moore
Rich Moretti
Wayne Morgan
John Page
Bill Pocilujko
Ed Rodriguez
Bill Sanderson
Dave Smith
Ed Sowa
Jerry Sumoge
Gregg Tarlton
Scott Thomas
Eric Treon
Stephen Wetterau
Jim Williams

Quality Custom Distribution, Groenz, KanPak, Q Performance

Mark Donahue
Fred Groen
Taylor Harbison
Doug Lorenz
Larry McGill
John Pecoraro
Melissa Vieira

Shop 'n Save, Save A Lot, Laneco, Lucia's

Marlene Gebhard   Darryl Long   Bob Patillo

Customers

Dan Cathy
Marion Gross
Zach McLeroy
Bob Nabil
Ed Ruby
Tim Yancy

Business Partners

Stephen M. R. Covey   Larry Senn   Douglas Wilson

And all others who bring *The Creed* to life at each of the Wetterau companies.

THE POWER OF A Creed

CONTENTS

INTRODUCTION	21
WETTERAU FAMILY LEADERSHIP	25
PART I: HISTORY AND EVOLUTION OF *THE CREED*	27
SECTION 1: THE WETTERAU WORLD — FIRST 100 YEARS OF UNCOMPROMISING VALUES	29
Chapter 1: Early Entrepreneurialism — Values from the Start	31
Chapter 2: A New Era and a New Company Creed	41
Chapter 3: A New Wetterau World — the Next Generation of Leadership Weaves *The Creed* Deeper into the Fabric of the Organization	69
SECTION 2: ADOPTING *THE CREED* INTO OTHER COMPANIES	93
Chapter 4: Blazing New Trails — Acquiring Quality Beverage and Quality Values	95
Chapter 5: *The Creed* in Action Enhances a Positive Company Culture at Quality Beverage and Opens New Windows of Opportunity	113
Chapter 6: Golden State Foods: A Tradition of Values for over 75 Years	129
Chapter 7: Going Beyond Company Borders — Sharing *The Creed* Outside GSF	155
Chapter 8: Continuing the Legacy	173

PART II: THE ANATOMY AND POWER OF A COMPANY CREED — 189

SECTION 1: *THE CREED* DECONSTRUCTED — 191

Chapter 9: We Believe in God and the Dignity of All People — 193

Chapter 10: Treat People as You Want to Be Treated — 201

Chapter 11: Successful Independent Business is the Backbone of Nations — 215

Chapter 12: Pledging Best Efforts to Ensure Mutual Success — 225

SECTION 2: CAN A CREED HELP YOUR ORGANIZATION SUCCEED? — 233

Chapter 13: The Need for a Creed — The Benefits of Instilling a Company Conscience into Your Culture — 235

Chapter 14: Top 20 Tips for Implementing a Company Creed — 259

CONCLUSION — 281

APPENDICES — 285

END NOTES — 299

INTRODUCTION

Over the years, many business experts have declared the value of a positive business culture on an organization's success. Even the best strategies won't succeed, they say, without a solid, *trusted* company culture. Not for the long-term, anyway. Time-tested studies continue to show that culture, along with strategy and structure, has a direct impact on a company's bottom line. A strong culture manifests itself in a number of contributing factors like employee morale and loyalty; resilience during challenging times; trust and strategic efficacy; as well as brand identity and competitive advantage.

Management icon, Peter Drucker, was one of the first to pit a company culture against its business strategy in his well-known line, "Culture eats strategy for lunch* every time." Though a provocative notion decades ago, *Harvard Business Review* writer, Nilofer Merchant, agrees with the premise. Representing a host of business analysts, she explains that "the best strategic idea means nothing in isolation. If the strategy conflicts with how a group of people already believe, behave or make decisions, it will fail. Conversely, a culturally robust team can turn a so-so strategy into a winner. The 'how' matters in how we get performance."

Likewise, University of California, Los Angeles professor Eric Flamholtz, author of the article, "Corporate Culture and the Bottom Line," underscored the impact of culture on long-term success when he said, "Your bottom line next year will largely be determined by your current strategies; your bottom line in the following years will be more influenced by your current culture."

Further, Robert Whitman, chairman of FranklinCovey, explains how an effective culture can create a unique, competitive advantage for a company: "Nearly everything about your organization — including your strategy, products, and systems — can be replaced, except one thing: the effectiveness of your people. Culture is the ultimate competitive advantage."

See End Notes.

Additionally, *Forbes* writer George Bradt notes that 83 percent of business mergers fail in large part because of incompatible cultures, despite their potential on paper. Larry Senn, founder and chairman of Senn Delaney, a leading culture-shaping firm, calls this "cultural clash" and claims that the success of a merger has more to do with culture than whether or not companies have exactly the right systems in place, which organizations tend to focus on the most.

Clearly, the power of a strong culture in an organization's overall health is evident. *So, what are companies doing about it? What steps are organizations taking to shape and actualize their culture or to revive and invigorate an existing one?*

This book highlights how one family of companies achieved organizational success by nurturing a robust business culture — not just temporarily or over a few years but over generations — and how it continues to thrive through its unique set of strong cultural values. The keystone of its constancy is a special "credo" of sorts, appropriately called *The Creed* — a philosophical values proclamation (different from a "company vision" or "mission statement" as will be shown) on which all other business activities and company behaviors are based. This simple, yet powerful philosophy is embraced and exemplified year after year, decade after decade by thousands of diverse employees from all over the world and from all walks of life.

How is this possible?

Take a look at the following pages to find out. This book will take you on a journey — through the voices of many — of how this unique creed originated, how it evolved over time to help companies succeed, how it expanded into various organizations, and how it is making a difference in the lives of thousands of people worldwide. It will define *The Creed* and illustrate why it works — how it serves as a "true north" for major decisions and as an anchor during challenging times. It will provide a glimpse into the characters and leadership styles of some of the key leaders of these creed-based organizations, how they direct and interact with their teams, and the impact (in their own words) *The Creed* has had on their associates, their customers, their suppliers, and other stakeholders. And it will demonstrate how by emphasizing humanity, *The Creed* continues to help companies and organizations stay focused on what really makes businesses succeed: *people.*

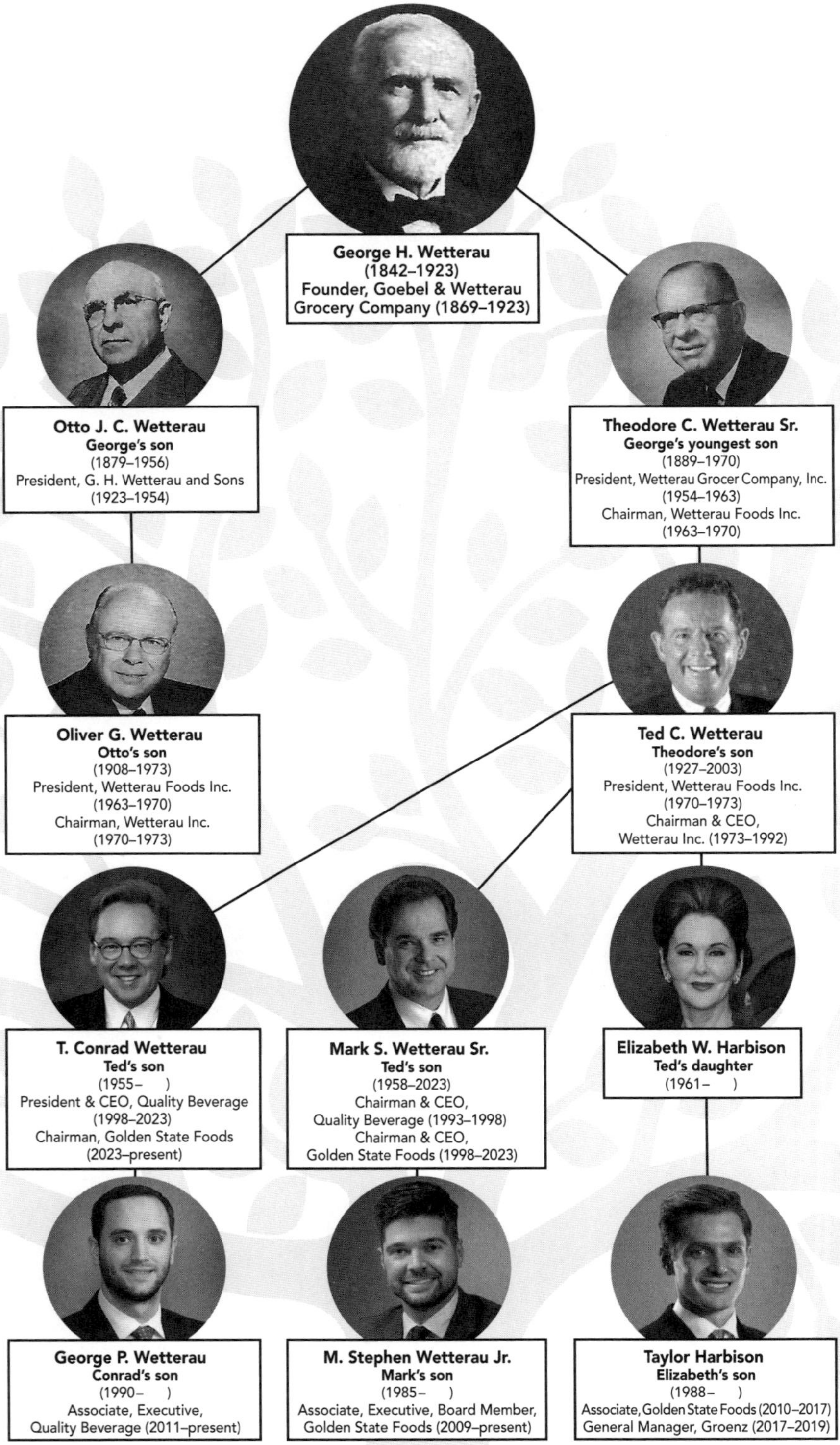

George H. Wetterau
(1842–1923)
Founder, Goebel & Wetterau
Grocery Company (1869–1923)

Otto J. C. Wetterau
George's son
(1879–1956)
President, G. H. Wetterau and Sons
(1923–1954)

Theodore C. Wetterau Sr.
George's youngest son
(1889–1970)
President, Wetterau Grocer Company, Inc.
(1954–1963)
Chairman, Wetterau Foods Inc.
(1963–1970)

Oliver G. Wetterau
Otto's son
(1908–1973)
President, Wetterau Foods Inc.
(1963–1970)
Chairman, Wetterau Inc.
(1970–1973)

Ted C. Wetterau
Theodore's son
(1927–2003)
President, Wetterau Foods Inc.
(1970–1973)
Chairman & CEO,
Wetterau Inc. (1973–1992)

T. Conrad Wetterau
Ted's son
(1955–)
President & CEO, Quality Beverage
(1998–2023)
Chairman, Golden State Foods
(2023–present)

Mark S. Wetterau Sr.
Ted's son
(1958–2023)
Chairman & CEO,
Quality Beverage (1993–1998)
Chairman & CEO,
Golden State Foods (1998–2023)

Elizabeth W. Harbison
Ted's daughter
(1961–)

George P. Wetterau
Conrad's son
(1990–)
Associate, Executive,
Quality Beverage (2011–present)

M. Stephen Wetterau Jr.
Mark's son
(1985–)
Associate, Executive, Board Member,
Golden State Foods (2009–present)

Taylor Harbison
Elizabeth's son
(1988–)
Associate, Golden State Foods (2010–2017)
General Manager, Groenz (2017–2019)

24

Wetterau Family Leadership
1869–2023 and Beyond

A Creed for All Generations

    As a family-driven organization, the Wetteraus often passed down leadership responsibilities and family names to their posterity, throughout generations of business ownership. As such, to better identify the various leaders of the Wetterau companies over time throughout this book, please refer to the Wetterau Family Leadership Tree on the opposite page.

    A family tree can be an indispensable visual aid to help sort out lineage in families that have recurrences of identical names in each descending generation, as in the case of the Wetteraus. This tree is meant to provide clarity in distinguishing between different family members and their respective roles in the Wetterau organization, to visually map the progression of leadership, to understand the transfer of responsibilities within the company, and over time, and to recognize the unique contributions of various individuals.

    The illustration includes birth and death dates, years of key leadership service in the various Wetterau companies, and relationships to other Wetterau family members and company leaders.

PART I

The History and Evolution of *The Creed*

SECTION 1

The Wetterau World — First 100 Years of Uncompromising Values

Photos (left to right):

1) Founder, George Henry Wetterau

2) Wetterau home in Richelsdorf, Germany, 1850: Otto Wetterau (George H.'s brother); George H. Wetterau (founder); Anna Wetterau (George H.'s sister-in-law); Schrader (sic) Wetterau, wife of Otto Wetterau with their two young daughters; Anna Regine Wetterau (George H.'s mother); standing on wagon: Otto Wetterau (Otto Wetterau's son, George H.'s nephew); seated on wagon: Johannes George Wetterau (George H.'s father)

3) George H. Wetterau's sons, George Jr. and Otto Wetterau

4) Wetterau Grocer Co. truck driver outside Hazelwood warehouse in the 1950s

CHAPTER 1

Early Entrepreneurialism — Values from the Start

"This philosophy [of The Creed*] that was personified by my grandfather 12 decades ago has been a source of inspiration for all who came after him."*

–Ted C. Wetterau Jr. (1927–2003)
Chairman and CEO (1973–1992)
President (1970–1973),
Wetterau Inc.

During the post-Civil War era of the 1860s, America was healing from its emotional and physical scars of a nation torn apart. But by the end of the decade, the country had regained much of its hope and strength and had again become the land of opportunity. River traffic on the Mississippi had evolved from shipping war supplies and emerged instead into the country's heart of trade and commerce.

During that time, 25-year-old George Wetterau had left Germany to make his way across the Atlantic to join his older brother, Otto, in St. Louis, where many other Germans had settled. In fact, William (Bill) Heimburger, who would later marry into the Wetterau family, had already set up a wagon and blacksmith shop in the area nearly a decade earlier. Heimburger and Son, Inc. was one of the oldest businesses in St. Louis, shoeing horses and providing wagons for traveling pioneers passing through.

Excited by the growing wholesale grocery trade in the river port city, George went to work for a local grocery wholesaler, J.F. Lauman and Company, while studying business at night school. A year later, Lauman retired, leaving young George with the opportunity to lead the business. Long on ambition but short on funds, George joined forces with merchant Frederic Goebel, and in 1869, the partnership of Goebel & Wetterau Grocery Company was born. They set up shop on the west bank of the Mississippi, near what would later become the south leg of the famous towering Gateway Arch.

From the start, George Wetterau had demonstrated his values of honesty, pride, and dedication in his business as he built solid relationships and a positive reputation in his budding company. A prominent St. Louis trade journal at the time, *Interstate Grocer*, later noted George's customer-centered approach to his business and encouraged retailers coming to St. Louis to visit this progressive company: "He is ever alert to the interests of those with whom he comes in contact, and is possessed of shrewd buying qualifications … ." These ideals served George well, enabling his grocery distribution business to continue growing. Laying a foundation for generations to come, these simple yet important values and ethics would serve as a base for future organizational cultures to thrive and businesses to succeed.

During the last quarter of the 19th century, America saw an increase in innovations and growth. At the turn of the century, the country was alive with trade and commerce. St. Louis became the fifth-largest city in the country, the "Gateway to the West." Goebel & Wetterau grew as well, delivering barrels and bags of groceries from their own horse-drawn

CHAPTER 1: EARLY ENTREPRENEURIALISM

wagons to retailers throughout St. Louis and selling staples to thousands of frontiersmen heading west toward a new life and beginning. Through their quality service and reliability, Goebel & Wetterau earned their reputation as a trusted supplier throughout the area.

Quick to embrace the technological advancements of the 1890s, George Wetterau pioneered practices that would become one of the hallmarks of his company. A newspaper account at the time described its headquarters as "one of the most modern wholesale grocery stores in the western country," and Wetterau was also among the first organizations in St. Louis to be part of the telephone system.

In 1899, Frederic Goebel sold his interest in the company to George Wetterau, and they dissolved their partnership. Subsequently, George formed G. H. Wetterau & Sons Grocer Company. That same year, three of George's eight children, sons Otto and George Junior and daughter Minnie, joined George in the business. As the wholesaler celebrated its 30th anniversary of growth and success, Otto, George Junior, and Minnie carried on the company's values that George Senior had established three decades earlier, as the business continued to thrive.

The 20th Century: Farms to Factories and Company Growth through Quality Service

After the turn of the century, the population had shifted as people left their farms and sought factory work in the cities. The automobile came to many American homes, and paved roads multiplied. Steamboats were replaced with trains and trucks, speeding up the food distribution process. George's youngest son, Theodore Carl, had joined Otto in the company and both were diligently learning the family business in the billing, shipping, buying, and sales departments, refining the skills they would need for future company leadership. Likewise, daughter Minnie put her financial abilities to work and was appointed treasurer of the company.

After 40 years of business, the Wetteraus had come a long way and achieved much as an organization, particularly technologically and financially. Revenues for G. H. Wetterau and Sons continued climbing. Though they were certainly adept in their skills and offerings, much of their success could be attributed to their growing reputation as an ethical family running an honest, reliable company.

The Roaring '20s, Stock Market Crash, and World War II: Wetterau Thrives through Generational Leadership

With the Spanish Flu and World War I behind the country, America was poised to embrace a new decade, one that would hopefully be filled with greater peace and prosperity. Indeed, Americans in the 1920s witnessed the standard of living begin to rise, along with hemlines. The family car made life easier, and the radio became a household necessity. Otto Wetterau was named president of the company in 1923, following the death of its founder, George Senior. Otto introduced many technological advances to the Midwest, including forklifts, trucks, and pallet loading.

To meet the needs of the organization's growing retail base, Wetterau expanded geographically throughout eastern Missouri. The roaring '20s seemed to be in full swing — until October 1929. Devastated by the crash of the stock market, the country began a decade of economic despair. It was the Great Depression, a time when survival meant pulling together to help family and friends.

After graduating from Washington University in St. Louis with a Bachelor of Science in business administration, Oliver ("Ollie") G. Wetterau, Otto's son and George Senior's grandson, joined the company in 1930 as an apprentice. He served in many capacities over the years in every department, including buying and store engineering. His keen interest in all phases of food distribution led Ollie to positions of greater responsibility. He was later elevated to vice president and eventually served as executive vice president, president, and chairman and chief executive officer of the organization.

CHAPTER 1: EARLY ENTREPRENEURIALISM

Meanwhile, responding to needs of struggling independent retailers during this period, Theodore Carl (known as "Mr. Ted") encouraged the business to strengthen its commitment by becoming one of the first organizations to join the Independent Grocers Alliance (IGA) in 1931. With sales just under $1.6 million that year, Wetterau not only survived the Depression, but actually thrived in its business. In 1938, the company made its first acquisition — a local wholesaler — then changed its name to Wetterau Grocer Company, Inc.

Happier Days Lead to Social Change — Wetterau Values Continue

The company proceeded to evolve through the battle-scarred years of World War II and the happier days of the 1950s. In 1954, Theodore Carl, "Mr. Ted," the youngest son of George Senior, was named the new president. Like his father before him, Theodore was dedicated to nurturing and strengthening the independent retailer by helping it keep pace with the larger chain stores, and in fact later served as a member of IGA's board of directors. Reflecting on the company's success some years afterward, Theodore revealed much about himself as a leader:

> *"Results come from dedicated people, from sustained courage, from the exposure and exchange of ideas, from opportunity jointly recognized and individually met."*
> THEODORE C. WETTERAU SR.

His philosophy enabled him to lead the company to nearly $25 million in annual sales by 1952.

That same year, Ted C. Wetterau Jr., son of the newly named president, was asked by his father Theodore, uncle Otto, and cousin Ollie to join the family business, which he did after some resistance. Despite his passion for retail, Ted was a devout Presbyterian and had always wanted to go into the ministry. So after his two-year military service in Korea and four years at Westminster College in Fulton, Missouri, where he earned a bachelor's degree in mathematics, Ted also spent two years in the seminary. (His college cohorts even nicknamed him "Rev," short for reverend.) But when asked by his dad for help, Ted ultimately felt like his calling was to support the family business.

"My uncle Theodore, Ted's dad, was a hell of a good salesman, and he definitely wanted Ted in there," recalled Fred Heimburger, fourth generation president of Heimburger and Son, who passed in 2019. Fred was Ted's close-knit cousin and supplier through Heimburger, which had evolved from a wagon-making company to a sophisticated transportation supplier, selling truck bodies and over-the-road trailers to Wetterau. "But he wasn't going to block him if he wanted to do something else."

Though Ted agreed to join the company, he was somewhat frustrated with the lack of vision that Wetterau seemed to have at the time, so his initial stint was short-lived. He decided to leave the organization and partnered with a business associate to operate two IGA grocery stores for two years. After that, he was again invited back to Wetterau Grocer Company, and he accepted the offer, initially working in store development and design.

With his experience as a grocery store employee, learning every aspect of the store — from meat cutting and produce to distribution — and his innate foresight for growing the business, Ted's unique leadership abilities and fierce determination helped him formulate long-term business plans for the company.

A strong supporter of the independent retailer, which was based on his own experience as a retailer owner/operator, Ted envisioned Wetterau as a comprehensive, full-service organization, capable of providing all of a retailer's needs. He devised an array of pre-designed stores from which retailers could choose and called this the "Packaged Store Concept." His creative approach redefined the role of a wholesaler and decided not only the direction for Wetterau's future, but the path the entire industry would follow.

CHAPTER 1: EARLY ENTREPRENEURIALISM

As the company sought to better serve their expanding customer base, Wetterau also built a new corporate headquarters in Hazelwood, Missouri. By the end of the '50s, sales had grown to more than $58 million.

Social change in the 1960s was also a time of change for Wetterau. As it continued to grow, the company once again underwent a name change, becoming Wetterau Foods Inc. in 1961. Later that year, the family took the company public with the issue of 100,000 shares of stock to support acquisitions and further growth.

By 1963, Wetterau Foods had hit $100 million in annual sales. That same year, after serving for more than 30 years in the company, Ollie Wetterau took the reins from Theodore Senior (who remained as chairman) to become president in 1963, carrying on the family tradition of leadership in the food industry. Furthering the Wetteraus' Christian values, Ollie empowered and trusted his teams, helping the company continue to thrive. As part of this growth, Wetterau pioneered additional programs to assist independent retailers to meet the challenges of a growing, competitive marketplace.

"Ollie and Ted [C.] were very close — like brothers," said former IGA president and lay minister, Dr. Tom Haggai, of the two cousins. Haggai was a long-time friend of the family, until his passing in 2020. He met Ted Junior at an IGA convention in the mid-1960s, and they became fast friends. "I was glad to just find a guy who really had those convictions," shared Tom, of his and Ted's common religious beliefs and business ethics. "What drew us together was our common faith." Ted later invited "Dr. Tom" to speak often at various Wetterau retailer conventions, prayer breakfasts, and other industry conferences. He and Ted would often discuss both spiritual and business philosophies, and he considered Ted a visionary leader. "They wanted to grow," related Haggai, of both Ted and Ollie's desire to expand the company, "and they loved to see [their employees] succeed."

Wetterau's 100th Anniversary

Wetterau continued to establish new businesses including Wetterau Finance Company and Creative Management Institute, to help retailers build and improve their grocery businesses. They also began to diversify the company by acquiring entities such as a commercial construction company (later named Wetterau Builders), Gateway Bakery Company (later named Hazelwood Farms Bakeries, Inc.), and Monarch Printing Company, along with multiple wholesalers in the region that served more than 450 combined retail stores in the Midwest and eastern U.S.

By the end of the decade, as it celebrated 100 years in business, Wetterau had become the third-largest food distributor in the country. Analyzing the company's acquisition objectives and growth strategy at the time, young Ted Wetterau Jr., who by now was serving as the company's executive vice president, cited healthy finances and location for its success, but added:

> "The third and most important objective of all, however, is people. We do not buy just warehouses or cases of canned vegetables, nor do we look to new inviting growth areas — unless we have people. We buy [companies for their] great management teams, we buy ideas and creative merchandising techniques."
>
> TED C. WETTERAU JR.

As the organization expanded, Wetterau continued to engage its customers, suppliers, employees, and their families in part through its regular open house-style luncheons that included facility tours, food tastings, entertainment, and inspirational leadership speeches. The company hosted many social gatherings, special events, and exciting trips for these groups to help rally them, celebrate benchmarks together, and share the organization's rich heritage and exciting growth.

One such event was a three-day celebration of Wetterau's 100th anniversary, which included a Mississippi River cruise, musical reviews, grand banquets, generous gifts (including a car giveaway!), and an evening

CHAPTER 1: EARLY ENTREPRENEURIALISM

at the St. Louis Cardinals' baseball stadium, where Ollie would receive the game's first pitch thrown out by Ted C. Catching the ball on the first bounce, Ollie later joked about not being "signed by the scouts," but continued in good spirits.

These events and activities became a hallmark of the Wetterau business culture and helped build and strengthen relationships of all Wetterau stakeholders, enabling business to flow more smoothly and efficiently into a new season of leadership for the company.

Photos (left to right):

1) The official Wetterau Creed

2) Independent Grocers Alliance (IGA)/Wetterau crest, representing the organization's strong partnership and shared support

3) Opening of the new G. H. Wetterau and Sons Grocer company at North 2nd Street and Monroe Street in St. Louis, Missouri

4) Ted C. Wetterau Jr. and Oliver "Ollie" G. Wetterau holding the St. Louis Metropolitan Council of the National Association of Investment Clubs' 1972 "Missouri Growth Company of the Year" award, presented to Wetterau Foods Inc.

5) Wetterau Inc. truck displaying recently updated logo in the 1970s

CHAPTER 2

A New Era and a New Company Creed

"We called it a 'creed' because 'we' believed it. It's interesting that Ted didn't use the word 'credo,' which is singular Latin for 'I' believe. That he used 'we believe' is critical, because what he was saying is that everybody who works for this firm now, believes this creed."

—**Dick Federer** (1927–2014)
Speechwriter and Creative Advisor (1980–1992),
Wetterau Inc.

A New President Formalizes the Company's Conscience

As Americans tried to make sense of the 1960s, Wetterau ended that decade on a high note, with solid revenues and strong relationships with its independent retailers and suppliers. It began the '70s with a name change from Wetterau Foods Inc. to Wetterau Inc., in order to better describe the newly structured company based on two major operating groups: Wetterau Food Services (its food wholesaling business) and Wetterau Industries (its retailer support services business).

Changes continued for the company following the death of Ted Senior in 1970, after his 60 dedicated years in the family business and food industry. Wetterau Inc. then named a new chief executive, Ted C. Wetterau Jr. as president, and Ollie transitioned to chairman of the board. After working in virtually every capacity of the business, Ted was well-prepared to serve in this new leadership position. He brought new energy, new ideas, and new approaches to the company.

"I have never met anybody who was so passionate about what he was doing," says Ted's longtime executive assistant Lois Laverty, who worked with him for more than 30 years. "He wanted to fulfill the goals of the company, to take care of the people and make sure everything was covered, and you don't do that by sitting back casually letting things happen. You have to have your hand in the pie, so to speak, and keep working on it. Ted had all these ideas about growth for the company, and he had a hard time selling them to Ollie and his father. They were like, 'What do you mean you want to do this [initiative]? We are fine just the way we are.'"

Ted's innovative management style advocated for additional acquisitions, expanding the company's service area throughout the East Coast. Sales continued to grow at a quicker rate to hundreds of millions of dollars in the early '70s ($720 million in 1975). Then after four decades of uninterrupted growth in earnings, Wetterau reached a milestone of more than $1 billion in sales in 1979. Among its many other achievements, Wetterau Inc. also became the largest distributor of IGA products in the world.

"It was a big deal," recalls Lois, of the billion-dollar sales achievement. "It was very exciting times working for a brilliant man who was so dedicated to his mission — and it wasn't for the money, because he would turn down raises. The board of directors would say, 'Ted, you've got to take more money so we can give the people under you more money.' Then he would say, 'All right.' But there was something higher that drove him. The higher way was providing opportunities for all the retailers and employees, making sure they were all improving and becoming inspired by what he said. He was a unique human being to work for, no doubt about it."

Earlier that decade, as Ted spoke to a group of Wetterau retailers, he projected that collective success and credited the fast growth within that era to the enthusiasm and achievements of the independent retailer:

> *The talented minds at Wetterau Food Services and Wetterau Industries have come up over the years with unique programs to stimulate retail sales, to improve profits, to create better service. Nevertheless, the retailer still has to put it all together and make it work. He can look at all the Wetterau programs — he can pick and choose what he wants — but his success and the ultimate success of Wetterau Inc. depends upon his enthusiasm. ... An enthusiasm born of the conviction that American businesses become great because of individual initiative. An enthusiasm that is the basis for our belief that Wetterau will indeed reach $1 billion by 1980. We will [achieve this] not because we are smarter than anyone else, not because we have the services and wherewithal to put a man in business. We will reach [this goal] because we have hitched our corporate wagon to a star. A whole galaxy of [retail] stars — 573 bright glittering reasons for our optimism in the future.*

Not only was this decade a financial benchmark for the business, but it was also a cultural milestone for the company. With the geographic growth, diversity, and leadership expansion, Ted felt that it was time to institutionalize the Wetterau values that had been quietly-yet-consistently demonstrated for more than a century. He thought the company was ready to go beyond unspoken behaviors of goodwill and declare more openly and directly the organization's philosophical approach to how they would conduct their business.

So in 1972, with input from his management team, Ted articulated this philosophy in the form of a credo of sorts, which he appropriately called "The Wetterau Creed." Those close to him recalled this time of its budding development:

"I remember when Ted came home one day with some scribbles of something on a scrap of paper," recalled his wife, Helen, before her passing in 2020. She was reminiscing about how Ted was always a "dreamer" and visionary of possibilities, who was never without his notebook. "I said, 'What's that?' and he said, 'It's our new company creed. How does it sound?' and he read it. And I said, 'It sounds lovely,' thinking it was the Golden Rule, which wasn't anything unusual to me. That had been my life. That was what drew me to Ted, and he was just expressing himself on that paper. So I asked him what he was going to do with it. And he said, 'We hope it's for all the people. Don't you think that would be wonderful if we were all trying to work towards the same goal, and consequently it will pull us all together?' I think it gave him a sense of security that as the company grew, all his team, all his people would all be together. He truly believed that. So I said, 'That's a great idea!' And it continued from there, not changing much from what was written on that torn-off scrap of paper."

The Wetteraus saw *The Creed* as a *philosophy,* which is a little different than a mission statement, a business plan, a set of values, or even a vision statement. ***Some liked to refer to it is the "conscience" of the company — a simple ideology of trust and mutual respect that permeated everything the organization did.***

(Original Wetterau Creed shown right.)

CHAPTER 2: A NEW COMPANY CREED

The Wetterau Creed

We believe in one God and the dignity of man.

We believe that people should be treated
as we would like to be treated, and this applies
to the welfare of our employees and their families,
to our suppliers and all with whom we do business.

We believe that successful, independent business
is the backbone of our country; that our success is closely
related to the success of our retail customers, and that
only by working together can the ultimate success
of both partners be assured.

We therefore, dedicate ourselves to work for our
mutual success and we pledge our best efforts always
toward the attainment of our common goal.

"We called it a 'creed' because 'we' believed it," explained Dick Federer before his passing in 2014. Federer was Ted's long-time childhood friend who worked with him on creative pursuits at Wetterau. "It's interesting that Ted didn't use the word 'credo,' which is singular Latin for 'I believe.' That he used 'we believe' is critical because what he is saying is that everybody who works for this firm now, believes this. I don't know if that was absolutely true or not, but he certainly had the right to say that. And that's where the name came from."

Before introducing The Wetterau Creed companywide, Ted first shared it with his broader management team. Darryl Long, 22-year Wetterau veteran, who led store development and operations, recalls the simple yet powerful presentation.

"Ted said, 'I have given this a lot of thought, and I have tried to reduce to a few words my feelings and embodiment of where I want this company to go and how I want this company to be viewed from the outside and felt from the inside.' Then he unveiled *The Creed*. He read it to us and said, 'You know, this is going to be our guiding light in the future.'"

When Ted and his leadership team shared this written creed with employees companywide, it was sent with a personal note from him as president along with Ollie Wetterau, who was serving as chairman of the board at the time. Ted also included a copy of *WFI* (Wetterau Foods Inc.) *Magazine,* showcasing *The Creed* on its cover (shown right).

CHAPTER 2: A NEW COMPANY CREED

To Our Fellow Employees:

Ted C. Wetterau   Oliver G. Wetterau

The Wetterau Creed, which is featured on the cover of this issue of WFI Magazine, *represents one of the most important pronouncements of corporate philosophy by top management. For a statement of this kind to be meaningful and effective at all levels of our company, it must first be communicated. Next, it must be accepted and become a part of the thinking of every member of the Wetterau employee family. Only then can the performance standard set forth in* The Creed *permeate the daily business life of each member of the Wetterau team.*

To serve as a reminder of the principles stated, we ask that you retain this issue of WFI Magazine *and refer to its cover from time to time. This way each of us can check on his own progress in fulfilling the intent of* The Creed.

As a reminder to all who are associated with our company, each division, subsidiary, office, and warehouse will be furnished with an attractive plaque rendering of The Creed, *which will hang in reception areas and warehouse entrances.*

Wetterau believes that when its creed becomes a vital part of each employee's daily business duties, it can result in continued progress and success — with the same progress and success that has stood the company in good stead over more than a century of operation.

Ted C. Wetterau
President

Oliver G. Wetterau
Chairman of the Board

Ted and Ollie recommended *The Creed* to each employee and encouraged them to try to incorporate it into their daily work lives, referring to it regularly.

Welcoming *The Creed*: A Familiar Philosophy

The company, customers, and suppliers alike welcomed the written Wetterau Creed because it was simply words that described the familiar tone and behaviors that had already been evident in the company for decades. Yet they saw value in formalizing it in writing. "They lived by it before *The Creed* was ever put on paper," said Fred Heimburger. "Anybody can write a creed, but you've gotta live by it. And they lived by it. It was just part of them. But it was a great step for them [to institutionalize it]."

"Instituting a creed wasn't a big jump from who Ted was or what we saw at Wetterau before," says Bob Crutsinger, former president and chief operating officer of Wetterau Inc., who was a customer (an IGA supermarket retailer) and a supplier (sold cash registers and counting machine equipment to the retail stores) before he became an internal employee. "But I still thought it was a good thing when I first saw it because I was a customer [at the time], and I wanted to be treated as loyal as possible, and they did. I was also a supplier calling on the company, and this creed further indicated to me that these were good people. Going down the road you have to make everybody [inside the company] understand that 'this is what we want to do; this is the way we act, and this is the way you are supposed to act.' *The framed Creed in the managers' offices wasn't just a decoration. The people at Wetterau tried to live by it because this was the way they were trying to run the business."*

Crutsinger, who was the first non-Wetterau president and chief operating officer when Ted eventually took over as chairman and CEO, adds that the Wetterau culture was quite different from the "rough and tumble" environment he had experienced at other companies and organizations. He describes Wetterau Inc. as "very first-class" in behavior, dress, and teamwork — "everybody is looking out for everybody else and you're all in this together."

CHAPTER 2: A NEW COMPANY CREED

Eight-year Wetterau (Shop 'n Save) associate, Bob Patillo, who served in a number of roles on the retail side of the company, agrees. "We treated suppliers like partners. And that was a major advantage for us. They still gave us deals because we treated them fairly, we didn't bad mouth them. We listened, and we didn't try to tell them how to run their job, and that's also very critical. To me, it's the employees first, followed by customers and suppliers. You have to be fair with all of them, and we were."

Patillo began as a zone manager, remodeling and converting acquired Kroger locations into Shop 'n Save stores and operating them in the Springfield, Illinois area, as the only non-union stores at that time. "*The Creed* allowed us to [operate without a union]," he says. "I had always worked with these tough unions, and I told [employees] when we hired them that [we weren't] going to have a union. We didn't need it. I had worked for them in the past and they weren't productive … but Shop 'n Save employees would be treated fairly. And they were. We were able to have an extremely successful operation, and we did it by treating people well, giving them a chance to grow by establishing policies and protocols that were fair, giving them all the rights they deserved. We always tried to have picnics, ball game tickets, and things like that for the folks. And we were always on a first-name basis. We spent a lot of time listening and talking. They knew we cared, and they felt like we were a part of their team. And that was the difference."

"It was so important for management to see that the organization wasn't just about profits," adds Andy Blassie, who served in various finance leadership roles for the company for 15 years.

> *"To have a creed, you are somehow promoting more than just raw profit and loss or earnings per share. … It promotes the well-being of everyone and assumes a long-term situation."*
>
> **ANDY BLASSIE**

Describing a creed as "a mission statement on steroids," Blassie, a devout Catholic, further likens a business creed to a basic construct of a religion's beliefs. "In the Catholic faith we have an apostolic creed and that is the framework of the Catholic religion. You believe in God and all the various tenants of the religion. To me, the Wetterau Creed was what we believed in and why it was so important that we try to live it every day. It was like the Wetterau religion."

"It was really like a religion," concurs Darryl Long, who served in store development and operations. "It is a belief, a feeling, and something that gives you warmth and strength."

"I was favorably impressed with it because it just seemed like the right thing to have," adds Lois Laverty of the initial impact *The Creed* made on her. "And to put it out there — how we are going to run this place — and what should and shouldn't be done, it just seemed so right."

"It kind of personalized the corporate environment and made people feel comfortable with each other, in all age groups," explains Blassie of how *The Creed* encouraged employee diversity that contributed to its success. "The younger people were given such an opportunity at Wetterau. We were growing, and that probably necessitated giving them that chance somewhat, but we brought in good people, young people in their 20s and 30s, who had a wonderful opportunity to progress quickly. In other companies you wouldn't even be a director [at that age], you know? Our growth was tied in with the fact that we had so many young people merged with the later generation — we were able to acquire so many divisions in short order."

Blassie goes on to say that Wetterau's Creed was not only emphasized as an important cornerstone of the company, but the associates truly lived it. "Customers were extremely important as well as our associates. I get a little emotional about that," he says reminiscent. "The way the company treated its people, to me, was the driving force behind why we were so close."

Associates, retailers, and suppliers alike appreciated the Wetterau Creed. "*The Creed* was amazing," says eight-year Wetterau associate,

CHAPTER 2: A NEW COMPANY CREED

Cathy Heimburger Cortright, who served in store development, point of sale, and supported the public relations efforts of the organization. "It really truly was the core of the company. I don't think it was required to be in all the offices, but it was in quite a few, whether they were big or small. Many retailers had it displayed, too. You would walk in to their little, tiny offices in their store and there was *The Creed*, right there. It really meant a lot to so many people."

"The retailers loved it," recalls Crutsinger, from an external perspective. "I [as a supplier] loved it because Wetterau didn't kick us around. They treated the suppliers with dignity, and as a result they got much better deals."

"Our retailers were just good people," added Tom Haggai, who served on IGA's board of directors beginning in 1972 and then as the organization's chairman from 1986 to 2016. "So they liked *The Creed*, and a lot of them put it in their stores."

"It was like a family," explains Merwyn Sher, a multi-store retailer in the St. Louis area, of the entire Wetterau team. "They treated us like friends." Sher bought groceries from Wetterau Inc. for six years and explains how that era was a highlight in his career: "It felt more like 60 years because of the type of relationship we had. It was easy because their culture was the same culture I was raised with. In retail I have to make my customers feel real good so they want to come in and buy groceries from me. And that's how Wetterau made us feel, like we wanted to [buy from them] and work with them. There were always challenges [in the industry], but they would listen outwardly and were very attentive to our issues."

Each week, Sher opted to hand-carry his company's check for the groceries purchased to Wetterau's Hazelwood distribution center instead of mailing it or messengering it because of the "unbelievable relationship" he had with the Wetteraus — one that extended beyond business into philanthropy. Conrad Wetterau, Ted's eldest son, ran the Hazelwood center at the time. Sher explains that he would visit with Conrad every Friday. "He had *The Creed* on the wall of his office, and we would talk about all the things we were involved in — from JDRF (Juvenile Diabetes Research Foundation), to helping children of military veterans, to setting up charitable foundations, and so forth. We all worked together," says Sher. "When you have a bond like that with somebody, you're there for each other. When things were tough, that's when *The Creed* really registered in my mind; things are written on paper and with good intentions, but actions speak louder than words. And I felt like I had known the Wetteraus all of my life. … They made us feel like we were part of the family."

Leading by Example: Putting People First

As the patriarch of the Wetterau Inc. family, Ted C. was also positively affected by institutionalizing *The Creed* into the organization and seeing the powerful effect it had on his associates. According to Tom Haggai, Ted's faith in God grew substantially through this process, along with his spiritual character. "It took on a whole new level of vitality," explains Tom, "because it seemed like every day he felt that God had done some miracle, and he couldn't let Him down."

So to show his gratitude, Ted would continually strive to set a positive example for his team and guide them the best he could. He was known for his personalized leadership and loyalty and for taking a concerted interest in people and showing them respect.

"Ted would be there first thing in the morning and sometimes stay until later in the evening, and he would ask about your kids, or your wife, or about your life," explains Andy Blassie, who acknowledges that Ted was dedicated to his own family while balancing the demands of work. "We included spouses and key customers at most of our annual events. We always remembered our retirees. And we were very active in the community, which Ted promoted. If you were at a certain executive level, it was encouraged that you serve on charity boards in St. Louis, from the zoo to the children's hospital to Juvenile Diabetes."

CHAPTER 2: A NEW COMPANY CREED

Haggai explained how people were top priority for Ted: "His people were it," he said. "Whenever there was an event [with his team or the retailers], Ted met every plane and shook every hand of each attendee as they arrived."

"The jet would land with 300 of his retailers and their wives," explained Dick Federer, "and as each one came off Ted would say, 'Harry, welcome to Hawaii! And by the way, you had a great week last week. Your sales were outstanding!' and then he'd cite the numbers and say, 'That's terrific!' How would you feel if you spent eight hours on that jet? You're all grimy and you want a shower, there's a girl throwing a lei over your head and all of a sudden, here's the boss — THE boss (not the division boss but the head of the supplier company) — knowing your name and maybe your wife's name and the sales you did last week. What a confidence-builder that would be! He'd shake your hand and your wife has this feeling like, 'Oh, I married a pretty good guy!' That's the way it was done."

Despite his high status and top-level authority, Ted was known for being very approachable and down to earth. "He wasn't a snob at all," added Haggai, providing a glimpse into his character and style. "One time as attendees were arriving at an event, Ted said, 'Drop what you're doing, the people are here!' typifying his enthusiasm for his team, and the priority that they were in his business and life."

During good times and bad, Ted was known for going to great lengths to make sure his people and others in need were taken care of, which was typical of how he led throughout his career. For instance, as a noted philanthropist who supported and led dozens of charitable organizations and efforts in the St. Louis area, it wasn't unusual for him to simply write a check for a substantial amount to someone in need. When his associates fell on hard times or needed some extra support, Ted would extend them special, low-rate loans. And when business wasn't at its best, he would give away his bonuses so his associates could enjoy more of a reward. "He'd say, 'They need it more than I do to make ends meet,'" explains Conrad. "Nobody really knew that. But he did it. They got a little larger bonus because Ted Wetterau threw some of his bonus in to make theirs bigger. Dad used to have this saying that 'if you take care of the people, the people will take care of you,' meaning not him personally but the bottom line and the balance sheet will take care of itself. He believed that sincerely. So he spent a lot of his time making sure the environment was right. If the environment was right and they were the right people, they would produce."

Finding and hiring the right people with the same Creed-based values was a continued effort at Wetterau. Andy Levy, a long-time Wetterau associate, who first oversaw security for the company and then headed up human resources, recalls the process: "We felt so strongly about what we believed in and the associates we surrounded ourselves with," he says. "When we would interview someone for a top job, the first thing we would do was put the Wetterau Creed on the table to see how they would respond to it." In Levy's case, his initial interview consisted of one key question: "Ted asked me, 'If you caught someone misbehaving, what would be your primary objective?' And I said, 'to maintain the individual's dignity.' That hit home with him, so we moved to St. Louis, and I started working for Wetterau."

Levy, who considers himself "a champion of the people," conducted a survey among the associates to see how they felt about *The Creed*. "It was a positive thing," he recalls, giving voice to the rank and file employees whose opinions weren't often solicited in that manner previously. But he notes that the results were somewhat mixed at first until people really understood the depth of commitment to the words of *The Creed*. "The end result though was that through the survey people felt that Wetterau was concerned about how they felt and how they were being treated," says Levy.

Eventually, as management began to talk about *The Creed* more often and to underscore its importance in word and deed, people increasingly realized that *The Creed* went beyond just lip service. "Sooner or later, everyone came into the fold because they saw how it affected everyone else," Levy continues. "They'd become like outsiders if they didn't buy into it or become

CHAPTER 2: A NEW COMPANY CREED

a 'believer.' It became contagious when you saw men and women who work together so wonderfully well, and who had the same feeling about themselves, their associates, and the company. It was a wonderful thing to see."

Eighteen-year Wetterau associate, Bill Pocilujko, who served in various management roles on the distribution side of the business, was one such convert. "The first thing I thought when I saw *The Creed* was, 'Wow, this looks really good [but] how phony is this?' I mean, how many businesses say, 'We believe in God?' But it didn't take long to realize that this is what these people believe in, and this is how they run their business. They want you to treat people with respect. And they do live *The Creed*."

Pocilujko recalls one Christmas Eve when he was working late at the distribution center and received a call from the gate guard saying that Ted Wetterau had just driven through the gate and was coming to see him. He met Ted in the parking lot and said, "Mr. Wetterau, how are you? What can I help you with today?" And Ted said, "I just wanted to come by and wish you and your family a Merry Christmas. You are always there for us, anytime we need anything, and I can always rely on you." This kind gesture impacted Pocilujko for years afterwards. "That man had better things to do on Christmas Eve, and I never forgot that. That's just how the Wetteraus are. Conrad and Mark [Ted's youngest son] do the same thing [in the business today]. They call periodically just to see how things are going with you. Most people in business don't do that."

"I had never worked for a company that had a creed like that," said the late Ed Sowa, in a discussion about *The Creed* shortly before his passing in 2009. Sowa was highly sought after for his expertise in managing difficult situations between unions and companies and noted that "believing in the dignity of man and taking care of our customers" was something that really impacted him. He was motivated to join Wetterau Inc. because he already considered the unions like family and sought to treat them as such. "It's a value system that says, 'We want to treat people right and take care of the customer,' which most of the other companies I had worked with didn't express. It was more about how much money they could make from them. They didn't care about 'giving the customer a fair deal.' It was all about making money."

Like Pocilujko, Sowa saw the Wetteraus' personal touch positively impact many people, including some union cynics, who were occasionally at odds with management, particularly during contract negotiations. "They personally took care of some people in the union who were sick," Sowa explained. "They provided airplanes and medical support, things the union didn't or couldn't do. Those cynics became believers because they had been touched by an angel. When you see company execs using their jets and sending people to [places like] the Mayo Clinic when they didn't have to, those people definitely became supporters of *The Creed*. They knew it was real. Their response to it all was, 'Hey, these Wetterau guys are okay. They're helping us with so many things, so they ain't all bad.'"

The one word Sowa said he would use to describe Wetterau Inc. and the Wetterau family is integrity. "They believe in people, and they always want to do the right thing. The right thing to them comes even before profit. I was not used to that. It was such an intricate value system there."

Seeking Perfection among the Imperfect

Many Wetterau associates emphasized that while *The Creed* was idyllic, it didn't automatically make things perfect at the company. The organization's leadership welcomed the expression of varying opinions and approaches to determine best practices for the business, and thus, got them in abundance. Formalizing *The Creed* in writing and institutionalizing it throughout the company helped associates work through their differences.

"Quite often, in any corporate headquarters, there can be some infighting," says Andy Blassie, of working through differences of opinions, priorities, and other issues. "But Ted would let people talk it out. Our management team understood that and respected each other. You could always disagree, but to the rank and file, we were together."

CHAPTER 2: A NEW COMPANY CREED

Former Wetterau Inc. Executive Vice President Jack Ryan, a 20-year senior leader at the company, reflected on *The Creed's* impact on Wetterau before his passing in 2012, saying that the team was "extremely happy" and "productive" most of the time, but *The Creed* helped during the difficult moments as well. "When you're involved in something that's gotten you off-track, if you read *The Creed,* it starts a big change [of heart] that helps everybody. It's not that you recite the whole thing, but it changes the course of something that is going bad and suggests that you get it straightened out," Ryan explained. "Honestly, if I were on the downbeat, had a problem, or wasn't happy with the way things were going, I would look up and see that thing on the wall and think, 'Maybe I ought to read that, just a couple lines of it,' and it kind of changes your approach to the problems. … People are going to disagree. Everybody disagrees [even] with their best friend or relatives or child or whomever [at times]. But what matters is being able to put things back together — to finally agree on the important things. When you're in trouble, you need something like a creed to help you get back on track."

And perhaps engage one's moral compass when faced with a fork in the road.

"If you joined the company and you consented," explained Dick Federer, "then the idea was that whenever you started to waiver, if you had a situation with an employee that you could go right or left on and no one would know [for example], Ted wanted to build within your conscience a system of morality where you would automatically go for the right answer. He believed that would be a moral prerogative you would discover, if you got into trouble. That certainly helped him as CEO. He knew it would give you great moral strength for yourself, your product, and your manpower, if you continued to believe [in *The Creed*]."

Reinforcing *The Creed*: Communication, Celebrations, and Awards

Part of what made the Wetterau Creed so unique and different from typical company vision or mission statements was the way its originator lived and breathed its philosophy. Ted frequently referenced *The Creed* in his business dealings and when directing his associates. "On many occasions, he would mention *The Creed* — whether it would be with management or meetings with a customer, he didn't have any hesitation telling them what we stood for," recalls Darryl Long, who says Ted's enthusiasm and belief in *The Creed's* universal principles were infectious. "He backed it up because he believed it. And you know it was contagious! It really was. I felt it like most everybody in the company did, and it just continued to grow and grow. It was sort of amazing."

Ted spoke regularly, often in an uplifting, even spiritual manner to encourage and inspire his people. Addressing his leadership team in the spring of 1976, Ted shared a message of positivity and a "can-do" attitude regarding achieving the company's goals. He concluded his remarks by referencing the words of *The Creed:*

> *I hope that as we go back to our divisions and back to our desks and back to dealing with people within our firm that we once again realize that it is so important to knock any part of the "can't" out of our life; whether it is with our children, with our wives, with our communities. Let us give them that positive attitude that we have and step forth with the courage that built this company today.* **With longer steps, with faster strides, with greater enthusiasm, and with God at our side there isn't anywhere that this company can't go by being the finest, the most aggressive, and a company that does believe in God and the dignity of man; that does believe that people should be treated as we would like to be treated, and this applies to the welfare of our employees and their families, to our suppliers and all with whom we do business.** *We believe that successful*

CHAPTER 2: A NEW COMPANY CREED

independent business is the backbone of our country; that our success is closely related to the success of our retail customer and only by working together can the ultimate success of both be assured. Therefore, let us dedicate ourselves to working for our mutual success and that we pledge our best efforts always to the attainment of a common goal.

"Ted took every opportunity to promote the importance of *The Creed*," says Andy Blassie, "and was disappointed if the divisions and the offices around the country didn't have it prominently displayed."

Mark Wetterau, Ted's middle child, agrees. "Dad was always very open about the *The Creed*," he recalls of his 16 years with Wetterau Inc. "He kept his religion and his true beliefs upfront. Rarely was there a speech that would go by that he wouldn't talk about his beliefs or his political views concerning what was happening in our country. He was very open on his positioning to the point that you've got to be careful today. But that was then, and he loved doing that. He talked about his beliefs and his philosophy a lot."

Along with the way Ted evangelized *The Creed* (and his beliefs embodied in it), Darryl Long makes another important distinction about why it was so unique, getting at the heart of its dynamism: "The emphasis Ted put on *The Creed* and just how important people were and how important their families were — whether it was executive leadership, middle management, or the person out there picking the orders — helped everybody feel *The Creed's* [power]. It gives you a sense of direction that can be nothing but good. I think [the spirit surrounding it] is really more powerful than what the words alone are saying. It's the feelings you get from it, and you can't put those feelings into words."

"Spirit of the Creed" Award

The way *The Creed* made Wetterau associates feel played a significant part in helping them do exceptional work for the company. One way Wetterau recognized that service was by instituting a "Spirit of the Creed" award, which recognized employees, partners, and retailers who exemplified *The Creed* in their roles and responsibilities at the company. Award-winners were nominated by their peers each year and were recognized at company shareholder meetings and annual events.

"It was such an honor to receive that award," says Bill Pocilujko, who as an initial Creed skeptic now views the philosophy as representing his own personal values and ideals. "I've always tried to treat others the same as I want to be treated and I try to go out of my way to help people."

"It shows what you can do with a [company] creed," said one of Wetterau's first board members, Stanley Simon, now deceased, who was affiliated with the company for several decades as a management consultant. "It was very inspiring to work with such inspiring people, which was demonstrated throughout the company."

Part of what helped *The Creed* become so well accepted and cherished by so many Wetterau associates was the way in which Ted reached out personally, both internally and externally, to his associates, putting into action the words embodied in *The Creed* — in addition to all the handshakes, one-on-one inquiries, and other gestures of genuine concern, Ted also wrote letters to individual associates and to his teams. These included Christmas cards that typically quoted Biblical scriptures, which he sent to Christians, Jews, and gentiles alike.

"It was an honor to receive them," said Stanley Simon, who was Jewish. He recalled that he had never gotten anything like them at any other time in his 50-year career. "These letters were about *The Creed*, which was the philosophy of the company," and that explains "why the business ran so well," he said. "So what can you say against *The Creed*?"

CHAPTER 2: A NEW COMPANY CREED

"We were a Christian-based company," notes Blassie, "but Ted never forgot about or excluded non-Christians in his Christmas message or whatever we talked about. Faith to the Wetteraus was very important. Ted knew who he hired, whether or not [faith] was a big part of their life. I believe today that there is a divine being who supports companies that make [spiritual values] a priority."

Dismissing the Naysayers

But not everyone was a believer, regardless of religion. Not long after Wetterau introduced *The Creed*, the *St. Louis Post-Dispatch* reported that a New York stock analyst had dismissed it as "having little importance in evaluating the company's financial standing." But what the analyst didn't realize, the newspaper reported, was that "he was treading not only on a family name but a corporate philosophy that the Wetterau folks say has been the key to four decades of uninterrupted profit increases and annual sales that have now reached $800,000,000."

Ted Wetterau dismissed the dismissal. "It may be old hat or corny to some, but we're not ashamed of [*The Creed*]," he told the *Post-Dispatch* reporter. And contrary to the projections of some, the business continued to prosper.

In 1972, just months after *The Creed* was introduced, Wetterau Inc. was recognized by the *St. Louis Globe-Democrat* as the "Missouri Growth Company of the Year." Responding to the *Globe's* acknowledgment, Ted explained that the success Wetterau was experiencing was in part because of *The Creed*: "Our goal is to help our supermarkets become one-stop-shopping centers in their market areas," he commented, of the fruits of his earlier vision, which became one of the key focal points of *The Creed*. "This is part of our overall program to help our retailers become the most successful in their communities. As they succeed, so do we."

True to his word, Ted stepped in to help IGA Inc. during a period of struggle, devoting nearly a year of his own time to the reorganization and strengthening of this system — this helped IGA become the third-largest retail food organization in the world. Ted later served as an IGA board member and eventually as its chairman. (Please see *Appendix A* for a detailed list of Ted Wetterau's industry and community service.)

Greed vs. Creed: How an Attempted Takeover in the '80s Helped Wetterau Soar to Greater Heights

Leveraging the high-tech trends and financial prosperity and stability of the 1980s, Wetterau experienced the most dramatic growth in company history during this decade. It acquired several key businesses, which helped strengthen its presence on the East Coast and became the largest wholesaler in the New England area. The company also expanded throughout the Southeast Coast, made a formal entry into retailing, and established a foothold on the West Coast. It also began servicing regional supermarket chains, which was somewhat of a departure from the original policy of servicing only independent grocers. The hope in this was to create a broader base for growth.

But all wasn't roses and cash cows for Wetterau during this prosperous era. In 1981, the company faced a challenge more difficult than anything it had encountered in more than a century in business: an attempted hostile takeover.

Early in the decade, the U.S. was experiencing a tough recessionary period — when low stock values were common in wholesale grocery organizations — and many public companies, including Wetterau, were vulnerable (despite it being one of the top performing wholesalers in the category). People could buy undervalued companies for less than their worth, break up the devalued assets, and make a profit by selling off the pieces separately. In Wetterau's case, even though the company stock was performing very well, its distribution centers were fully depreciated, so on

CHAPTER 2: A NEW COMPANY CREED

paper they appeared to be undervalued. As such, a prospective buyer could acquire the centers for cheap and spin them off for a large profit. Because of this, Wetterau Inc. risked losing its family-led company of more than a century to an owner of a major propane gas distributor, who sought to buy them out.

"It hit the papers on a Monday morning that they had bought a substantial percentage of our stock," recalls financial expert, Mike Waitukaitis, who was serving as the director of corporate tax and mergers and acquisitions for Wetterau at the time. The unfriendly attempted purchase was spearheaded by an ambitious individual who allegedly had ties with the mob. "He wouldn't even give us a call to tell us he had bought enough of our stock that he would have to report to the FTC [Federal Trade Commission] that he owned it. It was very hot stuff."

"Dad was very emotional at that time," recalls Conrad, who explains that Ted naturally had high hopes and expectations of his sons continuing to lead the company into future generations. "What really bothered us was this bully was going to come in and buy the company cheap because of the undervalued stock and in turn, he was going to sell off the pieces and break up the business to make more money. This was strictly a make-money play."

So Ted and his team had a decision to make: Either allow the raider to continue buying up the stock or fight to preserve what they'd spent generations building. He called on his sons to listen to his concerns.

"I'll never forget, one Sunday after church at our parents' house," Conrad recalls, "Mark and I sat down together in the study with Dad and Mom and Dad said, 'It's down to this: Do we want to roll over and none of us will ever have to work another day in our lives? We'll put a ton of money in our pockets and let this guy come in, and the odds are that he'll just take us over. There's a chance that we could try to stay at the company, but it might be messy, and we might ultimately not walk away with hardly anything.' We all agreed that we couldn't allow him to basically dismantle Wetterau and let all these families lose their jobs and for him to sell off the pieces just like junk to other companies and walk away with even more money. So he went to the board and they were supportive of Ted's recommendation to try to save the company, and we fought and we fought and we fought."

According to Tom Haggai, they prayed fervently about the matter. "I said, 'Ted, you and I have one agreement. God is on the throne,'" explained Haggai. "'If this is to be, then God already has plans. ... So I'm going to be praying for you.' And he said, 'I'm praying all the time,' and I said, 'I know that.'"

And they solicited the prayers and support of others, as well. Wetterau leadership, employees, customers, vendors, and other partners banded together to support the company during this taxing period.

Many recall those dark days...

"This guy was trying to intimidate us," says Waitukaitis of the corporate raider using unfriendly tactics, which included threats on Ted's life. "And everyone agreed that there was no way we were going to let that happen. ... We had the internal fortitude to stand up to this bully, and I think we did it pretty much collectively. Whether somebody recited *The Creed* or whether just because it was there sitting in the back of our minds, we worked together through it. We were a very good, tightly knit group."

"I think *The Creed* helped out a lot, in a number of ways," says Bob Crutsinger of the organization's group efforts in dealing with the attempted takeover. "People had confidence [in the company] that regardless of the fact that those days looked pretty bleak in the newspapers and the publicity was pretty bad, that we would be okay. ... Not everybody woke up every morning and read *The Creed* and knelt down and made the sign of the cross, but everybody knew that [leaning on our values] was the operating mode Wetterau was in and when we were in trouble, this is what we needed: we needed God."

Fred Heimburger recalled that *The Creed* helped rally all Wetterau constituents together, "and not just the employees, but the retailers, too — 1,600 that they serviced at the time," he recounted. "Some of the big ones and a lot of the smaller ones let it be known that if Wetterau was taken over, they weren't going to buy from the new entity. So *The Creed* really came into effect then because Wetterau's customers really knew that the associates were living by it. They wanted to support [their suppliers], and that tells you a lot about the company."

"It was definitely an 'all-for-one-and-one-for-all' kind of time," adds Cathy Heimburger Cortright. "It was really something and showed the loyalty of the employees as well as the retailers and people associated with Wetterau. The offer was on the table for the stock and people could have made a lot of money off that, and they pretty much held their cards close to their chest and stood up for the company."

"Ted's team pulled together and worked extremely well," adds Mark, who was just beginning his career at the company at the time. "They made some hard decisions. I was relatively early out of school watching this, but I saw the pressures, the fears, the decisions, and all the hard stuff that needed to be done in a very rapid fashion."

During this time, the team determined a strategy to acquire a company to better position the organization for success. So they purchased the grocery/retail chain, Laneco, which aided in the situation. The stock-to-stock (instead of straight cash) transaction between Wetterau Inc. and Laneco chairman and majority stockholder, Raymond Bartolacci, temporarily diluted the stock price for the shareholders, including the intended Wetterau raider, until Laneco was assimilated. So rather than wait for the stock to regain its value after the purchase and go through with the Wetterau buyout, the raider took the short-term profit from the millions of dollars in "greenmail" (financial blackmail or a premium fee on an average value) the Wetteraus ended up paying him for the stock he had accumulated, and ran. "It made him happy because he made money on us and pushed us against the wall. But we retained our company!" explains Conrad, in a relieved-yet-victorious tone.

Though it took several months of hard-fought battles to put the attempted takeover behind them, Wetterau began to bounce back from the threat and continued to thrive as usual.

Ted Wetterau attributed this hard-fought victory to the team's tenacity and dedication, all united in the spirit of *The Creed*, which others also acknowledged. Stanley Simon said that *The Creed* helped Wetterau get through challenges such as the attempted buyout because, "it's like any other type of faith. You have confidence because of your innate, internal strength." And perhaps a bit of karma came into play during the confrontation as well — some positive ROI from Wetterau associates in whom Ted had personally invested so much over the years.

The amazing way Ted and his team, along with associates, vendors, and all involved with Wetterau Inc. rallied around the company and helped it manage this unexpected disruption was no doubt because of *The Creed* and positive company culture Ted had helped cultivate through the years through those personal investments in his associates. Such cultures must already be in place in the good times if companies want to survive during times of disruption, explains change management consultant, Damian Menzies, CEO of the Australian-based consultancy firm, Choice.

"What separates some businesses from others at times [of disruption] isn't their action plan, but their organizational culture," notes Menzies. "The way that businesses build a work environment without the presence of disruption hugely impacts how well they manage when things suddenly start going south. … Companies who have a truly inclusive work culture [where] … there is diversity of thought … [and] a strong sense of belonging by all team members … [who] feel comfortable speaking up in the 'good' times, can help you more successfully weather the difficult ones."

What followed the '81 takeover threat was an ironic-yet-sweet reward. "The threat propelled Wetterau to greater heights," says Conrad. "We were more than a $1 billion company at the time, a benchmark that took us about 110 years to reach. Then we went on the fastest growth spurt in the company's history."

Wetterau made some changes to better protect the organization from future buyouts and enable added success. They got a little more sophisticated

CHAPTER 2: A NEW COMPANY CREED

with things like incorporating "poison pills" within the board of directors that would force any future bidders to negotiate directly with the board to help stop potential takeovers from ever happening again. Then Wetterau started buying back its own stock with a vengeance so management could control more of the company. And employee ownership was increased through an enhanced stock-option program. Wetterau also formed a real estate investment trust (REIT) company and moved the distribution centers and other entities into the REIT to better protect them.

"It was very, very aggressive," explains Conrad, of the asset protection strategies put in place. "We also wanted to accelerate company and employee ownership and stimulate performance as well with these enhanced stock-option incentives. And by doing that, along with executing our acquisition strategy, we hit the growth spurt. Within five years we were a $2 billion company; within 10 years we were at $5 billion; and then a year or so after that we hit $6 billion. It was just unbelievable. This growth spurt was second to none in both earnings as well as sales revenue and really built the company into what it was."

©1990 St. Louis Post-Dispatch

Photos (left to right):

1) Ted C. Wetterau, T. Conrad Wetterau, and Mark S. Wetterau featured in 1990 St. Louis Post-Dispatch story about Wetterau Inc. leadership succession

2) A few of Wetterau Inc.'s retail stores: Save A Lot, Shop 'n Save, and Laneco

3) 1991 Supermarket News article spotlights Conrad, Ted, and Mark Wetterau as the "new generation" of leaders at Wetterau Inc.

4) 1991 St. Louis Business Journal story about Wetterau Inc.'s steady financial climb, despite the attempted takeover

©1991 *Supermarket News*   ©1991 *St. Louis Business Journal*

CHAPTER 3

A New Wetterau World — the Next Generation of Leadership Weaves *The Creed* Deeper into the Fabric of the Organization

"[The Wetterau company culture] was defined by how you dealt with people every day. It's powerful because **The Creed** *created such a positive environment."*

–Darryl Long (1950–   )
Store Developer and Operations Manager (1971–1993),
Wetterau Inc.

    As the folks at Wetterau relished in their exponential success, they continued to adhere to their business strategy and, as a result, they persisted in their efforts to grow the company internally and acquired other companies as well. Wetterau became a conglomerate of businesses from insurance to financing and construction to manufacturing and distribution, underscoring the need for alignment through the company Creed.

"The Wetterau family and the organization didn't balk at taking risks," says Andy Blassie, 15-year finance leader at Wetterau Inc. of the company's 22 acquisitions over the years. "And our growth was tied to the fact that we had a model of how to grow and move our people out into [new] areas we purchased — to take our company culture into those organizations."

The Creed proved to be the enabler that helped newly acquired organizations feel comfortable joining this new company culture, knowing they would be taken care of properly. "They bought into our culture," says Mark Wetterau, as he recalls his early years at the company. "They loved what we were representing and standing for. It worked on the growth surge in that sense, and then it also really worked well with the customers to generate a level of comfort, with us being the middle folks as a consolidator and a full distributor into their supermarkets, which they wouldn't typically get with another supplier."

The synergy between Wetterau Inc. and the various companies it brought into its conglomerate was certainly a result of the way in which *The Creed* was being more deeply woven into the fabric of the organization. Indeed, Wetterau was innovating, evolving, and exponentially growing thanks to the influence of *The Creed* on its culture for more than a decade. Now, a new generation of leaders was getting ready to propel the organization forward.

Company Leadership Advances Strong Values-based Culture

With the attempted takeover behind the company, Conrad and Mark Wetterau stepped up and assumed a number of leadership roles at relatively young ages, determined to continue building a strong company culture around the principles set forth in the Wetterau Creed. After working on the retail side in supermarkets, Conrad served primarily on the distribution side, and Mark, who had spent some time on the wholesale side, took on retail.

CHAPTER 3: A NEW WETTERAU WORLD

"Mark and I both started out taking positions at Wetterau at a very young age and those opportunities were given to us, frankly," Conrad admits candidly. "There were guys who had been there 20 years who would cut their right arm off to have that position. So they knew we were being groomed and we were on an accelerated path, which was somewhat controversial for some people. There were some jealousies like, 'Why does he get that job and I don't?'"

In 1983, at just 28, Conrad was the youngest general manager to run a distribution division, but he was wise enough to demonstrate some humility, which seemed to connect with his more experienced subordinates. "I had a team around me that I inherited, many of whom were almost twice my age. And they're looking at me like, 'I know you're Ted's son, but you really haven't had that much experience.' I knew I was going to fail if I couldn't get these guys to buy into me [as a leader]. So I admitted I was just a kid who didn't have all the answers and said, 'I've been given a significant opportunity here, and based on how well all of us work together or not is going to determine whether we (and I) are successful in this venture going forward. You guys are all veterans in your areas of expertise — you're really good at what you do so all I'm going to try to do is set the goals [for the team] then lead the charge. But if we don't work together, we're going to fail, and I'm going to fail."

Conrad's "participating management" style of leadership proved effective, as he led the financially struggling division into profitability to win the company's coveted Chairman's Challenge Award (CCA) two of the three years he oversaw the division, the highest honor given to a team at Wetterau at the time. Nicknamed "Kid Boss," Conrad was recognized by his team with his own individual honor after their first CCA win in 1986. "They pulled me into my office and gave me this hat that said 'Kid Boss' on it, but they had put a line through 'Kid' and replaced it with 'Man.' I still have that hat. It was a big step for me at that age, knowing that I was finally accepted not for who I was, meaning Ted Wetterau's son, but for what I could do."

Just a few years later, Mark faced a similar trial on the retail side. He was challenged at a young age to take one of Wetterau's retail grocery store chains, which was running in the red, and make it profitable. At age 28, he had already led several individual stores and specialty departments to success and had participated in many of the company's mergers and acquisitions of various supermarket chains. So he was asked to step in and lead the entire retail chain as president and chief operating officer and shortly thereafter, take over as the chief executive officer.

"The biggest challenge I had was getting the team to believe in themselves, to believe in me, and to trust each other enough to take some risks," explains Mark. "So it was really about pulling the team together and utilizing the strengths each one of these folks had. It was very exciting and also very humbling."

Mark admits that part of this challenge was not seeing eye-to-eye with some of the leadership and getting proper alignment. "One of the executives struggled with my age and experience level, and was very loyal to the former CEO," he explains, among other issues. "So after a lot of conflict, we just decided that it would be best for him to go a different direction."

Once the new leadership was in place and had overcome the hurdles that hindered their unity, they really started to progress as a chain. Mark and his team incorporated more diversification of store departments and product offerings, and an enhanced customer experience called "We Care" motivated by *The Creed*. This bolder strategy — including more direct, head-to-head advertising — enabled the team to see positive results and increase trust in the process. "We developed the strategy that we all aligned to, we had a great team, and then we brought in *The Creed*, which helped enhance the culture of the business," recalls Mark. "This all helped us move that chain to all-time records, all-time highs."

In 1989 and 1990, Mark's team won back-to-back Chairman's Challenge Awards, which qualified them to compete for the inaugural Master Quest Award in 1990, Wetterau's "best of the best" in the wholesale, retail, and manufacturing divisions. They ended up winning that award, which was a great victory for the entire team, along with Mark, who had won more than just an award. He had earned the respect of his fellow executives for his leadership at another level, which prepared him for future opportunities.

"Mark's a born leader," says Duane Daniels, who worked in corporate finance for Wetterau and Shop 'n Save for more than two decades. "The Wetteraus made you feel a part of the team, and Mark is great at that. He would ask, 'How are your kids? Your wife?' rather than, 'Where are we on this project or those numbers?' Just those little attitudes made you feel like the Wetterau organization was your home. That's why we worked so hard. It was our second home. We wouldn't have done that if it was just a job. We [felt like] we had an ownership in the company, so we worked hard."

Indeed, Duane and many other members of management were actual owners of Wetterau Inc. and its family of companies through the organization's stock option programs. But clearly, their commitments ran deeper than just money. As Duane indicated, he and others felt like they were integral to the success of the organization through a true team spirit that permeated the enterprise.

As CEO of Shop 'n Save, Mark led the organization that was Conrad's largest distribution customer for several years. As such, they relied on each other for their mutual success. "We counted on each other constantly to have the right products on the right trucks on the right days," explains Mark, "and Conrad counted on me for sales."

Beyond the bottom line, Conrad and Mark also leaned on each other for moral support, regardless of their roles at the company. They both shared the stigma of being Ted's sons, so they mutually understood those unique challenges like no one else. "To make it, we had to be as good as or better than others," explains Mark. But they both agree that the challenge of having to prove themselves to the doubters made them work twice as hard, which in turn accelerated their growth and leadership abilities. This, they say, along with surrounding themselves with very good people, ultimately helped them prevail.

Ted's confidence in them never wavered. As he later explained during an interview with *The Wall Street Transcript*: "I've got two sons in the business and in very good spots, so they will help perpetuate the company," he said, expressing both executive and paternal pride in his sons' achievements and leadership potential. "I am very proud that they're extremely hardworking and bright and are growing quickly, handling major business units of Wetterau."

The Creed's Influence on Other Wetterau Companies

During the Wetterau Inc. era, the influence of the Wetterau Creed was felt and implemented into a variety of organizations related to the company. These included: Shop 'n Save, Save A Lot, and Laneco, three of Wetterau Inc.'s retail store chains that it acquired during the 1980s. Each company has its own sphere of influence, including employees, customers, suppliers, and the families of each.

Shop 'n Save: Teamwork, Recognition, and Charitable Service

When Wetterau leadership introduced *The Creed* into Shop 'n Save in the 1980s, it wasn't just to get buy-in from the management at corporate. They instituted it into the entire chain of about two dozen stores with all of their associates. Mark Wetterau, who was serving as chairman and CEO of Shop 'n Save at the time, hired one of his previous supervisors who had been managing a Shop 'n Save store, Marlene Gebhard, to join him at corporate. Together they introduced *The Creed* into the company. "We actually hung a copy of *The Creed* in every store, so every customer and employee could see it," recalls Mark of the 25-store chain, after introducing it to all employees. "It was a real positive, not only for the associates, but also for the customers," he recalls.

Decades later, *The Creed* has continued its positive influence on the Shop 'n Save business. "*The Creed* was always the base," says Marlene, who progressed to serve as president of Shop 'n Save for about eight years. By instituting recognition programs, sharing earnings with associates, celebrating employment anniversaries, and serving the community, Marlene lived the values of *The Creed* and helped ensure its influence would be felt throughout her organization. "One of the first things I did when I took over was get involved in several charities," she says, having sat on the boards of a number of local and national non-profit organizations. "I felt very strongly that we needed to be a part of the community, and not just for me to be involved, but we needed the associates to be involved."

As a result, Shop 'n Save employees have supported a variety of charitable organizations over the years, including Special Olympics and the St. Louis Crisis Nursery, which helps stop child abuse. Their creative fundraisers range from Shop 'n Save trivia nights, which at one event raised tens of thousands of dollars in a single evening, to inter-store competitions that have raised more than a hundred thousand dollars over time.

Marlene explains that she learned many of her methods and the spirit in which to institute them from her days at Wetterau Inc. "When you get people enthused about something, and then you incent them and make it a contest and get everybody rallied around it, you can't lose. You *cannot* lose. And some of it was based on what I learned from Mark and Ted Wetterau and the team. We always had some kind of contest going to keep everybody excited about business."

Another way that the company sought to "pledge their best efforts" as noted in *The Creed*, was through their "Store of the Year" and "Mark of Excellence" recognition programs. The "Store of the Year" recognized the location that beat their budget by the most metrics in such areas as expenses, labor, and sales. The store director won a trip to virtually anywhere they wanted to go, and the assistant director won a bonus cash prize, as did the stores themselves. Then each month, a drawing was held where employees could draw down on that money (in smaller increments).

The "Mark of Excellence" cleaning program was aptly named after Mark Wetterau, who's known for his high degree of tidiness. "Our standards were high in terms of cleanliness, and we wanted them to remain high," explains Marlene. "So every month, certain staff members went out and did a cleaning inspection in the stores. The location with the highest score got to keep a coveted traveling trophy called the Mark of Excellence for 30 days. Every store wanted to have it so it moved around from location to location. [The stores] took a lot of pride in winning it, and the customers got cleaner, brighter stores, so it was a win-win!"

The Shop'n Save leadership team also instituted anniversary celebrations for employees who had been at the company at least five years. Marlene says that these gatherings gave everyone the chance to get to know each other on a more human level and were an important part of the company. "Those things are just vital to the survival of an organization," she explains. "They're what can take a large business and make it feel like a family business. And the Wetteraus were truly masters at it. And I think that it all stems from *The Creed*."

A Deeper Journey

Duane Daniels, who served as vice president of finance at Shop'n Save, agrees with Marlene. "Treat others like you want to be treated," he says, as the basis for success. "Keep faith in that. And keep your creator in it." A religious man, Daniels says that *The Creed* was always important to him while at Wetterau Inc. and at Shop'n Save, but it means even more to him as he's gotten older, so much so that he still has an elegantly framed Creed in his home today. "Your journey becomes deeper," he explains, "especially when you have kids. It felt good to work for a company that put values forth and wasn't afraid to show it, wasn't afraid to speak out. People have to realize that in the business world you don't have to jump and stomp on others to get ahead. Sometimes I think you've just got to let things go and not carry that burden."

"When you treat [employees] with dignity and respect, especially in the stores, they want to work harder for you," adds Marlene. "When you set a standard out in the store, associates want to live up to that standard because they know it's important to everyone in the company. So having something like *The Creed* as your base, and your employees know you live it, can help everyone reach [for the highest ideals] and reach for them together."

CHAPTER 3: A NEW WETTERAU WORLD

Wetterau Inc. Success: Exponential Growth after 120 Years

By the end of the 1980s, as Wetterau celebrated its 120th anniversary, it operated 24 modern food distribution facilities servicing 2,600 retail stores (and 3,000 institutional customers) in 28 states; five general merchandising centers operating in 38 states; and three bakery production plants. These facilities included single-store and multi-store operators and regional chains. Wetterau also ran hundreds of its own retail stores including Shop 'n Save, Save A Lot, and Laneco.

Company subsidiaries and operating divisions provided support services that included industrial development and commercial construction, insurance protection, transportation services, management development and skills training, communication services, financing and leasing, along with data processing and management information systems. Wetterau was thriving in every way, like it never had before.

Conrad and Mark both continued to progress in their leadership responsibilities and eventually advanced in the company. After spending several years overseeing the food distribution groups, Conrad was promoted to senior executive vice president and chief administrative officer at Wetterau Inc. Concurrently, a number of years after overseeing the retail and industry groups, Mark was elevated to president and chief operating officer. Both continued to grow in leadership ability and achievements.

"I think what made Mark and Conrad better business leaders as they grew [in their respective roles] was learning to value [the opinions of others] and surrounding themselves with people that would help them become better," observes Marlene Gebhard, Mark's former supervisor on the retail side, who eventually served as president of Shop 'n Save for nearly eight years. "They both allowed people to speak whatever was on their mind, and they made their decisions based on their input. And I think that's a sign of a remarkable leader."

Many Wetterau associates saw positive leadership traits of Ted in both Conrad and Mark, indicating that they consistently worked well as a team. "The two of them would have been great as co-presidents," says Andy Levy, who worked with both Mark and Conrad in various capacities. "One picked up where the other left off. They made a good team. There was a lot of love and a lot of loyalty in the Wetterau family. They respected loyalty and they paid it back with loyalty. That was the glue that cemented the company for many years."

Considering the cohesiveness within the Wetterau family and within the company, it's no surprise that along with Mark and Conrad, Ted was recognized countless times for his outstanding leadership and achievements throughout his career in business as well as his extensive philanthropic service. One of those honors included the American Academy of Achievement's prestigious "Golden Plate Award" for exceptional vision and accomplishment in Computerized Food Distribution in 1974. Many more industry and community service awards would follow and by the time he passed in 2003, Ted would be recognized multiple times for his exemplary leadership in the food/grocery industry and for his faithful service to the community.

One of the most significant honors Ted received was the prestigious 1990 Herbert Hoover Award from the National-American Wholesale Grocers Association (NAWGA) for significant contributions to the food industry and to society. This was one of the highest honors bestowed on an executive in the supermarket business at the time.

"Ted Wetterau is someone whose name is synonymous with success in the food industry," said Julian Leavitt, former NAWGA chairman and president of Sweet Life Foods, when he presented Ted with the award. "He is renowned for his personal achievements which had far-reaching effects on the very essence of high ethical and moral standards, a sense of responsibility to family, community and country, and has served as an example to many, not only in the grocery industry, but to countless others in the business community. ... The accomplishments and contributions of Ted Wetterau have become a sort of beacon for young people just entering the grocery business, and as an inspiration to those involved on a day-to-day basis." (For a complete list of Ted Wetterau's awards and recognitions, please see *Appendix A.*)

A Turn in the Road: Sensational Success to a Bittersweet Sale

After 122 remarkable years of growth, prosperity, and exemplary values established by company founder, George Wetterau back in 1869, Wetterau Inc. grew to $6 billion in annual sales by the early '90s. It became the third-largest wholesaler in the industry, the tenth-largest retailer, and the largest frozen dough manufacturer in the country. The leadership and associates alike couldn't have been more proud of the progress that each had a hand in bringing to the organization and of the way they achieved their success — with ethics and values.

> "There were so many good times and so many fun things that happened, just a great esprit de corps. We were like a band of brothers who watched out for each other. We loved each other, and we had a great deal of affection for one another. Everybody had everybody's back."
>
> ANDY LEVY

"Ted seemed to operate on the premise that anything is possible as long as we work hard enough and do the right thing," observes Lois Laverty. "That's obviously what caused the company to be so successful — he was inspired by the fact that if you are diligent enough, nothing is impossible. A lot of people limit themselves and say, 'I can't do that much; I can't go that far.' But that was not Ted's way of looking at things. It was quite inspiring to watch a person like that make things happen. And there were so many dedicated people that would go right along with what he said we should do. It was wonderful. Even if you are just the assistant, it's still inspiring."

In his signature style, Ted credited the company's success to the associates' loyalty to *The Creed:* "Another reason for the success of our company is an unwavering adherence to a carpet philosophy, a philosophy rooted in simple human kindness and respect for our customers, suppliers, and our coworkers," he explained in a 1989 corporate video called "Wetterau World." "This philosophy was personified by my grandfather 12 decades ago and has been a source of inspiration for all who came after him. Our philosophy is contained in the words and spirit of the Wetterau Creed. [But] *The Creed* by itself is merely words. The men and women of this company who live by those principles put life into those words and put meaning into our work."

"There's no question that *The Creed* was a significant piece of the success of the organization," says Mark, "in the sense that it attracted great people, it enabled us to understand how to work with each other, and it attracted outstanding customers. It allowed trust to develop quicker between us and the customer. It really postured Wetterau as a public company differently than others in the same category in which we worked."

Many employees viewed working at Wetterau as a deeper experience beyond just going to a job. "[The Wetterau company culture] was defined by how you dealt with people every day," explains Darryl Long, 22-year Wetterau Inc. veteran, who led store development and operations. "It's powerful because *The Creed* created such a positive environment. It wasn't like getting up in the morning and putting a coat and tie on because you have a job. It was more like putting on a coat and tie and dancing out of the house because you love what you are doing. And you can't wait to deal with the people you're dealing with, and you can't wait to do something good. It just affected you every day. *The Creed* was the embodiment of what you stood for and what everybody you worked with stood for. It just created such a positive environment," says Long.

CHAPTER 3: A NEW WETTERAU WORLD

The Creed impacted more than just those who worked at Wetterau, Long goes on to explain: "Our customers were happy and they were growing [because of it]. And it permeated my family [as well]. How can you measure the value of something that includes not only the employees and the customers but all of our families? Because of what I carried from *The Creed* my family knew I wasn't getting up just to go to work — they knew it was a part of my life and something I looked forward to. As a result, if I needed to do something last-minute [at work] I didn't need to hang my head — my family supported me because work was an extended part of the family, they were helping me do it. And not only my wife and kids, but my parents. It was amazing!"

"I always felt like I was a very important part of the company," says Debbie Thompson, who served as Mark's assistant at Wetterau Inc. and later at Wetterau Associates for several years. "And I think everybody felt that all the way down to the warehouseman who drove the forklift. [Leadership] had a way with names and they remembered everybody. They lived *The Creed*: 'Treat others the way you want to be treated.'"

Debbie says those examples inspired her to improve personally. "There's no doubt that *The Creed* made me a better person because I saw how the upper echelon treated people and I thought, 'I can do that. *I can do that!*' I did volunteer more and still do volunteer. …*The Creed* has helped me to really look at people, more than just superficially and have compassion for them."

"If you work for a company that has a creed and the philosophy that it holds, over time you want to live that creed," explains Duane Daniels of how it affected so many Wetterau associates personally, including him. "It goes into your personal life and everything else. … It's a fundamental belief that you start living and becomes a mindset, a feeling. It's about integrity, fairness, and the values that you want to have. It was just the way we went about doing business."

This way of conducting business, by being true to the company's "conscience" embodied in *The Creed*, seemed to pay dividends year after year and decade after decade. "What Wetterau did right was they surrounded themselves with good people," adds Duane, "people who shared the same vision, who shared the same philosophy [of *The Creed*]. Those who didn't, didn't last long. ... The bottom line was 'treat others like you want to be treated.' That extends to the whole business relationship. That's how they ran the company. That was the key."

Despite all the success within the company, however, the tide outside it was turning in the industry. In the late 1980s, the "big box" warehouse retail trend was on the rise and the independent retailer was slowly diminishing. "We had all these distribution centers to service independent retailers and some of our company-owned retail chains, but we didn't have enough money or the expertise to buy a bunch of chains throughout the country to support all those warehouse divisions," explains Conrad. "We also had all these great businesses: Save A Lot, Shop 'n Save, the frozen dough bakery business, Laneco, and others. So the bottom line was we were unclear about the future of the wholesale warehouses, because the independent retailer was becoming extinct."

With Ted's oversight, Mark, the newly appointed president and chief operating officer, was asked to lead the charge to evaluate the company and determine a new strategy for Wetterau Inc. With the help of investment bankers and private equity firms, Mark, Conrad, and the company's leadership team evaluated many options for more than a year and ultimately determined a strategy to sell off the food distribution/wholesale side of the business because it was low margin, and its customer base was slowly deteriorating. They would spin it off to one of the bigger industry players and then restructure the company in food manufacturing, with its retail and food processing entities, which represented the piece of business with the greatest growth potential in revenue.

The board of directors approved this strategy, and the company began to execute it. "But at the end of the day, no one wanted to buy the food distribution/wholesale business for the same reason — the dying independent retailer," recounts Conrad. "However, there were a number of interested parties that wanted the entire company because of all these jewels we had."

CHAPTER 3: A NEW WETTERAU WORLD

Wetterau received a generous offer from a large, national distributor that wanted to purchase the whole entity. The merger would enable Wetterau Inc. to keep the organization — and its values — intact. "When the offer came in, the decision had to be made," recalls Mark. "So we took it to the board, which determined that it was in the best fiduciary interest of our shareholders to let the whole company go."

"Dad was convinced that bucking a negative trend in this business was not good for the long-term," adds Conrad. "So as much as we wanted to continue to be a part of it, if we couldn't redesign Wetterau, we all believed the best thing to do for our shareholders was to maximize stock value by moving forward with the sale of the company."

After much deliberation and counsel, and while they were at the top of their game serving more than 2,750 supermarkets in 29 states, the board opted to sell Wetterau Inc. in 1991. The buyer (which Wetterau prefers not to reference by name herein) claimed a desire to perpetuate the deeply engrained values and rich culture that had permeated the Wetterau family of companies for generations, and Ted, Conrad, and Mark would remain leaders in the new entity, along with support from many of their fellow associates.

"It was a big acquisition for [the buyer]," explains Mark, of the bittersweet decision. "You had the number two and number three wholesalers in the U.S. coming together, forming the number one in the country — in the world, basically."

A match made in heaven ... or so it seemed.

Culture Clash

Despite extensive due diligence beforehand, champagne celebrations, and a hopeful horizon, what seemed like a win-win partnership on paper soon turned to a sour reality. After the deal was done, it didn't take long to see that the cultures between the two businesses would clash, and the integrity of *The Creed* would be compromised.

"There was such a difference in the culture of that organization at the time and the quality of our folks at Wetterau," recalls Mark. "Their associates were bright and very sharp, but a lot of these people were 'eight-to-fivers' and it was more about their paychecks. It wasn't about the belief in the business itself and what they were trying to do. Wetterau folks truly believed in and loved the business and yes, it was a paycheck, but really felt like an extended family."

"There was a philosophy [within the purchasing company] that everyone was replaceable," explains Bill Pocilujko, who worked for the new entity for three years. He says associates were required to re-interview for their jobs periodically. "You always felt threatened. Instead of negotiating union contracts they would tell the membership that they had two weeks to decide if they wanted the proposed offer or they would be replaced. It really gave me a better understanding of different values [outside of Wetterau]." From a retail perspective, Merwyn Sher describes it as "a betrayal — the company changed from being your partner to somebody you didn't even know. It was a completely different feel."

Duane Daniels, who worked for the new entity in various leadership roles for a few years after the sale, explains that part of the problem was that there weren't any feelings within the new company at all. "It was all very matter-of-fact," he recalls. "It was just all business. They didn't have a personal side to them. There's some good with that, but there's also a lot of bad." Communication, for instance, was ineffective according to Duane. "They didn't know how to communicate the benefits of changes and why we might want to do something different. They didn't try to sell us [on a new or different idea], they just came in and told us we were doing it."

Compared to the warm, family-like atmosphere at Wetterau, it's no wonder that Conrad describes the new purchaser as "a big, cold machine, a very arrogant company," and explains that the culture gap between the two organizations soon proved to be too much to overcome. *The Creed* was no longer a priority and wasn't visible (literally or figuratively) in the facilities. Philanthropic efforts, which had been part of the Wetterau legacy for decades, were dismissed as "non-contributors" to the financial bottom line. Christmas parties were halted, along with the signature Wetterau trips — deemed unnecessary by the new entity. And many talented people from Wetterau were either let go or left the company on their own.

"It was a bad time for everybody," explains Darryl Long, one of the few Wetterau managers retained at the new organization, "because we just loved who we worked for [at Wetterau]. We loved the company, felt that we were a part of it, that we had influence and that our voice was heard. And we knew those days were going away."

Darryl witnessed valued artifacts, including the framed Creed wall hangings and legacy photos tossed out, so he secretly picked them out of the garbage and distributed them to Ted and other Wetterau executives. He adds that while he actually made more money at the new company, he would have gone back to Wetterau in a heartbeat, "because money isn't everything."

"We felt like they lied to us, like they deceived us and weren't following through with what they had agreed to," adds Conrad. "Dad was hurt severely by the way things were handled. He wanted to believe they would be true to their word — he always gave people the extra benefit of the doubt, that second chance, sometimes that third chance — so he was really disappointed." Conrad recalls that "it wasn't a healthy situation for [Dad, Mark, or me] to be a part of. It was like we were just puppets, and they were trying to use us as Wetteraus to help get the transition done. And we didn't feel comfortable, like we were trying to be something we weren't. Obviously, Mark and I said we didn't want to be a part of that. So Mark left first, then I left about six months later, and finally, after another six months or so, Dad got the hell out of there."

"They were radically different," observed mergers and acquisitions expert, Brent Baxter, of the two cultures as he took part in the transition. "The national [U.S.] data actually says that 60 to 70 percent of all acquisitions fail to achieve the objectives of the acquirer. And overwhelmingly the number one reason for failure is cultural mismatch or lack of cultural fit. On paper, they were very similar companies: grocery wholesalers, selling independently to retailers, they both owned some grocery store chain businesses," Baxter continues. "But in the day-to-day operations they could not have been more different. Wetterau was a relationship-driven company, a values-driven organization. And [the acquirer] was very empirical, very numbers oriented, and my perception is that they understood that and were very intentional in imposing their culture on Wetterau. To say it more bluntly, [they were intent on] eradicating or eliminating the Wetterau culture. Both [companies had] successful performances, so I don't want to draw necessarily a complete judgment about right or wrong, but there is very little question in my mind that what appeared to be very similar businesses were run in radically different ways."

Baxter goes on to explain that mergers and acquisitions in general are often "all about numbers and present values and spreadsheets." The ability to assess culture or why a company is actually successful is a much more intangible thing. "But it's really what drives the value of any company," he adds.

Underscoring Baxter's point, some analysts claim that the merger failure number is even higher with cultural incompatibilities. *Forbes* writer, George Bradt, claims that 83 percent of business mergers fail in large part because of incompatible cultures. "When you merge cultures well, value is created. When you don't, value is destroyed," says Bradt. "While some will suggest other factors — silly things like objectives and strategies and implementations — they are all derivative. The game is won or lost on the field of cultural integration. Get that wrong and nothing else matters."

Larry Senn, founder and chairman of the world's first culture-shaping firm, Senn Delaney (now part of Heidrick Consulting), calls this "cultural clash" and claims the success of a merger has more to do with culture than whether or not companies have exactly the right systems in place, which organizations tend to focus on the most.

But in Wetterau's case, it wasn't all for naught. There were certainly many learnings and even warnings that helped prepare Mark and Conrad Wetterau for the next step in their future. "When you're buying a business, you've got to be aware of what you're acquiring," explains Mark, having since experienced numerous mergers and acquisitions. "And it's really, truly understanding not only the acquirer's strategy and structure, which is the great people, but truly understanding the culture and how it fits within the culture of your current organization. If it doesn't fit, it's an alarm. If you still want to go through with the deal because the people are so good, look at it as an enhancer for your organization. But be careful not to be too hasty. Take your time because at some point, you'll end up with one culture surviving over the other. You can't have multiple ideologies."

A New Dawn: Wetterau Associates

After the disappointing "merger," the Wetteraus took some time to take stock and regroup. "We thought, 'Now what are we going to do?'" recalls Conrad, "[but] we started to mend," and he, Mark, and Ted set up a new office in Brentwood, Missouri where they launched their newest venture: Wetterau Associates, LLC.

As the first to head out on his own, Mark took the lead on establishing Wetterau Associates. One of the first steps was to bring in Debbie Thompson, his long-time executive assistant at Wetterau Inc. to provide support during the organization of the new entity. A few months later, Mark asked Mike Waitukaitis, a strong financial expert with proficiency in mergers and acquisitions — who had worked for more than a decade for Wetterau Inc., to join him. Together he, Mike, and Debbie created a business plan and an acquisition strategy for the company.

"Mike could not have been a better partner because of his personality," explains Conrad, who orchestrated his own departure from the acquirer and joined the new Wetterau team six months later. "Mark and I are more volatile, and Mike is a very even-keeled guy and can handle the egos of the two of us," he says with a laugh. "It just works. Mike, Mark, and I have never had a cross word as partners. It's been a good relationship now for decades."

Mark concurs: "Mike is just an excellent partner, a great compliment to Conrad and me. In the early foundational stages of the company, once the business plan was established, Mike was critical in helping execute the strategy that had been set forth. He was key in leading the analysis of the industry and the deals that were out there, and because of his unique background and excellent track record with Wetterau Inc. and PriceWaterhouseCoopers, he was able to not only be a great representative as a lead negotiator, but he was extremely effective on the accounting side and the legal side of these deals," says Mark. "He was a real good balance for Conrad and me as we mainly focused on the business aspects and where we were going to go with the company, so the success of Wetterau Associates is equally attributed to him."

"We're a good match," agrees Mike, of the long-term trust that has existed among the team for more than 40 years. "They wanted to grow via acquisitions, and I felt flattered, frankly, that they came to me and made me that offer."

Once Ted had fulfilled his commitment to work for 12 months to help transition the entity that had purchased Wetterau Inc., he was able to walk away from the failed acquisition and join Wetterau Associates as an advisor. Nearly a year after its inception, Ted was finally free to unite his talents with those of the new Wetterau team, where he consulted and advised the ambitious, up-and-coming group.

So with *The Creed* back on the wall and its power and efficacy still alive and well in their hearts, the small-yet-mighty team at Wetterau Associates ventured on to new frontiers.

CHAPTER 3: A NEW WETTERAU WORLD

Wetterau Incorporated

The 1869 Club: Gone but Not Forgotten

With the launch of Wetterau Associates, Wetterau Inc. was not to be forgotten. Many mourned the loss of their beloved company that had enriched their lives for decades, even generations. Naturally, the associates kept in contact with each other to the point that shortly after the sale in the early '90s they started the "1869 Club" (honoring George Wetterau's 1869 founding of the original company), which continued for years.

The group held two major events a year: an annual Christmas party and a summer golf outing, both in the St. Louis area and both well-attended. Even subgroups like the accounting and data processing teams established their own reunions, continuing them even after Ted's passing in 2003. The Wetterau Retiree group, which was established before the company sale, also continued to meet.

"They all longed for some connection to those people during that [Wetterau] time frame," recalls Andy Blassie, who says he went through a grieving period when he left Wetterau. "When you loved it as much as I did it was like your family had died and you had to adjust.... It was a large company, yet it was the wonderfully small family values that allowed a big company to stay really close," something that intrigued outside observers. "We built a core of relationships that was unusual, over and above the running of a business," said Ted to Margie Manning, a reporter at the *St. Louis Business Journal* in 2002, just a year before his death. In her report, Manning wrote about the executives' careers beyond Wetterau Inc.: "They have stayed friends, getting together at the 1869 Fellowship Group," commenting on the unique bond and camaraderie that they shared.

"I believe what goes around comes around," explains Darryl Long, who later ran Lucia's Pizza, a company that he had acquired with Wetterau Associates and former Wetterau consultant, Brent Baxter, of Clayton Capital Partners. Though the company has since been sold, Darryl says he sought to perpetuate *The Creed* during his leadership of Lucia's and continues that promotion today in his current business dealings. "You treat everybody as you want to be treated, and long-term it comes back around, it really does. The whole experience enriched my life, including the numerous times we got together after the company was sold. We all talked about our time at Wetterau. We're proud of it and we miss it. We talk about the next time we can get back together. It's just powerful stuff, it really is. So I try to recreate it where I can."

"The Wetterau days were phenomenal," adds Bill Pocilujko, who later transitioned into Golden State Foods, a Wetterau Associates company. "There was no other way to put it. Everybody cared for everybody. We have such great memories, and I wouldn't change a thing."

SECTION 2

Adopting *The Creed* into Other Companies

Photos (left to right):

1) Quality Beverage company logo

2) Wetterau Associates partners, Mark Wetterau, Conrad Wetterau, and Mike Waitukaitis sharing a toast with one of their customer's products

3) QB truck displaying one of the brands (Budweiser) of its customer, Anheuser-Busch/InBev

4) Conrad and Mark Wetterau demonstrating their partnership in front of Quality Beverage's Creed

CHAPTER 4

Blazing New Trails — Acquiring Quality Beverage and Quality Values

"The Creed is a powerful enabler for us to align as an organization to help our associates and customers succeed."

–**Mark Wetterau** (1958–2023)
Chairman and CEO, Golden State Foods (1998–2023)
Chairman and CEO, Quality Beverage (1993–1998)

"It's a part of what we represent. It's a part of who we are and how we try to live our lives within the framework and the walls of our companies every day."

–**Conrad Wetterau** (1956–   )
Chairman, Golden State Foods (2023–present)
President and CEO, Quality Beverage (1998–2023)

While parting ways with their intended merger was not the most pleasant experience, it gave the Wetterau family an opportunity to start fresh — with their values, through Wetterau Associates. With *The Creed* as their frontrunner and firm foundation, the new partnership — Mark, Conrad, and Ted Wetterau and Mike Waitukaitis, along with the support of executive assistant, Debbie Thompson — blazed a new trail of possibility, creating opportunities for themselves and others that would enable even greater success.

"We probably worked harder than we ever had," recalls Mark of the new start-up. "We're talking a 'seven-day burn!' We also didn't have a lot of money at the time, so if we couldn't make this new entity work, we thought we were going to have to go get 'real jobs!'" he says with a laugh.

Despite the uncertainty, the team remained optimistic and encountered a number of business opportunities in a variety of forms. These included various distributorships, retail stores, pharmaceutical ventures, and others — some of which came as a direct result of *The Creed* in action.

After evaluating several opportunities, Wetterau Associates opted to greenfield three Save A Lot retail stores in the Carolinas and later sold them. At the same time, the team was invited to bid for an Anheuser-Busch (AB) distributorship in New England that was coming up for sale. Established in 1986, Quality Beverage (QB) was a thriving distributor owned by the Moran family, who had been in the beer business since 1936, and who also owned another AB distributorship that serviced the entire state of Rhode Island. The Morans were contemplating a change of ownership and Wetterau Associates was one of several companies considered for the purchase.

"We wanted to turn the company over to someone who had similar core values as we had," explains Tim Moran, the eldest son of the family, who comes from generations of devout Catholics. Like the Wetteraus, the Morans also sought to treat their associates with dignity, respect, and even "reverence," as Tim's father, John, encouraged. "We love people. The employees are the ones who make things work," says Tim, who served as president of Quality Beverage for nearly a decade during the Morans' ownership and encouraged an open-door policy. "You can direct them all you want but unless they buy into it, it's not going to work. So we empowered our employees to make decisions. And we wanted someone who was going to be involved with them day to day, someone who knew how to deal with people."

When the Morans decided to sell the QB business, there were several interested parties which they evaluated, but the Wetteraus stood out from the start.

"It just made sense," explains Tim, "with leaders like the Wetteraus, who wanted to continue the way the company had been run as a family business. They're people who understand people, how to empower people, and say, 'job well done!' and be down there with them [on the floor], and not just sit up in their hallowed office."

After a few months of due diligence on all the contenders, the Moran family opted to go with the Wetteraus, in large part because of *The Creed* and the Wetterau example, which demonstrated their deeply held values. "Tim Moran was open about how impressed he was with our creed," recalls Mark. "He told us that the Morans knew we would take care of their people and that we would take care of their business they had worked so hard to build." So once they agreed on the price, Quality Beverage became a Wetterau Associates company in September of 1994.

"The Wetterau family was just really great," says Tim, of the negotiation process. He acknowledges that it can be a challenging transition for employees, especially when former leaders had been so involved with them on a daily basis and were well-respected. But in this case the transition was smooth because of the common philosophies and leadership approaches among the owners.

"I can't say enough about how [the Wetteraus] handled the whole thing," says former Quality Beverage Vice President and General Manager Tom Nicholson, who was initially recruited to the company by Tim Moran in 1989, and who also made a pitch with a partner to purchase the company. "It was just aces, really."

"The [Morans] were very good, and it was tough to hear, 'We're being sold! Where do we go from here?'" says former controller and current

Executive Vice President Ted Audet, a four-year employee at the time who is still with the company more than 30 years later. "And then we end up with Mark and Conrad who were just great. Both sides just kind of hit it off, and we worked really well from the get-go," he says. "We were very fortunate."

Perhaps the Wetteraus were so effective in their leadership style with the Quality Beverage team because not long before, they had been on the other side of the table with the Wetterau Inc. purchase. Maybe they understood a little more clearly how those who were being bought out might feel and they developed a unique sense of empathy. "An organization reflects the head," adds Audet. "And the Wetterau family, they're just good people. And they told us that the employees are pretty darn important. [So we concluded that] they were good enough and got behind it."

With positive feelings all around, Mark, Conrad, and Mike Waitukaitis headed for QB's headquarters in Taunton, Massachusetts and brought with them experience and expertise in the sales and distribution business, which they had managed at Wetterau Inc. Mark headed up the organization as chairman and chief executive officer, Conrad led as president and chief operating officer, and Mike served as chief financial officer. All three leaders served on the board of directors, along with Ted Wetterau, who acted as an advisor to the board. Tom Nicholson remained Quality Beverage's general manager and oversaw sales and marketing. "We all found our niches and just kind of took our roles," explains Conrad. "It was a little crowded, but we were all so thankful to be there and were excited about the new business we owned on our own."

Photo (next page):
Conrad and Mark Wetterau take an equal seat at Wetterau Associates, as they partner together, along with Mike Waitukaitis (who took the photo).

Sibling Rivalry?

Conrad and Mark Wetterau had served together for many years prior to acquiring Quality Beverage. They pledged the same fraternity in college, worked closely together at Wetterau Inc., and of course spent time together as a family. But could two highly competitive brothers who were establishing themselves as leaders in their own right work effectively together in this new, small company, where there wasn't quite as much elbow room?

Considering some of their shenanigans growing up, it might be hard to imagine. As teenagers, the brothers brought new meaning to the term, "sibling rivalry." They wielded their young prowess through an array of debates and disagreements, drag racing each other in their self-built cars, and even battling in an occasional fist fight.

"We fought all the time," admits Conrad, of their high school years. "We punched each other, and I threw a bamboo spear at him one time that almost put his eye out," he says with a hint of pride regarding his accuracy. "Another time I was chasing Mark through the house because he did something to aggravate me, and he grabbed the door and slammed it right as I ran full speed into it," which left Conrad with a bump between his two black eyes.

The behavior was somewhat typical of many young brothers perhaps, who were competing for their place in the sun. But possibly the most cutting was a prom-night fender bender that really made the sparks fly, maybe because it involved something so close to their hearts: their beloved cars!

"We were both going to the prom and I've got my girlfriend in my car, and Mark was in his car with his date," shares Conrad. "Then all of a sudden, Mark stops in the middle of these big speed bumps and I slammed on my breaks and rammed right into him. We both got out of our cars, our girlfriends are still inside, and we're screaming at each other at the top of our lungs in the middle of a subdivision!" Mark still laughs about that one. "That was some night," he grins.

While both admit to some teenage bickering and competitive antics, eventually the brothers worked through their adolescent differences to become two of the most effective sibling partnerships in business. "We became really close," says Conrad, of their relationship over the years. "It really started with Dad." Conrad and Mark both credit Ted for encouraging cooperation among them, as he made it a point to take them to special dinners and sporting events, and on trips. "He'd talk to us about how important it would be if the two of us could really work together without internal jealousies or egos," Conrad continues. "He said that if we could just set those aside, that our strengths could complement each other, and we could be far greater collectively than we could be on our own."

The brothers listened and nurtured the relationship. They spent more time together. They even started a small partnership in their 20s around their shared passion for cars called MarCon Limited — a collector car ownership business. They began by putting in $5,000 each and started buying, rebuilding, and selling cars. Everything was 50-50. They've since bought, sold, and rebuilt dozens of cars and the bi-coastal business continued until 2023.

"There's just a strong respect and deep love we have for one another," says Conrad. "We park our egos at the door when it comes to business and we try to do the right thing. And I wouldn't trade that for anything in the world. I'd give up all the business, all the success, everything, to keep that relationship."

Mark certainly agrees. "Conrad's my best friend," he says. "We talk almost every day. He advises me when I need it and I do the same for him. But we respect each other enough to allow one another to make our own decisions as the leaders of our own companies. We don't tell each other what to do. We just give our opinions and then allow each other to make our own decisions. We have a very strong relationship, and it means a great deal to me."

CHAPTER 4: BLAZING NEW TRAILS

> "It's not that we don't have arguments, because I think that's healthy," adds Conrad. "But at the end of the day, we work together on whatever the decision is that needs to be made. Selflessness is really the key. And we're brothers, we're blood, and we're best friends."

Growing Quality Beverage and Rolling Out *The Creed*

As it turns out, they all could work together — quite effectively, in fact. Under Wetterau Associates' leadership, Quality Beverage quickly grew from being one of the largest independent Anheuser-Busch beer distributors in Massachusetts, to the largest in the state, and eventually in the entire New England region. And the influence of *The Creed* lived on. But before they formally introduced *The Creed* into QB, Mark, Conrad, and Mike alluded to it during their first meeting with all the employees.

"It was out on the loading dock," recalls Tom Nicholson of the employee gathering. Many Quality Beverage associates admired the previous owners and were skeptical of the new ones. "They mentioned *The Creed* and told the people that it was how they wanted to do business at QB, which actually put us at ease because when they said they wanted the Golden Rule, [even though] it was all words at that point [and] they hadn't proven it yet, at least you hear it and think, 'Well, maybe this is a good thing. I'll give it a chance.'"

"We did it right out of the box," says Mark, of the importance of sharing their values with the associates earlier than later, even before the official roll out of *The Creed*, which would need management input and approval. "*The Creed* is a powerful enabler for us to align as an organization to help our associates and customers succeed," says Mark, "so it was important to get it in front of the associates as soon as possible to assure them that we had a philosophy similar to the former owners. We were excited to build upon what the Morans had already established."

Conrad says that bringing up *The Creed* early (within the first few months of their new ownership) was just doing what they had been taught. "We talked with Tom and Ted [Audet] about what *The Creed* was at Wetterau and went through it together, explaining that we needed to develop some sort of philosophical road map for the company. 'It doesn't have to be exactly what it says here,' we told them, 'but we need a statement bold enough to convey that this is how we want to live our lives within the walls of Quality Beverage. And here's the starting point: the Wetterau Creed. Now, how can we adapt this into our company?'"

Audet recalls how they gathered the leadership together and went over it. "They presented *The Creed* to us to see if we wanted to change it," he says. "But they didn't tell us that their dad and his management team had written it [back in the early '70s]," which he found interesting. "And I thought, 'I can live with this.'"

As a person of faith, Audet adds that *The Creed* felt comfortable to him personally, and it also seemed to align with the existing company culture. "We do this all the time already," he says about what he thought when he first heard it, wondering why QB needed something in writing. But he soon realized that "if you're looking through that prism of 'what's the right way to run our business?' then [a written creed] seemed to be a good idea."

"To me, the biggest thing in *The Creed* is about doing things the right way," explains Tom, who resonated with *The Creed* from the start. "And the fact that we were dealing with so many independently owned retailers as customers that we care about, it really was a perfect fit in that way."

So the leadership team agreed to incorporate the Wetterau Creed into Quality Beverage virtually as it stood, with just a few minor edits. "It actually integrated almost exactly," says Conrad. "We didn't have to make hardly any changes because it fit the QB business model, which was no different than a distribution center at Wetterau Inc., and because the independent retailer is the backbone of QB. We had very little chain business in our market at the time; it was primarily independent retailers, so it just made sense to leave it pretty much the same. We [simply] called it the Quality Beverage Creed instead of the Wetterau Creed."

The only minor updates that were made were to its first line: "We believe in one God and the dignity of man" was changed to "We believe in one God and the dignity of *all people*." While it was commonplace during Ted Wetterau's era to interpret "man" or "mankind" as generic for men and women, Mark and Conrad and their leadership team felt more comfortable modernizing it to "all people" to avoid any misinterpretations.

Additionally, the language of "one" God earlier in that line was omitted two decades later. This was done to represent a broader inclusion of various religious philosophies that still maintained a belief in God, however those faiths defined it.

(Quality Beverage Creed shown on next page.)

The Quality Beverage Creed

We believe in **God** and the dignity of **all people.**

We believe that people should be treated as we would like to be treated, and this applies to the welfare of our employees and their families, to our suppliers and all with whom we do business.

We believe that successful independent business is the backbone of our country, that our success is closely related to the success of our retail customers, and that only by working together can the ultimate success of both partners be assured.

We, therefore, dedicate ourselves to work for our mutual success and we pledge our best efforts always toward the attainment of our common goal.

Rolling Out the Quality Beverage Creed Companywide

Once the language of *The Creed* was agreed upon by the leadership team, it was time to share it with the entire company. Months of preparations were made before the actual rollout. *The Creed* was printed on signs, plaques, new business cards, and even ceiling danglers, which were displayed throughout the office and the warehouse. Then at the kick-off of the company's new fiscal year in 1995, the leadership introduced it to all the associates.

"It was during a breakfast event in the warehouse with all the employees," says Conrad. "Mark and I explained the history of *The Creed* and how our father and his management team instituted it into the company, and how it helped the organization succeed. We talked about carrying on this tradition [at Quality Beverage] in the spirit of the Wetterau Creed. And then we unveiled it."

"It was exciting to finally get to that point," says Mark, of officially implementing *The Creed* into the company. "Overall, we felt like it was very well-received and accepted because of all the prep work over the prior months, so it wasn't a big surprise to them. Making it official seemed to really energize the associates and move them to the next level."

But there was still a bit of trepidation about *The Creed* among some associates. "I think the first sentence probably scared some people right off the bat," recalls Vice President and Chief Operating Officer Steve Doherty, a 43-year employee who had been with the company for about 14 years at the time. "When you bring God into anything these days, everybody tries to be so politically correct that you can't [really talk about it]. God to you may be different than God to me, so really it's just a word for whatever you're using to identify what your faith is."

Once the employees understood that *The Creed* is broad enough to encompass many faiths, Doherty says that it helped remove the "guess work" for existing and new employees — many of whom came from different backgrounds — about what was expected from them at the company. "As you're walking up the stairs [in the lobby of our building] and you see

The Creed, you know, 'This is what we want to do. This is what we believe the company should be.' It's like a road map or as Anheuser-Busch put it, 'guard rails.' *The Creed* is sort of like guard rails as to how we'd like our people to be here in the company and out in the world. You read it and there's nothing in it you haven't heard before from your parents or your church or your school or whatever. But especially when change is occurring (like company leadership and ownership), you look at it and say, 'You know what? It's not a bad thing.'"

Walking the Talk

It didn't take long to move beyond the words into action. QB employees began to see that the leadership did indeed, walk the talk. "Their actions every day really did show it," explains Tom Nicholson, of the examples that Mark and Conrad set. "They are very sincere. The way they get along with each other and all those around them, and the way they make time for people — they really do have [*The Creed*] in them." Speaking to that point, Conrad has said this about the way *The Creed* has been woven into the fabric of the company and into the Wetterau family: "It's a part of what we represent. It's a part of who we are and how we try to live our lives within the framework and the walls of our companies every day."

"You learn by example," says Steve Doherty. "Ninety-nine percent of the time we get a good example from these guys living *The Creed*, so I try to follow their precedent with my people, and then the next level of managers does well by their people, and it just sort of works. There are no huge mood swings around here. And if you get treated right by your bosses, you're going to do the extra things it takes to make sure your little part of the world gets taken care of the right way."

"I try to treat people like I want to be treated," says Tom Clark, former director of operations at QB, who says that he respected *The Creed* when he first joined the company in 1998. "If I respect the people who work for me, then they're going to give me respect, too."

Higher Productivity through the Golden Rule

Those leadership examples soon flowed throughout management and the rest of the company. Managers and supervisors would often arrive early just to visit with their teams and see how they were. They made time to talk with them about their work and their lives. They showed appreciation for good effort and overtime and rewarded their employees accordingly. True to Ted Wetterau form, they even extended modest loans, in some cases, to associates in need.

"It's the Golden Rule: treat people the way you want to be treated," says Tom Nicholson. "That alone to me is *The Creed*. And we do that with our people. I think that's why you see associates around here all the time [even beyond work hours]. … I just think that you get a lot more done by working with your people and being fair and honest with them."

"You just get so much more accomplished," says Steve Doherty, when it comes to problem-solving and addressing issues. "And it can work everywhere. It can work supplier to wholesaler, or wholesaler to retailer. It can work retailer to customer. It can work employee to employee." Nicholson emphasizes how much this meant to Quality Beverage retailers: "I think they took *The Creed* to heart when they read the sections of it that applied to them. To find that [the new leadership] really did want to work with them made them want to work with us."

Communication and Resolving Issues Fairly

Even when there are issues, Doherty says that *The Creed* can serve as a subtle reminder that they can be solved in a civil manner. "There's always going to be some problem somewhere," he explains. "Communication, execution, something, but there's no reason to blow a gasket over it. We're going to fix it somehow by dealing with people the way that we like to be talked to."

Steve incorporates specific strategies to deal with communication issues. "Most every week I write [a note to myself] — 'Listen and relax' or something like that," he shares candidly. "So when somebody comes in here and there's a problem, I don't try to fix it before I have all the information. When I was a [young] supervisor, I went off half-cocked more times that I can remember. I don't like people doing that to me when they don't know what the whole situation is. That's one of the things I've learned from Wetterau leadership is to get all the information you can in a timely manner and then make a decision based on that. And there are very few screaming matches in this building about anything. People's tempers go up and down now and then depending on the situation, but it is a very friendly environment, a very professional company."

"We see examples all the time of people [living the Golden Rule] in our employees and their families and our suppliers and even our vendors," adds Ted Audet, citing examples of partnering with the unions and QB's banks, for instance, openly, fairly, and equitably during financial transactions or when negotiating salary contracts. He encourages forthright transparency during these types of negotiations. "Don't beat around the bush," he says, of good news or bad. "If we're having a problem with the banks or the unions, then we try to tell them the way we want to progress. The truth will set you free."

Anheuser-Busch's Wholesaler of the Year Award

The fruits of *The Creed* in action went beyond the internal organization. Customers also took note. For instance, just a few years after instituting *The Creed* into Quality Beverage, the company won Anheuser-Busch's 1996 Wholesaler of the Year Award for the Northeast Region, a prestigious honor from the beverage giant. The award recognizes the system's best all-around wholesaler for a given year. "It was really a strong validation for *The Creed's* positive effects," says Mark, of what can be accomplished when associates align together with common values. "The entire team performed so well and was very deserving of that honor. We were really proud of all of them and appreciated the recognition from our customer."

CHAPTER 4: BLAZING NEW TRAILS

Leadership Changes and "The Main Thing:" How a Mission Statement Relates to a Creed

In the late '90s, Mark and Mike moved west to lead a newly acquired Wetterau Associates company, Golden State Foods, while remaining on QB's board of directors. As president, Conrad then took on the role of chief executive officer at QB. The company continued to move forward and with that progress, Conrad felt the need to simplify the focus for employees.

"I read the book, *Monday Morning Leadership* [by David Cottrell], and it was all about trying to keep things simple in your company," explains Conrad. "The simpler it is, the easier it is for people to follow and not screw up."

The Creed was already providing much of that simple guidance for the folks at QB, but Conrad felt that instituting a mission statement into the company would make it even easier for top leadership and associates alike to stay focused on the company's vision. So in 2004, the QB management team instituted "The Main Thing" of Quality Beverage, a simple, straightforward mission statement that company associates seek to achieve, along with the ideals of the QB Creed. The Main Thing, which focuses more on the vision for the company, has three main tenants:

1. Increase sales.
2. Provide exceptional service.
3. Build value and create opportunities.

Supporting direction within The Main Thing includes:

- Do it right the first time.
- Accept individual responsibility.
- Always look for a better way.
- Treat others the way that you want to be treated.

"It's basically our mission statement," explains Conrad, of the interplay between The Main Thing and *The Creed*. "It's very simple and very straightforward and it ties in with *The Creed*. But it is different. It's *what* we want to accomplish as a company, while *The Creed* is *how* we want to live our lives."

Main Thing
OF QUALITY BEVERAGE

- Increase Sales
- Provide Exceptional Service
- Build Value and Create Opportunities
- Do it Right the First Time
- Accept Individual Responsibility
- Always Look for a Better Way
- Treat Others the Way You Want to be Treated

"The Main Thing is great because it is so simple," says Tom Nicholson. "It is easy to keep the team focused on it, in addition to *The Creed*. *The Creed* is about our ideals and *how we* do things, but The Main Thing is *what* we do. So it clarifies things. But the biggest part [that's included] in both is 'treating others the way you want to be treated.'"

"Both The Main Thing and *The Creed* give Quality Beverage employees something to aspire to," notes Steve Doherty. "Both of them are pretty high standards, and I think if you hold yourself to them, you're not going to get it every time, but you will have something to strive for. It's a constant, continuous effort that reminds everybody about how we should do things."

With the QB Creed front and center supported by The Main Thing, Quality Beverage was on its way to continued growth and expansion. Enhancing its company culture of dignity and respect continued to be a top objective of its leaders, which helped sharpen the focus of the organization more keenly on what's most important — people.

Photos (left to right):
1) Mark and Conrad Wetterau present the 1997 "Spirit of the Creed" award to QB associate, Dot Fogerty, who went on to win it two more times after that. The award in Taunton is now called the "Dot Fogerty Spirit of the Creed Award" after her.

2) Truck and driver from Williams Distributing, a QB acquisition

3) QB team earns Anheuser-Busch's 1996 New England Wholesaler Sales Team of the Year Award: Michael Buffer (celebrity ring announcer); Tim Brown (Anheuser-Busch); Paul Doherty (Anheuser-Busch); Conrad Wetterau (Quality Beverage); Mark Wetterau (Quality Beverage); Pat Stokes (Anheuser-Busch).

4) Quality Beverage headquarters in Taunton, Massachusetts

CHAPTER 5

The Creed in Action Enhances a Positive Company Culture at Quality Beverge and Opens New Windows of Opportunity

"Because of the Wetteraus, at a time when we could have lost everything, we instead achieved a life-long dream. And we get our cultural DNA from the Wetterau Creed."

–David Fields (1970–   )
Founding Partner and CEO (2010–present),
Wormtown Brewery

New Acquisitions: Consolidated Beverages and Williams Distributing Co.

In 2006, Wetterau Associates acquired the majority ownership of another Anheuser-Busch distributorship, Consolidated Beverages, LLC of Auburn, Massachusetts, and in 2013 Quality Beverage purchased the remaining ownership. This merger transformed QB into one of the largest independently owned beer wholesalers in the New England region. But one of the primary enablers of the purchase was QB's Creed in action.

"I had been observing [the Wetteraus] from a distance," says Ronnie Fields, one of the Consolidated Beverages owners and its equity agreement manager, who was considering a change in partnership. "I could see what their business creed was and that they were the real deal. They weren't just investors. I saw their involvement. I saw the kind of people they were — they treated their [associates] well. And they were always nice to talk to. The conversations were always great. So I always hoped to be able to do business with them some day."

Over the course of a decade or so, Conrad, Mark, and Ronnie had developed a friendship, as they operated businesses in neighboring areas. They bought and sold cars together with Ronnie's son, David Fields, and they rode motorcycles together and occasionally hung out on weekends. So when it came time for the Fields to evaluate their partnership in Consolidated Beverages, they turned to QB. "My dad said to me, 'Call the Wetteraus,'" recalls David. "he said, 'Conrad, Mark, and their team at their core are people you can lean on and trust with the leadership and guidance that we need. They're the sharpest, most capable team in the industry right now.'"

"It had to be the Wetteraus," remarks Ronnie of why he had encouraged David to give them a call. The Fields had many viable suitors for the business who would have loved a shot at it. "[But] there just wasn't going to be anyone else," he says.

Unlike many AB distributors, Ronnie had not been a generational owner of Consolidated Beverages, but rather earned the opportunity from Anheuser-Busch, whose leadership invited him to purchase it in 1985 from the original founder after Ronnie had worked for AB for about a decade. So the Fields needed some guidance from someone with experience buying, selling, and running successful businesses of this nature. Without knowing

CHAPTER 5: *THE CREED* IN ACTION

what role, if any, the team would play, Conrad offered Wetterau Associates' assistance to the Fields. "That's the epitome of *The Creed* [the Wetteraus live by]," says David. "No gain, just selflessness; a willingness to reach out and help someone when needed."

Even though Mark and Mike were busy leading Golden State Foods in California, they joined Conrad, Ted Audet, and Tom Nicholson, and with Mike's expertise, worked with the banks to help the Fields determine a fair market price for their company. After a series of events over the course of a few months — because of the deep trust that had developed through the years between the Fields and the Wetteraus — Ronnie and David offered Wetterau Associates an opportunity to join with them and buy out another partner for shared ownership of the company.

"This was a life-changing event for us," says David, who explains that due to the complex nature of the deal, they actually had a lot to lose, including the company itself. "We needed guidance. And we had all the information in front of us because of the Wetteraus." As the team celebrated the transaction, Ronnie announced that after observing Mark, Conrad, and Mike and getting to know them better over the years that he knew some day they would all be partners "because of the way they are."

This was very moving to Conrad, who says, "I'm prouder of that than anything we had done with that acquisition. That to me was as big of a compliment as anybody could ever pay. Here's an outsider who didn't know much about us really, other than what he observed, and yet he came back and said, 'Someday, I was hopeful that we would have an opportunity to do business together.' So I think that speaks for our training and what we stand for and what *The Creed* stands for because that's just how we live our lives."

"It's been a great partnership," says Ronnie, who describes it as "perfect — a great marriage, where everybody's happy." Complimenting the Wetteraus on their exemplary standards and ethics in 2015, he said, "It's too bad they're not running this country! Their ethics are beyond reproach."

"We were fortunate to find and work with these outstanding individuals with a philosophy of treating people well," adds Mark. "Because the Fields really did believe in those ideals, and they demonstrated it. Then we were blessed to have David step in as the general manager of Consolidated Beverages, which created continuity from father to son. With the beliefs in line and this seamless continuity, it made for a great partnership moving forward."

Due to the trust and solid relationships that continued to grow as partners over the years, when the Fields were ready to sell their remaining portion of the Consolidated Beverages partnership in 2013, they again turned to the Wetteraus with the opportunity. It didn't take long for the two parties to agree on price, and the transition was completed that year. "We have an enormous respect for the Wetteraus, who have implemented *The Creed* into all their companies, as well as into their families," adds David. He says he tries to emulate the principles of *The Creed* in his current company, Wormtown Brewery, his entrepreneurial dream made possible by the Consolidated Beverages partnership sale. "Because of the Wetteraus, at a time when we could have lost everything, we instead achieved a life-long dream," he continues. "And we get our cultural DNA from the Wetterau Creed."

Quality Beverage is currently Wormtown's largest supplier in central/eastern Massachusetts. David says that this alliance epitomizes the "mutual success" that *The Creed* encourages. "It just shows the synergy of our partnership," he explains, of the mutual growth of both companies in Taunton, one of the fastest-growing areas of the region.

In 2019, Quality Beverage acquired another regional distributor, Chicopee, Massachusetts-based Williams Distributing. With this purchase, QB grew to service more than 130 cities and towns throughout Massachusetts, delivering to over 3,200 retail-licensed accounts each week. The company employs more than 250 associates and ships millions of cases of product each year. Quality Beverage is the single-largest stand-alone beer distributor in Massachusetts, as well as the state's leading supplier of Anheuser-Busch, InBev, and Constellation Brands products. In 2023, QB's territory represented 45 percent of the state's geography and more than 50 percent of the malt beverage market share with all their collective brands.

"We have a wonderful portfolio, and we want to continue to build on that," says Conrad, about the growth the company's acquisitions have enabled. In order to manage the growth, QB has upgraded its operational systems, increased its brands, and multiplied its SKUs. "The business has gone through a huge transformation since '94, when Mark, Mike, and I [first] came in here to where it is today."

"The great things Conrad and the QB team have been able to accomplish over the years underscore the strength of that team to deliver the highest quality service to its customers," explains Mark. "Not only is it evidence of the power of teamwork, but it's also evidence of the power of *The Creed*," which is inherently about alignment on multiple levels, striving for the highest ideals."

Quality Growth and the "Spirit of the Creed"

As Quality Beverage continues to grow, *The Creed* remains a prominent motivator through an array of characteristics, programs, and practices throughout the company. For instance, similar to the recognition award at Wetterau Inc., QB has celebrated its own "Spirit of the Creed" award for more than two decades. Deemed the "most important award" by the QB leadership team, this annual honor recognizes two individuals (hourly and salaried) who best emulate *The Creed* for a given year. Peer-nominated then blind-selected by senior management and previous winners, the "Spirit of the Creed" award is cherished by its recipients.

"There's a lot of pride in winning this award," says Steve Doherty, who won it in 1999, explaining that it helps elevate behavior, unite employees, and underscores employee buy-in of *The Creed* in general. "It's a pretty cool thing to get your name up there and be recognized. It is a big deal. When associates hear about the good works that the award winners do, which have been illuminated by their peers, it emphasizes *The Creed's* credibility."

Charitable Service

Regarding matters of the heart, QB leadership and associates alike volunteer their time, talents, and treasure in a variety of ways for dozens of charitable organizations and causes. These include the Taunton Chamber of Commerce, Easter Seals, Toys for Tots, Boys and Girls Club of Taunton, and Dana Farber Cancer Institute, along with many others. They serve on boards, chair capital campaigns, and support organizations that their associates are passionate about.

"Being involved in the community and giving back is very important to us," says Conrad, following in the Wetterau family tradition — which has been inspired by *The Creed's* precepts to treat others the right way — as well as the example set by Anheuser-Busch. "We try to keep the money in the marketplace where we do business, and let it affect the communities that give back to us."

Conrad has personally served in leadership roles or supported a variety of charities, including Juvenile Diabetes Research Foundation (JDRF), Dana Farber Cancer Institute, Jimmy Fund (a branch of Dana Farber that focuses on children with cancer), and the Rodman Ride for Kids, which is the third-largest bicycle ride in the United States. He has been honored with a number of charitable awards, including a special recognition from JDRF for Man of the Year, after he started their first corporate campaign. "We're all active in the community, and we give a lot of stuff away," says Ted Audet. "And we try to treat people the right way." For instance, in 2019 QB received Easterseals of Massachusetts' annual Team Hoyt Award for their years of unwavering commitment to supporting individuals with disabilities. Likewise, Conrad, who chaired their annual fundraiser gala that year, accepted the award on behalf of the team and was also recognized as Easterseals' Man of the Year, the organization's highest honor. (For a complete list of Conrad Wetterau's awards and recognitions, please see *Appendix B*.)

CHAPTER 5: *THE CREED* IN ACTION

Teamwork, Camaraderie, and Family

Whether it's non-profit or for-profit service, one thing that's evident in the Quality Beverage leadership team over the years is the positive team spirit and camaraderie that exists among them. They all agree that *The Creed* continues to play a key role in that positive culture.

"There's definitely a comfort zone working here," says Steve Doherty, of the culture overall. "Ninety-eight percent of the people get along. Nobody's trying to cut your legs off to get ahead and nobody's trying to come in and make you look bad. It's not that kind of business culture."

"The people who work for me are very good," says Tom Clark. "That's the main thing. They're loyal to me, and I'm loyal to them. But you've got to produce. It's not like a job where you just come and go through the motions. You don't do that here. My people know what I expect, and we all do our part. Nobody's better than anyone else. We're all treated the same. And I think that goes a long way towards us all getting along and working well together."

The common sentiment is that QB's culture is one of cooperation and support, where people make efforts to get along. The leadership is approachable and works to respect others at each level. Extra hours worked are often rewarded. And both leadership and associates agree that success is a team effort, which is all driven by *The Creed*.

Tom Nicholson, who recently retired after a stellar 40-year career with QB says it wasn't easy for him to leave such a positive culture. "I just loved making a difference, trying to do something that mattered," he says. "I loved the people [and still do]. I love the fact that hundreds of families are making a living out of QB. It provides good-paying jobs and a great working environment for its people."

Since Tom's retirement, Ted Audet has taken over as executive vice president and chief operating officer. For many years during his tenure, he has recognized his fellow associates who exemplify the QB Creed with a special commemorative coin that says, "Thanks for doing the right thing."

Associates, retailers, and customers at all levels have been recognized for going the extra mile in their roles, taking special care to train someone effectively, or going out of their way to help other associates in a unique way. "It's *The Creed* in action," says Audet, who explains that it helps everyone become better together, every day.

"They definitely follow *The Creed*," says Tom Nicholson, of his former colleagues. "You probably wouldn't survive at Quality Beverage if you didn't."

And not just at work. It's clear that many QB associates "take *The Creed* home with them," in terms of its positive effects on their ethics and character, as well as influencing their families. *The Creed* has permeated the Audets' lives to such an extent that Ted's daughter, Andrea, actually created a college presentation about it. "She said, 'Dad, I did this whole thing on *The Creed!*'" shares Ted, of her enthusiasm.

"It's part of our culture, part of my culture," says Conrad, as he explains how *The Creed* has not only penetrated the company over the years, but how it's affected him personally. "It's part of who I am and what I stand for; it's part of how I try to live my life every day. It's a guiding light for how I run my businesses and my personal life."

And clearly a part of many QB associates companywide.

Low Turnover and Greener Pastures

It's possible that the company's low turnover rate is an indication of the general appreciation for and value placed on *The Creed* and all of its manifestations throughout the organization. "Most of the time, you'll find in any of the businesses that Mark and I have been involved in, there's very little turnover," explains Conrad of QB's lower-than-average exit rate. "Once they make the cut and they're on board, usually they don't want to leave because they realize how special it is. Sometimes people who have lived within our culture and *The Creed* for many years have aspirations that things are better somewhere else, and they leave us. Then they come back and say, 'Do you have an opening in the company anymore? Because I really thought the grass was greener on the other side and it isn't at all. I was spoiled, and I really didn't know what I had.' That has come back to us a lot over the years."

Steve Doherty has noticed similar trends: "We've had a number of associates for whom the grass did not turn out to be greener, leaving a very nice job to go somewhere else. We had a guy within four working days call back and say he made a mistake, and ask if he could come back to work for us. We've had others who thought they were going to make a lot more money, and it didn't pan out the way they wanted it to — in order to make that money, they had to do things they didn't think were ethical or moral."

Working through Its First Strike and Rebuilding Trust

Despite Quality Beverage's positive track record, the company has faced opposition along the way, challenging the long-held unity of its associates and leadership. In 2017, QB faced its first-ever strike in Taunton during labor negotiations with its local Teamsters union. During the 21-day strike — which was politically motivated by top union leaders seeking power — 45 drivers and warehouse workers surrounded the QB headquarters in Myles Standish Industrial Park, protesting the terms of the company's five-year collective bargaining agreement.

Leaders of QB were dismayed that their union employees rejected the contract proposal, offered in good faith and approved by elected representatives of the Teamsters. After all, their annual salaries and benefits were highly competitive within the company's stable, values-based culture.

About 10 days into the strike, the union and company representatives sat down for discussions. But they couldn't reach an agreement at this stage, so the strike continued.

Then during a final round of talks, with some help from union leadership, Quality Beverage was ultimately able to ratify a contract that was satisfactory to everyone for the entire term of the agreement. QB leaders said the pact was "well balanced, comprehensive, and addresses the needs of labor and management on a range of important issues, while ensuring the long-term viability of Quality Beverage."

"We always try to do the right thing for our people," explains Conrad, constantly seeking to take the high road. "We understood that this was a political strike driven by two top union managers, so we held our ground and didn't hold any animosity towards our people. In line with our Creed, we continued to demonstrate good faith during our talks at the table, and once we were aligned, we put it behind us, stayed positive, and moved forward together as a united team."

Turning the Page

During its near three decades of Quality Beverage ownership and leadership, Conrad, Mark and Mike have been fully dedicated to enhancing the culture and vitality of the organization, while working to dynamically grow the company. Whether it has been through productive day-to-day business activities, effective contract negotiations with the union, community leadership and service, or simply though the camaraderie of its team, this special organization has achieved a remarkable amount together with its upbeat company culture, solid ethics, and a bright spirit — the spirit of the QB Creed.

But in 2023, as this book was going to print, Wetterau Associates felt it was time to close their chapter with Quality Beverage. Following deep discussion and evaluation, the company was sold to the Martignetti Companies of Taunton, Massachusetts, New England's leading wine and spirits distributor, the fifth largest in the United States. At the time of sale, QB serviced approximately 3,200 accounts with a portfolio of more than 400 brands.

CHAPTER 5: *THE CREED* IN ACTION

"For almost 30 years, it has been one of the great joys of my life to own and lead this incredible company of incredible people," says Conrad Wetterau, as the outgoing president and CEO. "Soon my chapter will end and a new one will begin with the Martignetti family, who will continue leading with our common values. I feel confident that we have put all of our people in the best of hands going forward, ensuring Quality Beverage's future, financial strength, positive culture, and ability to grow."

"We are excited to add Quality Beverage to our company and to welcome their talented team," says Carl and Carmine Martignetti, principals of the Martignetti Companies. "We have known the Wetterau family for nearly three decades and have admired the values and commitments they have practiced every day in their company with employees, customers, and suppliers. We are committed to build upon that legacy and to provide new growth opportunities for the company and all those associated with it."

Mark Wetterau also commented on the likeminded culture of the Martignetti Companies and Wetterau Associates, which he says made the transition a smooth one. "We greatly appreciate our common values, people-first culture, and how they will continue on at Quality Beverage," says Mark. "We are grateful for the efforts that the Martignetti family have made to carry on these important standards and ideals at the company, which have made our organizations successful."

QB and the Next Gen: George Wetterau's Namesake Continues the Legacy

More than 150 years after George H. Wetterau ventured out into his first business in St. Louis, his namesake, George P. Wetterau (George Senior's great-great-grandson), continues the family legacy through his role at Quality Beverage.

"It's a huge responsibility," says George P., of not only continuing the family's good name and business reputation, but to effectively carry on the ethical tradition of *The Creed*. "It's important to me, and it's on my shoulders to keep the culture and the philosophy of *The Creed* going forward into the next generation."

Indeed, he stands on tall shoulders, as he joins leaders both past and present, who have so effectively led this charge. But despite that he's Conrad Wetterau's youngest child, nepotism has not necessarily paved him a royal path to the top. George was young when he first joined QB, spending summer breaks during his college years at the company in the garages, mopping floors, and taking out trash. Before joining the family business full-time, Conrad wanted George to get experience away from Quality Beverage. So after graduating from college, George worked in sales for an Anheuser-Busch branch in Boston, where he sold craft beer to distributors. When he later joined QB full-time in 2011, George worked on the trucks and helped drivers with their deliveries. Once he mastered those basics, he moved on to sales in both the Auburn and Taunton locations, meriting his own junior sales route and then working his way up to sales execution coordinator, overseeing sales analytics and growth. He later served as sales team manager, supervising other sales reps within a specific territory. This earned him a promotion to

CHAPTER 5: *THE CREED* IN ACTION

director of corporate marketing and eventually led to his current position as vice president and general manager of the Taunton division. Both roles are part of the company's senior steering committee.

"It was really important to [Conrad and Mark] that I work from the bottom up and honestly, that was the best thing they could do for me," he explains, "because a lot of people respected me for that, instead of just coming in as an adult and taking over a management position."

While George is incredibly proud of his heritage and appreciates the opportunity to be a part of the family business, he doesn't broadcast the fact that he's the boss's son. In fact, he'd rather be known for his own accomplishments, especially when it comes to his new role and responsibilities. "I'm really excited to see what I can do with this role and just prove to everyone I can help the company grow and get better," he says enthusiastically.

George's humility certainly aligns with the principles of *The Creed*, which he says mean more to him now as a working adult. He recalls his dad often sharing the Wetterau family history and the importance of *The Creed* during his employee speeches and various meetings, underscoring its relevance at the company. "I've really grown to appreciate it and have a better understanding of what *The Creed* is and what it stands for," he says.

Treating People Fairly and Equally

One aspect of *The Creed* that particularly resonates with George is treating people equally and fairly. "That's something my dad really instilled in me, even as a young kid," he says. He shares how he's seen inequality around him outside of the organization, especially amidst the current political climate, and tries to go out of his way to spend extra time on selected accounts that might need his help by extending a hand to retailers with displays or rotating coolers or sending them a special jacket or gift to let them know they're important to the company. After all, "their success is our success," he says. "And by working together, it can ultimately mean the success of both partners."

This attitude of working together for the advancement of all partners permeates the associates at QB, according to George. "I can just see it when I'm out there in the trade with the guys and how they carry themselves and

Photo (left page): George P. Wetterau, great-great grandson of George H. Wetterau

communicate with the retailer and other accounts. There's teamwork there. In the facility, we're all very close-knit — it's an all-around good atmosphere. That's part of the reason why we have people who stay at the company for 20 or 30 years. It's not always the pay. It's the climate we create that makes the difference."

Unique Competitive Advantage

George observes that the QB Creed is a unique competitive advantage in the trade, as well. "Not a lot of companies have a creed or even much of a mission statement," he explains. "So having that kind of foundation gives us an advantage over the competition. If people are having an issue with an account or a hard time with something, they can relate back to *The Creed* and maybe it will help them have a better understanding or a different point of view on what they're handling. It makes you reflect back and think, 'Did I do this right?' or 'What can I do differently?' or 'Did I treat him or her fairly?'"

When it comes to *The Creed*, George says that other partners are taking note, as well — literally. During QB visits, customers, vendors, company leaders, and other visitors recognize the value in the QB Creed. "Almost always, people are taking notes [during our company overview presentations] and tell us they think it's awesome," he explains. "Even top leaders say it's something they can relate to and wonder how come they haven't thought of something like this to instill into their company."

As George looks to the future of QB and all the Wetterau companies, he acknowledges the incredible legacy of his family's past with honor, respect, and responsibility. "It makes me really proud," he says, of the opportunity to be a part of the effort to continue the Wetterau legacy. "Maybe that legacy will include my daughter or one of my kids some day at one of the Wetterau companies. So I'd definitely like to keep *The Creed* going. Whether it stays the same or evolves over time, [it's important] to keep its philosophy going strong for years to come."

Photos (left to right):

1) GSF Founder, Bill Moore

2) The GSF-McDonald's business began on "a handshake and a promise."

3) GSF Chairman and CEO, Mark Wetterau, next to the company's Creed and Values

4) Former GSF Chairman and CEO, Jim Williams

CHAPTER 6

Golden State Foods: A Tradition of Values for over 75 Years

"I think one of the real underpinnings of our success is The Creed. We didn't have a creed in my day, but we had our Values, and we lived by them. And it's very refreshing to see GSF carry on [with those Values], and expand them, [including] the consistent care of people, the customer, the products, the services, and how we present ourselves. And I think if we stay on track, live The Creed and Values, and continue to take care of our customers, GSF will go on forever."

–**Jim Williams** (1939–   )
Chairman and CEO (1977–1998),
Golden State Foods

Post-War Beginnings: Big Dreams, Small Profits

As Quality Beverage continued to thrive, Wetterau Associates encountered another "golden" acquisition opportunity in the foodservice industry — Golden State Foods (GSF), which had been rich in its own values, ethics, and culture for many decades.

Founded by Bill Moore in post-war 1947, GSF was established on the principles of honesty and integrity, where Moore had demonstrated dedicated customer service and encouraged upfront, forthright business from the start.

On a small G.I. bill and a heart full of dreams, Moore set out to build his humble meat supply business in Los Angeles. Described by his wife (and initial secretary), Mary, as "a born salesman," Bill hustled meat off the back of a paneled truck for little more than a living wage. Soon he was known in the industry for positive relationships and following through on commitments.

"Bill was a meat man through and through," says former Golden State Foods Chairman and Chief Executive Officer Jim Williams, of Bill's hard-working personal style and three decades of leadership. "I think he was happiest when he was smokin' a cigar, with either one or two phones to his ear negotiating — buying meat cuts, cattle, or whatever the case may be — he enjoyed that side of it. He was truly a meat man. And he was a good one, very good; great personality, very good with people. You know, Bill didn't have too many enemies, to be quite honest. He was a good guy and we hit it off pretty well."

Moore built his business serving a variety of local hamburger stands, restaurants, hotels, and even theme parks. But he was particularly enamored with a new restaurant operation started by two brothers, called McDonald's, in the Southern California area. "A guy I met came to me and said, 'Geez, have you seen that hamburger stand in San Bernardino?'" recounted Bill in a 1975 interview about his first encounter with the new and revolutionary quick-serve process the McDonald brothers called the "Speedy Service System." "He said, 'Man, you gotta go look at that thing!' So, I blew out there and sure as hell, there were these long lines of people. I couldn't believe what an operation the McDonald brothers had going."

CHAPTER 6: GSF — A TRADITION OF VALUES

McDonald Brothers, Ray Kroc, and a New Partnership on a Handshake and a Promise

Moore knew that he had to have some of that business. So, he tenaciously tried selling to the McDonald brothers, with little initial success — despite the amiable relationship he had built with them, particularly Maurice "Mac" McDonald — during the early 1950s.

Then, the former milkshake-equipment salesman, Ray Kroc, came onto the scene in the mid-1950s with his vision of franchising the revolutionary McDonald's restaurants, and Bill eventually landed some McDonald's business from him later that decade. On a handshake and a promise, Moore and Kroc began what would become a life-long business relationship to supply the fast-food leader.

Moore began supplying a few independent restaurants in San Bernardino and Downey, which eventually grew into more. With this new service came higher standards. Moore quickly learned that McDonald's insisted on higher food quality and consistency than others, standards that would ultimately revolutionize the industry. And Bill delivered. From there, a 70-year partnership with McDonald's was born.

After a few years, Moore and Kroc kicked things into higher gear. Moore gained the business of multiple McDonald's stores throughout Southern California, while still servicing other customers, and GSF began to expand the business and its signature quality service even beyond the golden state.

"Bill Moore cared about everything that went on — not only what happened in the business, but he cared about the people," explained Ed Ruby, a 38-year McDonald's owner/operator and Southern California purchasing chair, who has since passed away. "That has always been the hallmark of Golden State Foods."

Ruby related a story about one of his relatives that illustrates Moore's dedication and the GSF way: "When my brother-in-law, Bill Brownstein, opened up his first [McDonald's restaurant] in Hacienda Heights,

[California], he found himself short on meat," said Ruby. But Moore delivered — literally. "Bill took all the meat [the restaurant required] and threw it in his Cadillac and delivered it and put it in his basement personally. *That's* caring."

Bill's reputation of customer dedication and care, along with higher quality standards, enabled GSF to grow year after year. As the company consistently prospered, its values continued to be demonstrated along with that success, decade after decade under the leadership of Jim Williams, who at Bill's request started as a young meat associate in 1961. "When I went to apply — or talk to Bill," Williams recounts, "he said, 'I want you to learn the meat business, and someday you'll be president of the company.'" At the time, GSF was a $3 million enterprise with about 30 employees. "So Bill introduced me to the general manager and the manager says, 'Well, if you're gonna get in this business you should learn it all, so why don't you start by cleaning beef coolers,' which I gladly did."

Williams' enthusiasm took him well beyond the beef coolers and he proceeded to learn every aspect of the business, including running the grinding room, overseeing patty operation, boning cattle, driving trucks, supervising the transportation department, and then earning his stripes by selling hamburger. He was an example of hard work and dedication, and like Moore, always put the customer first.

"Jim was very much like Bill Moore," added Ed Ruby, comparing Bill and Jim's relationship to a father and son. "That's how Bill basically treated him. And you could trust anything Jim Williams told you."

"J.W. (as his friends call him) is a wonderful person," says Mark Wetterau of his relationship with Jim Williams. Mark, GSF's third chairman and CEO, relied on Williams for support when he took over the lead at GSF and often referred to him as his "West Coast Dad" after the passing of his own father, Ted Wetterau, in 2003. "He is very forthright; you're going to hear what he has to say. He makes himself crystal clear on his points. At the same time, he's got a nice touch. He's a very caring person. He understands the fact that the success of any organization is directed through its people, and that's the greatest asset an organization can have."

Within a few years, after recognizing early on Jim's ability to establish and maintain quality customer relationships, Moore assigned Williams to the McDonald's account. "Jim was very much a delegator, but he stayed very close to the business, very close to the customer," continues Mark. "He is a special individual in that he really built extremely strong relationships with our customers."

GSF and McDonald's: Common Values and High Growth Years

The '70s and '80s were high-growth years for Golden State Foods, as they supported McDonald's with its burgeoning U.S. and international expansion. GSF broadened its meat business into liquid products, dairy, produce, and distribution, building numerous manufacturing plants and distribution centers around the country. In order to infuse cash into the business to support further expansion, Bill Moore and his management team leveraged the opportunity to take the company public in 1972.

Just a few years after this transition, Jim Williams took over as president and CEO in 1976 and then as chairman and CEO in 1977. In 1978, after more than three decades of successfully leading the company, Bill Moore passed away. With his passing and the company's public status, there was some concern about GSF's vulnerability. Some wondered if it would be sold and who would control it. "GSF was a major part of McDonald's growth back then, and [McDonald's] wanted to continue that relationship," explains Jim.

So with McDonald's support, Jim and his management team, as well as Bill's wife, Mary Moore, managed to raise the substantial funds required to take the company private again in 1980. "We wanted to make sure everyone was taken care of," explains Jim, "McDonald's, our associates, and of course, the Moore family."

By the end of the '80s, GSF had grown to a $1 billion company. During this time, it had also formally instituted in writing what Williams and his team called the "GSF Values:"

1. Treat others as you would like to be treated.
2. Make the best product.
3. Provide the best service.
4. How you look is who you are.

These ideals closely aligned with McDonald's standards of quality, service, cleanliness, and value and were what Jim says he had watched Bill Moore demonstrate throughout his leadership, explaining why he felt it was important to officially document and publish the Values.

"GSF's Values have been consistent over time," said Rich Moretti, a 25-year associate and former GSF chief financial officer in a 2006 corporate video prior to his passing. "Its products and processes have changed and evolved, but its core values have really remained in place. And that's why we've been so successful over the years."

Golden State's values continued to fuel additional growth and success during the 1990s. The company expanded throughout the U.S., then internationally into the Middle East and Australia, serving dozens of countries around the world. In addition, the company broadened its produce and baking ventures and continued to grow its other businesses in meat, liquids, and distribution. By the end of the '90s, after nearly four decades of exemplary service to the company, Jim Williams determined that it was time to pass the baton to a new leader and move on to another phase in his life. So in 1997, as the world anticipated the turn of a new century, for the first time in GSF's history, the $1.3 billion company went up for sale. Jim had a big decision to make: Who was going to lead the company, which he had spent nearly 40 years of his life building, into the new millennium?

CHAPTER 6: GSF — A TRADITION OF VALUES

The GSF Purchase: A Match Made in Values

The chance to bid on Golden State Foods came up rather unexpectedly for Wetterau Associates, when Mark and Conrad received a phone call from a former Wetterau Inc. executive, Tom Loggia, who was consulting with McDonald's at the time. "It was just one of those fortunate opportunities," says Mark. "Tom mentioned that there were two companies coming available in the system, one of them Golden State Foods, and asked if we would be interested." The conversation was encouraging, recalls Conrad: "He said that GSF was something 'you and your brother should look at because it's right up your alley.'"

"It was like a match made in heaven," explains Mike Waitukaitis, who describes the commonalities of GSF with the Wetterau companies. "Our major divisions at Wetterau Inc. were wholesale [including distribution]. We also had retail operations, so we knew how to run grocery stores. And then we also had a bakery, so we baked products for use in our customer stores. We had 'been there, done that' in manufacturing, wholesale, and retail, which [made us] a great match with Golden State Foods."

Yet despite all the business similarities, the catalyst for starting the whole negotiating process was the two companies' shared values and similar business cultures. "The enabler for [Wetterau] to even get the opportunity to bid for GSF and then ultimately receive the business was *The Creed*," explains Mark, who recalls the details of the deal.

"*The Creed* was actually one of the initial key elements [that brought Wetterau] in as a bidder," says former GSF president, Dick Gochnauer, who joined the company in 1994 and continues to serve on its board. "All of us were interested in new partners and owners with the same sense of principles and values that we had."

Jim Williams was obviously keen on making a synergistic transaction. "I felt we certainly had a responsibility to … leave the company in the hands of somebody who had the same values, but more importantly who was going to continue on with what McDonald's expected the company to do," he explains. "I think the character of the people involved played a role," adds Waitukaitis. "[Jim and his team] saw Mark, Ted, and Conrad and said, 'Yeah, these are the kind of people we'd want to turn the business over to.'"

Because McDonald's had a critical stake in what happened to GSF, the leadership team there took a close look at Wetterau Associates as well. "They did their homework," Waitukaitis continues, "because they had a say too, and [concluded that], 'Yeah, these guys check out. And not only do they check out, it turns out that they're in wholesale, retail, and manufacturing already.' So it was almost like a marriage made in heaven." Jim Williams agrees: "When I ran into the Wetterau family, I saw a lot of synergy and I thought, 'You know what? This is a pretty good marriage.'"

"Certainly, the very strong values that were attached with GSF, the focus and the energy toward the independent operator, the constant emphasis on excellence in running better operations, keeping the bar high — these were all something that really attracted us to the company," says Mark.

"We saw a management team that was professional, driven, hard-working, and dedicated, and that's what impressed us more than anything," adds Conrad. "Because the bricks and mortar are only the surface of the company. What drives the company are the people."

So after about a year of courting, lots of due diligence, and with McDonald's blessing, Wetterau Associates and its seasoned food industry business financier in the transaction, the Los Angeles-based Yucaipa Companies, submitted their proposal.

"The Wetteraus at that time were not the high bidder," noted Ed Ruby of those vying for the GSF purchase. "But Jim [Williams] was more interested, I've always felt, that we get the right person running it for the restaurants and for the operator community and for [corporate] McDonald's, than all that additional money he could have gotten. [In the end], I think [selling to Wetterau Associates] was the best decision he ever made for me."

"It was the right value for the relationship we spent all our life building," says Jim. "I mean, I was there 39 years, and we certainly didn't want to see that disrupted. And to be quite honest, if we hadn't found the Wetteraus, I might still be there, who knows!"

So the "proposal" was accepted and Wetterau Associates acquired Golden State Foods in 1998. The acquisition brought in veteran food industry executive, Mark Wetterau, to lead the organization into the new millennium as chairman and chief executive officer. Jim Williams remained on the board and certainly maintained an active role in the company, particularly during the transition. Ted and Conrad Wetterau also joined the board, along with Mike Waitukaitis, who served as chief financial officer and board member. "We couldn't have done the deal without this team, including Yucaipa," adds Mark. "We hadn't gone through large, private equity deals like this one, so we relied on Yucaipa's experience a great deal."

"I look at our investment in Golden State Foods as a home run," says Ron Burkle, managing partner of The Yucaipa Companies. "Not only did we improve the health of the company and create superior returns for all stakeholders, but more importantly we had the good fortune to work with Mark Wetterau and his incredible management team. [They] were tremendous partners and never wavered in their focus on not only doing well but doing good for those who were counting on us to make this venture successful. I would welcome any opportunity to work with the GSF management team again."

New Leader, New Creed

Once the transition was complete, Mark Wetterau hit the ground running in his new leadership role as chairman and CEO. With Mark's move to Southern California, Conrad continued to lead Quality Beverage in the Northeast as president and CEO, with Mark as its chairman, and Mike Waitukaitis serving on the board.

Mark engaged his GSF management team in making key decisions, such as what the company vision and values would be. "We had a vision as a team, where we wanted to go, and we built a team around that strategy," explains Mark. "And then along with that we pulled in the strong culture that had been within Golden State Foods and started to build on that. And that's where, taking what Jim had established with the GSF Values, we came in and added *The Creed* to the organization."

Dick Gochnauer explains why *The Creed* was important in making the leadership transition easier for GSF employees: "Jim Williams was a very values-centered leader, and he not only had the Values, but he walked the talk," he says of Jim's leadership and positive relationships with the associates. "So there was a high degree of trust that Jim had with the employees built up over decades because he'd been around and hired most of them. Well, Jim was leaving, and we had new owners, which made us ask: 'Should I be worried? What's going to happen to the culture?'"

"We were nervous," says 31-year associate, Lisa Gottlieb, GSF's corporate treasurer. "Not gonna lie. We were so afraid, because we didn't know who was going to buy the company and what they were going to do with it. But then we found out it was the Wetterau family with Yucaipa. And it was such a joy. We hit the jackpot! Mark and his father Ted, his brother Conrad, and Mike Waitukaitis all came in [to the Irvine office], and they were so sweet. They were so genuinely friendly. They were great leaders, but they were friendly. They had a sense of humor. And they had great values, especially with their creed. So we knew we were going to be okay. We knew that they would take GSF to the next level. We were primarily focused on McDonald's at the time, and with Mark's vision, we knew we were going to grow with more customers and do it in the right way."

"What *The Creed* did, and what Mark and the senior team did by leading with *The Creed*, was to take the GSF Values up another level," continues Dick. "[This said to us], 'not only do we support the Values, but [this creed we are giving you] is the basis by which [the Values are] underpinned and provides a broader view of those Values as they play out in our belief system.' When you lead with this, and you say it and look people in the eye, [the employees begin to say], 'I think they mean it; I think they believe this stuff,' and then when Mark Wetterau walked the talk, it made the transition easy."

"Since this company is so widespread, and we're dealing in 40 to 50 different countries around the world on different continents, we felt it was very important that we had something to clarify the Values, and that's where *The Creed* came into play," says Mark, implementing Ted's original intention of *The Creed* on an even broader scale. "So when our folks are over in Egypt, Australia, China, or any of the many other regions of the world we're in and the managing director needs to make a decision that will move his operation forward — our company forward — and he gets confused at times, he can fall back on and read *The Creed*, read the Values, which helps him make that proper decision."

The Values and *The Creed* are the foundation for the associates at the GSF family of companies to aid them in important management challenges, Mark further explains. "When I look at our team's approach over the years, it's really been more about people carrying the torches themselves, in allowing them the freedom to make those decisions that they have been so well trained in doing. I don't need to constantly look over their shoulder because the Values and *The Creed* are really sitting on their shoulders to guide them to make those right decisions."

But *The Creed's* introduction into GSF did not come before some lively discussions with the company's management team. "We did have a good debate [centered] around the questions: 'What if everyone doesn't believe in God? Does this mean that I can't work here?'" recalls Gochnauer. "And our response was, 'No, this isn't a litmus test to say if you can work here or not. It's more of a statement of beliefs, and it's broader than that. It goes into 'the dignity of all people,' which is a statement of how we act and our value system."

Former First Lady of California and GSF Advisory Board Member Sharon Davis notes that *The Creed* is actually pretty courageous: "It's brave in a way because I think you don't see [such declarations] in companies today. They're so worried about being politically correct and maybe offending somebody. So to put [God] front and center and let people know upfront where you stand on your beliefs is brave. It's a bold statement." Davis goes on to say that in this day and age, where so much is done for show, that some could assume *The Creed* is nothing more than window dressing. "[But] *The Creed* was implicit [at GSF] before we ever saw it in writing — we got the sense from working with the Wetterau family how they approached their business. So even before they put it in all their facilities, it was [already] part of who they were. It really is woven into the fabric of this company."

Certainly, the other principles in *The Creed* fit nicely with GSF's business dealings and complimented the Values that were already in place.

> "Our belief in the value of small businesses, and our role in supporting that [is significant]. The majority of jobs in the U.S., around two-thirds, are created by small businesses, and enabling them to be successful and supporting them is a good healthy thing for the economy."
>
> DICK GOCHNAUER

By introducing the idea of *The Creed* at Golden State Foods, Mark seemed to be on the verge of taking the Wetterau philosophy to an entirely new level. But before fully instituting it into the company, it was important for the management team to evaluate *The Creed*, along with the Values, to ensure their relevance at GSF. Over the course of several months a few changes were incorporated.

One of the first changes to be made, as was the case with the Quality Beverage Creed, was in the first line of the Wetterau Creed that states, "We believe in one God and the dignity of man." It was edited slightly to read, "We believe *in God* and the dignity of *all people*." Mark and his team felt

CHAPTER 6: GSF — A TRADITION OF VALUES

more comfortable modernizing it to "all people" to clarify and avoid any misinterpretations about women being excluded in that statement.

The next change was made in the second phrase, "this applies to the welfare of our employees and their families, to our suppliers … ." It became, "this applies to all our *associates*, their families, *our customers* and suppliers … ." These changes reflect the respect and equality of the employees as equal associates and include customer awareness.

Another line, "We believe that successful independent business is the backbone of our country …"was updated to fit GSF's growing international business beyond the U.S. and thus currently reads, "We believe that successful independent business is the backbone of *nations* … ."

Additionally, the line, "that our success is closely related to the success of our customers …" was tightened up to send a stronger message about GSF's role and perspective on customer service and how it defines success. As such, it currently reads, "our success is *dependent upon* the success of our customers … ." Continuing on in that line, "both" partners was changed to *"all"* partners to emphasize that there are more than just two partners in the GSF sphere. This includes the heretofore-mentioned customers, suppliers, other business partners, and each of their families.

Concluding *The Creed*, the final word was altered slightly from "goal" to "goals," indicating that the company's objectives are many and perhaps multi-faceted and ever-increasing.

Other minor grammatical edits were also implemented, but the overall message remained consistent.

(Golden State Foods Creed shown on next page.)

The Golden State Foods Creed

We believe in **God** and the dignity of **all people**.

We believe that people should be treated as we would like to be treated, and this applies to all of our **associates**, their families, **our customers** and suppliers and to all others with whom we do business.

We believe that successful independent business is the backbone of **nations**, that our success is **dependent upon** the success of our customers, and that only by working together can the ultimate success of **all** partners be assured.

We, therefore, dedicate ourselves to work for our mutual success and pledge our best efforts always toward the attainment of our common **goals**.

Likewise, one line in the long-held GSF Values was also changed. "How you look is who you are" was altered to read "Maintain the highest standards," which broadened its meaning beyond personal appearance to the cleanliness of trucks, buildings, and other elements of the company.

"Once we got *The Creed* completed, we started to discuss it as a management team," says Mark. "Do we buy it? We made the changes, but do we buy into it?" He recalls that there was a near-perfect consensus among the team except for one "non-believer" who drug his feet a bit on it. "It took some time, and we were patient," notes Mark, who explains that they all agreed that 100 percent alignment was required before rolling anything out. "Through lengthy discussions and listening to different points of view, ultimately we were able to come to an agreement and have 100 percent support," Mark adds about the alignment process, which took about a year.

Communicating *The Creed* and Enhancing the Culture

Once there was solid consensus among the company's top leaders, it was time to share *The Creed* with associates companywide. So over the course of several months, it was methodically introduced to employees at all levels throughout the organization, along with GSF's new strategy and structure.

Mark Wetterau personally toured all the facilities and in conjunction with the local facility leaders, conducted "town hall" meetings for associates on all shifts (a practice Mark and his team had instituted at Shop 'n Save years earlier). During those meetings, management asked associates to consider *The Creed* as an enhancement to the GSF Values, with which they were already familiar. *The Creed* and updated Values were displayed together on facility walls, employees' desks, GSF business cards, the company website, promotional videos, and other collateral.

More importantly, the spirit of *The Creed* and the Values started to come to life, as they were mentioned more and more in meetings companywide as a guiding ideal for GSF and all its associates.

Mark and his executive team helped keep the importance of *The Creed* and Values top of mind by continuing to conduct the periodic town hall meetings with associates at all levels around the world, while seeking to exemplify the ideals embodied within them to the best of their ability.

As Golden State Foods continues to grow and welcome new associates, the executives still share the history, evolution, and importance of the company's Creed and Values and foster a dialogue with the associates about these ideals. Associates have been receptive to the visits and many have been positively impacted by the message, increasing their pride in the organization.

"Mark came into town for his Creed and Values tour," recalls Chad Hopkins, a former 13-year associate at the GSF Sumner, Washington distribution center. "When he talked about all the billions of dollars of assets and equipment and everything else [and then emphasized] that our people are the most important asset, that was so meaningful to me, showing that *The Creed* and Values are alive and well at GSF."

Sherrie Homer, a prior 12-year associate at the same facility, agrees. "From the time I started with GSF, I can honestly say that it continues to surprise me how alive and functional our Creed and Values are within our decisions, within our team, within our teamwork. And that's something that makes me very proud."

Mark continues to reach out to associates through special "Breakfasts with the Chairman" events, and various round-table discussions, where each associate has the opportunity to talk directly to him about whatever is on their mind. Mike Waitukaitis recalls accompanying Mark to some of them early on. "It's probably hard for some of those people to open up to the chairman of the board," he explains, looking at it from the associates' point of view. "But eventually they do, and I think that speaks volumes about what we are. [That kind of caring] gets down to the warehouse or production floor: 'Hey, I had breakfast with Mark Wetterau, and we spent an hour together and when I wasn't afraid anymore, I actually asked him some questions. [This kind of personal contact] emphasizes the fact that we don't work in a vacuum."

CHAPTER 6: GSF — A TRADITION OF VALUES

Patience with Skepticism

Although *The Creed* and Values were largely well accepted, of course everyone didn't fall in line immediately. Some associates had to be converted, which took time. "Some people who really loved Jim Williams were skeptical of the Wetteraus when they came in and took over," explains Bill Pocilujko, who started GSF's Centralized Leasing Corporation (CLC) in 1999.

A skeptic himself at first of *The Creed* at Wetterau Inc., where he had worked previously, Bill could spot similar initial doubts among the GSF family. "Some guys would say things like, 'Mark's a young guy, who does he think he is? What kind of show is he trying to put on?' They were struggling with the change in leadership overall. But I can tell you that a year or so later, these same people admitted that [they felt differently about it]. They'd say that Mark had really 'proven himself,' like it was a test or something, that he really walked the walk and talked the talk. Today, not many people within GSF challenge *The Creed* or the Values."

Former GSF driver, Jerry Sumoge from the Portland, Oregon distribution center illustrated this in a letter he sent to Pocilujko regarding the company's charitable efforts and leadership: "When Jim Williams turned GSF over to Mark Wetterau, many of us were suffering from a form of 'separation anxiety.' We knew Mr. Williams as a hard-working, straightforward man who had a history of dedication to his company. We did not know anything about Mr. Wetterau, and it kind of 'scared' us. Then 9/11 happened. Mr. Wetterau announced a plan to contribute to the suffering of New York. He even said he would match any contribution we would make to NY relief. His gesture to provide support to those in need was an act of compassion and kindness. We knew then that Mark Wetterau was going to be an 'okay guy' at GSF."

"I was in our Cairo [Egypt] facility on September 11," explains Larry McGill, a 25-year senior executive, now retired, who served in a number of leadership roles, including managing director of GSF Egypt. "As soon as the Trade Towers were hit, not minutes afterwards, I got a call from Mark Wetterau. He asked me, 'How's your family?' not how the buildings were or how the trucks were, but how my family was. So, I would say that that defines Golden State Foods. It comes from the top; it's all about our people. And that was the defining moment for me at GSF."

The Creed emphasizes that it's more than just business, notes Mike Waitukaitis. "It also talks about families, and I think Mark understands that if you've got a family situation you need to take care of, go take care of it. In fact, he'll probably help you if he can! He believes in families. In fact, the first thing he'll [usually] ask you is, 'How's your family?' Usually not, 'Did we make our budget?' I mean, business is important; it's important to make money, otherwise you might as well do something else. But family is also important, and Mark doesn't forget about people or families." Mike goes on to explain that the spirit of *The Creed* and the way those values permeate every part of your life, if you let them, are all-encompassing: *"It almost becomes part of your nature. It becomes part of what you do and how you do it."*

Former long-term Phoenix distribution associate, Rene McNary can attest to this. Just a year after starting with GSF, her 7-year-old son had a stroke while on vacation. "I called the office the day after they had admitted my son into the hospital," she recounts. "They got in touch with HR and within hours, GSF arranged a rental car and a place to stay at the Ronald McDonald House near the hospital. This was a very trying time for us, and it was wonderful to have the support of a great company and have less on our plate to worry about. This, to me, is what *The Creed* and Values are all about. Our son has since graduated with honors from college and is well into a successful career."

Sharon Davis aligns with the associates' assessment of the common sentiment that Mark Wetterau cares about families. "You see it in the way he conducts himself, the way he talks about the customers, our suppliers, and the people who work in this company — his dedication to them is beyond the bottom line. He doesn't just speak [about] *The Creed*, he lives it. It seems

CHAPTER 6: GSF — A TRADITION OF VALUES

to come from that higher place. It's a real 'lead-by-example' style. And everybody in this office needs to embody this same style... because they are also ambassadors for the company," says Davis. "You want everybody who goes out with a GSF business card and *The Creed* printed on the back of it to exhibit that creed. It lets people know your faith, not by what you say but what you do."

GSF associates at all levels have taken note of the dynamism of the Wetterau leadership style and the active role *The Creed* and long-held Values of the company have played in defining a business culture dedicated to doing the right thing — from hiring, to daily behavior, to defining successful performance. Dave Smith, a 24-year human resources director for GSF in the Southeast U.S., now retired, is one of those people who appreciates deeply just how relevant in today's world that leadership and those ideals are:

"When I think about *The Creed* and Values of our company, and I share them with family and friends, they always look at me and say, 'Oh, those are [just] words, right?' And I'm able to tell them, 'No, those are deeds, and it's something we truly use as a screen in our daily decision-making.' And for that I am very, very grateful and just [so] proud to have been a part of Golden State Foods."

"The dignity and respect Mark extends to our associates up and down the organization throughout the many locations we operate goes above and beyond," explains 16-year GSF associate, Frank Listi, former senior executive vice president and president of global food processing and current board member. "It is one thing to write and speak to the Values and Creed. But walking it daily has defined who Mark is and has encouraged others to do the same. We worked side-by-side through both challenging and rewarding times. Our relationship was built on trust because he is trustworthy, and hopefully I've earned the same with him. There rarely is a day that goes by without me saying a prayer of thanks for the experiences that he affords me — and all the GSF associates."

"We're a 'people-first' company," says Mike, referencing Mark's priorities as Golden State Foods' CEO and the trust that permeates the organization. He mentions how GSF seeks to incorporate Steven M. R. Covey's "Speed of Trust" philosophy, which teaches that gaining employees' trust enables companies to accomplish more, quicker. "Mark grew up valuing people," Mike continues. "Ted taught him and Conrad how to do that, and you can see it in them."

According to an ethical leadership case studies project conducted by Ohio University in 2020, which examined four companies in recent history that faced ethical dilemmas, moral leadership is a better indicator of the long-term health of a business than short-term profits and margins: "Companies that exhibit ethical leadership practices generate goodwill with consumers, protect their assets, and increase value for shareholders, while unethical leaders can put the entire organization at risk for short-term or personal gains."

Jim Williams agrees. He explains that every outstanding company has strong leadership behind it, which places serious stock in moral and ethical values. Those values protect not only the bottom line, but the people who help create that bottom line. "Every company that's successful and has a strong leader has got their own values, if you will," says Williams, "and they've got their own 'smell' when you walk in the door, and it's always a good one. And I think the aroma at Golden State Foods is a fine perfume."

Wetterau Inc. veteran, Darryl Long, recognized this familiar "scent" right away during a business trip to GSF in 2000. "As soon as I walked in, I just felt it," he explains, of his visit to one of the company's Southern California distribution centers. "Unless you've been out there and seen a lot of what's going on, you can't really appreciate [that feeling]. I felt it when I was at Wetterau Inc. as well. [That feeling isn't at GSF] because Mark is there preaching it, it's just there with management, with the people in the distribution center, and it just grabs you, and you totally realize what it's all about."

"I think one of the real underpinnings of our success is *The Creed*," adds Jim." We didn't have a creed in my day, but we had our Values, and we lived by them. And it's very refreshing to see GSF carry on [with those Values], and expand them, [including] the consistent care of people, the customer, the products, the services, and how we present ourselves. And I think if we stay on track, live *The Creed* and Values, and continue to take care of our customers, GSF will go on forever."

Lucia's

Lucia's Pizza: A Tasty Wetterau Spin-off

In 2001, Wetterau Associates partnered with Darryl Long, a long-time Wetterau store developer and operations manager, and former Wetterau Inc. consultant, Brent Baxter, of Clayton Capital Partners to acquire Lucia's Pizza in St. Louis, a small frozen pizza manufacturing and distribution business that serviced various supermarkets in the Midwest. Wetterau tasked Darryl with running the 20-year-old company that specialized in a unique St. Louis-style cheese blend. Thrilled to be back in business again with the Wetteraus, Long ran Lucia's, along with some other business ventures, including Fromage, a cheese spread and meat alternatives company for pizza for more than a decade. Greatly valuing the positive culture he gleaned from *The Creed*-based Wetterau family of companies, Darryl naturally wanted to continue those ideals within this new business environment.

"*The Creed* embodies how I feel," Long says of the philosophy that was implemented on day one at Lucia's. "It's how I wanted to conduct myself on a daily basis, and it's how I wanted everybody at the company to feel — like they were a part of a family and not have their legs cut out from under them tomorrow. That's what it's all about."

Like Ted, Conrad, and Mark Wetterau and other Creed-based leaders before him, Long sought to openly share *The Creed's* philosophy and how it galvanized the company's objectives with all of his employees. "One of my goals was for associates to feel comfortable as they talked to people on the street about the company and be able to say, 'I work at Lucia's Pizza Company, and I freakin' love it!'" he says. "Feeling proud about where you work is just as important as making a dollar. Yes, we have to make money to pay bills, but if there is something going on that we can do a better job with, let's talk about it," Long continues. "I wanted everybody to feel proud of where they worked. I wanted their families to feel good about it. It's just the way it should be. The Lucia's Creed was one of the most powerful tools I had [to achieve this]."

Over the years, Lucia's grew in size and scope and eventually changed ownership. Today, it's a national company, including brands like Sophia's gourmet flatbread pizza, Oasis Mediterranean cuisine, and Argus Brewery pizza, a Chicago-inspired pan pizza. But for Darryl, running that business with *The Creed* as its base was a dream come true. He believes that there will always be good feelings surrounding *The Creed*-based company culture he worked so hard to create at Lucia's: "I think there will be a day down the road when everybody will look back and say, 'That was a good place — a freakin' good place to work!'"

CHAPTER 6: GSF — A TRADITION OF VALUES

ARGOS
FAMILY OFFICE

Argos Family Office: A Wealth Management Company Decades in the Making

Established in 2007 in St. Louis, Argos Family Office is a wealth management advisory firm for a select group of ultra-affluent families. But the richness of the organization's foundation was actually built on *The Creed* in action, years earlier.

In the early '90s, Paul Vogel was a busy staff tax associate at Price Waterhouse and was assigned to the Wetterau Inc. account. At that time, there was also a partner, senior manager, manager, and senior associate on the account, so he was definitely the low man on the totem pole.

One day, the partner on the account was looking for any associate who worked on Wetterau Inc. Apparently, Ted Wetterau had called Price Waterhouse and wanted a meeting that afternoon. The senior manager, manager, and senior associate were all out of the office, so the partner took Paul with her to the meeting at Wetterau Inc., where he met Ted for the first time.

"During the meeting at Ted's office, he began asking the partner various questions, including those quite technical in nature," recalls Paul. "He asked one question the partner answered incorrectly. When she finished her answer, Ted turned to me and asked, 'Do you agree?' I am not sure why he chose to ask my opinion on that particular question (maybe I looked at my shoes or I winced). I paused for a moment and thought to myself, 'I am surely going to be fired,' but I told Ted I did not agree with [the partner]. I explained to him that her answer had been the firm's thinking, but I had written a research memo on this topic, and it had obviously not made it up the chain to her.

"As we left the meeting, I wondered, 'How am I going to explain to my parents that I just got fired for making a partner look stupid?' Once we got outside, the partner said two things: 'One, never lie to a client; and two, never let a partner look that stupid again.'"

Even though Ted had not met Paul before, he clearly knew the position he had put him in. By the time he and the partner arrived at their office, Ted had already called the managing partner and asked him to make sure Paul was not fired or reprimanded for what had happened. He explained that he had asked Paul a direct question, and Paul had given him an honest, direct answer, even though it was going to put him in a bad spot. Ted said that forthright honesty was a quality Price Waterhouse would want in its employees. "*The Creed* says to 'treat others as you would want to be treated,'" explains Paul. "Ted did that [for me] even though he didn't know me at all, and there was absolutely no obvious benefit to him at that time in doing so." Paul continued to serve on the Wetterau account for his entire tenure at Price Waterhouse.

Fast forward to 1997. Paul was hired by Arthur Andersen as a practice leader for its Family Wealth Planning practice in Dallas/Fort Worth, but upon leaving Price Waterhouse he had signed a non-solicitation agreement, which prevented him from telling Ted (still a Price Waterhouse client) what he was doing. Nonetheless, Ted reached out to him to continue the partnership. "He called me at home one evening to discuss moving the Wetterau business to Arthur Anderson with me," shares Paul. "I explained I had a contract that prevented me from taking clients. Ted said he understood, but asked if I would be available to talk later, and I said yes. Later that evening, the office managing partner from Price Waterhouse St. Louis called to say that Ted had called him and wanted the Wetterau business to follow me. He said he would agree if I would assure him I wasn't taking any other clients. I assured him I was not, so Ted moved the Wetterau business."

Then in 1998, Paul got another call from Ted, who sat on the board of directors of a small bank that was planning to start a trust company. Ted told the bank that Paul should start the new trust for them and run it. He said the only caveat he gave the bank was that if Paul took the job, he would be allowed to continue as the Wetterau's personal tax advisor and attorney. Paul took the job and built the trust company into what it is now, Enterprise Bank and Trust, a public company.

"During my 10 years at Enterprise, Ted and I talked often about his desire to create a Family Office for the Wetterau family," recounts Paul. "I still have the memo I wrote for Ted about the concept. Unfortunately, Ted passed

CHAPTER 6: GSF — A TRADITION OF VALUES

before he saw it come to fruition. In 2007, a couple of my Enterprise clients approached me about starting a Family Office for them. I was intrigued and explained to them that two families were not enough to build out what they wanted. I approached Mark and Conrad about being one of Argos' founding families and owners, knowing they were aware of the conversations I had with Ted, and they agreed."

Today, Argos has 11 client families and may add one or two more over the next several years before closing permanently to new clients. They continue to operate with the high values and standards that gave birth to the organization years ago — the principles of *The Creed* exemplified by Ted and Paul over the years of their trusted relationship.

Photos (left to right):

1) Established in 2002, the GSF Foundation helps children and families in need in the areas where GSF associates live and work.

2) (Inset) Established in 2010, the GSF University is Golden State Foods' in-house leadership development program, offering hundreds of online and in-house courses annually.

3) Chairman and CEO, Mark Wetterau, presents the 2011 Chairman's Challenge Award to Conyers, Georgia team leaders, Wayne Morgan and Brian Dick.

4) (Inset) GSF's Golden Spirit Award program, established in 2002, recognizes associates who go above and beyond the call of duty as they exemplify one or more of the company's Values in their everyday roles at the organization.

5) News media tells the story of GSF's Creed-based culture and success.

©2012 OC Metro

CHAPTER 7

Going Beyond Company Borders — Sharing *The Creed* Outside GSF

"*The Creed* is not just our ethos internally, it's our public image, our brand in the community."

—**Bill Sanderson** (1954–   )
Chief Administrative Officer (2017–2020)
Chief Financial Officer (2011–2017),
Golden State Foods

Once *The Creed* was introduced inside Golden State Foods, the leadership and associates began to share it outside of the organization as well. They carried it throughout the industry to their local restaurant owner/operators, purchasing committees, suppliers, and other business partners and communicated it more proactively to the media and to the public in general.

As GSF grew into a top supplier for industry icons, becoming one of the largest private companies in the U.S. and one of the fastest-growing private companies in Southern California, others began to take notice of *The Creed*. Mark Wetterau was repeatedly invited to speak publicly about GSF's Creed and the positive impact it was having on business and company culture. Soon, Golden State Foods became known throughout the community for its rich, values-based environment of enthusiastic, caring people driven to perform at high levels of excellence.

In fact, GSF even began to get fan mail about its creed as a result of increased media coverage and public awareness. After being featured in A&E's 2008 television program called "Modern Marvels: Fast Food Tech," about the quick service restaurant industry, GSF received a vast positive response, including a letter from a viewer applauding the company's values stance and its positive impact on society.

"I was watching the part about Golden State Foods and how they supply McDonald's, and it came to me that you guys really do feed a lot of people. A whole lot of people," wrote Mark Cooper from Sedalia, Missouri in his fan letter. "So I thought I'd check you out on the Web. The first thing I noticed was your witness, your statement that you believe in God and in treating others fairly. Good for you! This world would be a far better place if more people and corporations held that belief and lived/operated in a more serene and confident manner. There's nothing like the belief in God to keep people treating each other well."

Cooper's letter is not unique. It's just one of numerous emails, comments and positive messages saluting *The Creed* and GSF's candid declaration about its values and high standards. Many express appreciation for GSF's courage and boldness in stating upfront its divine belief in a higher power and its commitment to treat all its stakeholders with respect, with the common goal of mutual success for all. In fact, the positive impact of the GSF Creed and the principles it manifests continues to attract people who are passionate about its values and who can evangelize the company's culture, brand ID, and its contributions to the community.

The Creed Serves as a Filter for Attracting Values-driven People

GSF's growing reputation as a values-driven company has evolved into a screen that helps attract people who are passionate about helping the company reach its goals and achieve its purpose. Applicants who resonate with the company's ideals are enthusiastic about joining the organization and those who aren't, typically fall out of the screening process.

"Making a public proclamation about what you stand for in an organization creates a filter or gate for those that either believe in it [and] aspire to it, or those that don't, and that's proven to be true here," explains Bill Sanderson, a former 19-year senior executive who's served in a variety of leadership roles at GSF, including chief financial officer and chief administrative officer.

"What I find is that the people who actually make it to a specific role at GSF most often are those cut from the same cloth as the rest of us here at the company," he continues, "and are really not only attracted to, but held together by *The Creed* and Values. It creates a self-filtering mechanism for those who want to be open and transparent, and who are passionate about the customer. Those who are collaborative and treat each other with dignity and respect and are great in working with teams come here. Those who want to win in a different way, who like to work in environments where there's a culture of 'I can only win by you losing,' don't fit," says Sanderson.

"It's remarkable to me to see the number of people we hire and onboard who align with *The Creed* and Values," he continues. You would think, just based on the law of averages, that we would have pockets of people of a political nature who aren't a fit for GSF. But it doesn't seem to be the case. I think those words on the wall are a big part of that."

Sanderson goes on to characterize *The Creed* as the company's "ethos," which permeates the business culture internally and externally, significantly contributing to its brand identity. "It's our public image, our brand in the community. When you meet someone at a business event or other activity, and they already have an impression of you, it is a responsibility for us as associates to be sure we communicate that image in the way we behave. Because [that brand] is a very positive impression, and they expect you to conduct yourself in a certain way, so it keeps you on your game."

Once an outsider, Sanderson appreciated how *The Creed* and Values were discussed and exemplified when he was considering joining the company full-time. He had experienced companies that had "fast and nefarious" morals, as he describes it, and wasn't willing to compromise his own ethics to accommodate them. Conversely, Bill had also led businesses with more positive cultures similar to Golden State Foods, and knew that this type of environment was what he was seeking. Bill observed in his first week as a new consultant to GSF, both short- and long-term employees referencing *The Creed* and Values in various meetings.

"They would pull up a phrase, a line from *The Creed* primarily, and reference it in the conversation we were having, and use it as a guidepost or a mantel by which a decision was to be made, or a filter by which a strategy or a plan was being put together," he explains. "That was just awe-inspiring to me, to see what I knew I was attracted to as words on the wall or on the back of the business card, be truly put into daily practice and into people's business lives and have it be valued as an important guidepost for decisions that were made — it just impacted me tremendously."

Once Sanderson had been at Golden State Foods for nearly two decades and had served in some of its most senior roles, he saw even more clearly how *The Creed* is a powerful tool for the company. "I think it's a key differentiator," he says, explaining that many people who interview for jobs at GSF tell him they have seen similar attempts at company values statements, but they're really "just words on the wall" or that "nobody really knows it or lives it." They then want to understand how it's different at GSF. Bill explains that "it's not just about having a creed, but it's about *owning* it; it's the buy-in, it's keeping it front and center, it's living it. It's got to be something that's held in the highest regard by everybody, each and every day."

A Journey of Values for a GSF/QCD HR Leader

Group Vice President of Human Resources Melissa Vieira was struck early on with how authentic *The Creed* and Values are at GSF and its family of companies. "When I first began interviewing with GSF, I was quickly made aware of *The Creed* and Values and even saw them in action during interviews," she explains. "In the back of my head, I thought they were too good to be true. However, since joining the company in 2015 I have seen *The Creed* in action on a day-to-day basis and am frequently reminded about what it means to be a part of the organization, particularly in a leadership capacity."

Melissa reveals just how inspired she's been by the efforts made by associates at all levels to demonstrate *The Creed* and Values in their responsibilities at the company. "No matter what their role in the organization, our associates and leaders continually try to place our people first, ensuring that they are supported, cared for, and treated fairly," she observes. "Over the last eight years, the volume of examples is too many to count. Although it is truly apparent in times of great tragedy, it is also evident in the everyday decisions. While we are certainly a for-profit company, our decisions are rooted in steadfast principles that place our people first."

Vieira shares a few examples that have truly stood out for her during her tenure at the organization. "Just a few years ago, one of our associates was diagnosed with cancer and was notified he would need to wait to begin treatment due to scheduling conflicts. Not only did his leaders ensure he and his family had the time and space to seek care, but our Chairman and CEO Mark Wetterau quietly reached out and connected him with a specialist who could begin treatment right away. The associate recovered into remission and frequently shares how grateful he is for Mark discreetly supporting him."

Photo (above): Melissa Vieira, Group Vice President of Human Resources

Melissa goes on to explain how during the COVID-19 pandemic, *The Creed* and Values really shone through. "GSF immediately formed a committee to ensure that associates had key details needed to work safely to protect themselves and their families," she explains. "Leadership also decided against sweeping job elimination when volume had severely declined. And I saw them personally support associates and family members who were devastated by the disease," Vieira notes. "Courageous leaders made difficult decisions to assure the stability of the business but also protect the livelihood of associates."

Finally, Melissa points out how the GSF Creed and Values impact stakeholders beyond its associates. "On a daily basis, I observe our leaders thinking through decisions that will support not only associates, but our customers, suppliers, and other business partners so that we can preserve the long-term relationships and trust we have built," she says. "It's important that our words match our actions, and it is evident every single day that our Creed and Values do both."

The GSF Foundation: An Extension of *The Creed*

One way GSF associates actively exemplify the company's creed is through their leadership and dedication to helping others in need and improving their communities through the GSF Foundation. A natural extension of *The Creed*, Golden State Foods launched its employee-run charitable organization in 2002 with a mission to *improve the lives of children and families in need, in the areas where GSF associates live and work, through personal involvement and contributions.*

The non-profit organization was established to rally the existing altruistic spirit of the company's employees, who had been serving and leading out in charitable organizations such as the Ronald McDonald House Charities (RMHC) for decades. The idea was to provide some structure and corporate support to their efforts but enable the local associates to run the Foundation.

"It was a dream come true," says Mark Wetterau, of the launching of the Foundation and serving as its chairman. Having come from a family

CHAPTER 7: GOING BEYOND COMPANY BORDERS

heritage of philanthropy and giving back to the communities that enabled their success, Mark says he tries to encourage others to give back "twice or even three times" what they gained from them. He, himself, has been chairman of the St. Louis V.P. Fair and the Second Harvest Food Bank of Orange County and has served on dozens of other charitable boards, chairing many of them. (Please see *Appendix C* for a full list of Mark Wetterau's charitable service.) So when he came to GSF, Mark was thrilled to be able to build upon the associates' charitable spirit and help them achieve even greater impact in their communities.

"It's all about enabling GSF associates at all levels to lead out and make decisions of where the money goes, versus just the CEO or executives donating on behalf of the company," explains Mark, of the Foundation's unique purpose. "It's about empowering associates to sit on boards, chair events and campaigns, and have a say about how the mission of the Foundation is executed in their communities, and experience first-hand the joy of giving back to others in need."

In its first two decades, the Foundation has raised more than $61 million to help millions of underserved children through more than 850 children's charities and schools in the U.S. Upwards of 80 percent of GSF associates consistently participate in the Foundation through its 30 (and counting) local committees throughout the country, where they provide financial donations and/or volunteer service. GSF associates' level of participation is one of the highest rates in corporate America. One hundred percent of associate donations go directly to help those in need in their local communities.

"The good works, generous hearts, and giving hands of our GSF associates are really what make the Foundation so special," says current GSF Foundation Executive Director Tess McAnena. "And it's inspiring to see the many ways our associates give back, whether it's through shoe donations to a child who's never had their own pair, backpack donations to young students in need, feeding a hungry family that's fallen on hard times, or financial donations from their own paychecks."

At the time of this writing, the Foundation has impacted millions of children and families through mass contributions of shoes, backpacks with school supplies, newly built bikes, and food, including millions of meals for the underserved. Associate volunteers have dedicated nearly 300,000 hours of service in addition to their ongoing financial donations.

GSF Corporate Executive Vice President and Chief Administrative Officer John Page, a 19-year associate who serves as chairman of the Foundation's board of directors and chaired the Foundation's 2012 Associate Campaign, further defines why the Foundation is so unique:

> *"It's almost a way of following the associates home and extending* The Creed *and* Values *into where they live. This giving communicates that we don't just do well to do well, we do well to do good in the communities."*
>
> JOHN PAGE

Mark concurs: "When you find you're able to improve the quality of life of even one individual, that's incredible. But when you put thousands of associates who are focused on helping to make a difference in the community, *that* is a powerful force."

"Whether it's cooking a meal at a Ronald McDonald House or delivering shoes and backpacks to the kids who need them, it's great to be involved," explains Lisa Gottlieb, 31-year associate and chief financial officer of the Foundation. "We're so fortunate to be able to work for a company that enables us to serve others in our community as part of our roles here at the organization."

In a letter to GSF associate and managing director of CLC, Bill Pocilujko, who chaired the 2018 Associate Campaign, Portland, Oregon-based veteran driver Jerry Sumoge wrote: "The fact that the GSF Foundation even exists, along with RMHC, sets us apart from many of the other fast-food restaurant [suppliers]. The GSF Foundation enables us to provide support for our local communities, especially the children who face poverty with their families."

CHAPTER 7: GOING BEYOND COMPANY BORDERS

Indeed, many GSF associates consider their involvement in the Foundation to be one of the highlights of employment at the company. "The best part about being here for me has been the interaction with the GSF Foundation and making a difference in the lives of young children,"

golden state foods FOUNDATION gsf
Changing Hearts, Changing Lives

IMPROVING THE LIVES OF KIDS AND FAMILIES IN NEED – IMPACT SNAPSHOT

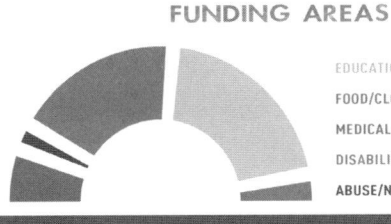

CORE PROGRAMS: — SINCE INCEPTION —

- 167,354 BACKPACKS DONATED
- 29,997 PAIRS OF SHOES DONATED
- 9,206 BIKES DONATED
- 6,180 COATS DONATED

2,814,060 MEALS FUNDED FOR FOOD-INSECURE FAMILIES SINCE 2020

TOTAL VOLUNTEER HOURS — 294,333

FUNDING AREAS

100% of ASSOCIATE CONTRIBUTIONS go to KIDS IN NEED

- EDUCATION/CULTURE (41%)
- FOOD/CLOTHES/SHELTER/ (37%)
- MEDICAL/HEALTH (15%)
- DISABILITIES (5%)
- ABUSE/NEGLECT (3%)

| 2002 YEAR ESTABLISHED | 30 NATIONWIDE COMMITTEES | 80% OF ASSOCIATES SUPPORT GSFF | $60M+ RAISED SINCE 2002 | 850+ CHARITIES AND SCHOOLS SUPPORTED | SCAN ME |

WWW.GSFFOUNDATION.ORG

shares Donnie Little, former 14-year Garner, North Carolina distribution associate. Donnie has participated in a number of charitable activities including fundraisers, shoe giveaways, and backpack donations.

"My involvement makes me feel like a better person for the things the Foundation allows me to do," says 27-year associate and Risk and Benefits Vice President John Murphy, now retired, who led the instigation of the organization's shoe donation program more than a decade ago.

"It's the icing on the cake," says Bill Sanderson, of being able to work for a company that lets its associates give back to their communities that have contributed so much to their success. "It's a way for us to bring the face of GSF into the community … and as we engage our families in this service, they're also able to learn and see first-hand how joyous it is to give to someone in need, rather than just to receive." Bill knows from personal experience of this truth. He has served as a local committee chair in Irvine, California, and spearheaded a number of community-wide fundraisers, including an annual gala event called "Good News for Kids," which raised nearly $1 million over five years and increased awareness of the needs of local children.

"It's really a privilege for me to be able to work for a company that gives away money to help children and families," adds Vera Hunter, former chair of the Seattle, Washington committee. "It's like a dream come true for me!" Indeed, the GSF Foundation has stood as a special manifestation of the company's Creed and Values and continues to grow and positively influence others year after year, heart after heart.

Shared Values, Shared Programs, Shared Responsibility

In addition to the GSF Foundation, Golden State Foods has also implemented a number of corporate programs and initiatives over the years, as further extensions of *The Creed* and Values, such as:

Awards and Recognitions Programs

- The **Golden Spirit Award**, established in 2002, which recognizes associates for going above and beyond the call of duty as they exemplify one or more of the GSF Values. More than 1,000 associates are recognized with these awards every year.

- The **Chairman's Challenge Award (CCA) and Best in Class Awards (BIC)**, the highest form of recognition at GSF, the Chairman's Challenge Award recognizes the best all-around achieving facility team each year. Established in 1999, the CCA is awarded from winners of the Best in Class Awards, which recognize the top-performing facility teams in manufacturing, distribution, and other areas of the organization.

- The **Innovation Award**, bestowed periodically on those customers and GSF teams that demonstrate creativity or ingenuity in moving the business forward towards better service. In effect since 2000, this special award inspires inventiveness and imagination in GSF stakeholders to work and achieve together as teams, while living *The Creed* and Values.

Educational and Advancement Programs

- The **GSF University**, established in 2010 as the company's in-house leadership development program, helps take associates to new heights. The university offers hundreds of online and instructor-led courses annually, continuing the learning of thousands of associates at the company each year.

- Financial support for **college education**, as well as annual scholarship programs for associates' family members.

- **Succession Planning and Associate Development**, which evaluates all leaders and associates annually to determine successors, enabling GSF to promote from within and avoid gaps in customer service. From 2018 to 2019, GSF averaged 24.5 percent of internal promotions in the U.S., which according to the World at Work Salary Budget Survey is substantially higher than the industry average of 8.6 percent.

Strategic Goal-planning Process

- The **Strategic Planning** process, which sets the company's strategic direction every three to five years. Driven by GSF's Strategic Planning Council, this disciplined process enables the company to effectively plan according to its 5 Pillars: people, quality, growth, social responsibility, and financial security — all founded on *The Creed* and Values.

Diversity, Equity, and Inclusion

- The **Diversity Council**, which helps the company maintain balance and equality. In 2022, GSF was more than 76 percent diverse among its associates in the U.S. Women and ethnic minorities represented more than 83 percent of food processing associates; 69 percent of distribution associates; and 39 percent of management partners. Additionally, approximately 10 percent of U.S. associates had a military background. The company has received customer recognition for its outstanding achievements in this area. (Please see *Appendix F* for Diversity, Equity, and Inclusion Award recognition.)

Culture of Caring

- **Prioritizing Health and Safety**, underscoring the company's care and concern for all associates. GSF goes beyond traditional benefits and safety protocols to comprehensively support its valued employees, so they can safely and productively be their best.

- **Charitable giving**, through the GSF Foundation, the company's associate-run-and-funded non-profit organization (detailed earlier in this chapter), as well as substantial, ongoing corporate giving to an array of worthy causes. Over the years, Golden State Foods has donated millions of dollars to support those in need throughout the world.

Progress Evaluation

- **Associate and Customer Surveys**, focus groups, and annual reviews enable the company to assess strengths and opportunities, and track progress as a global, regional, and local organization. GSF has been soliciting company associates every 12 to 18 months since 2000. More than 98 percent of associates participated in its 2021 survey, which, according to the Qualtrics World Norms database — the largest database of employee survey projects across all major industries — is not only well above the industry average of 80 percent, but is truly best in class. Likewise, the company's customer satisfaction surveys are administered every few years to key customers throughout the world. Many customers specifically applaud GSF's values, integrity, and deep, long-held customer relationships, while providing areas of opportunity. The company has earned multiple customer awards and recognitions for their excellent results. (Please see *Appendix F* for the complete list.)

Each one of these programs and initiatives is about further developing all associates as professionals and supporting their communities at this "Plus-1" company — as Mark Wetterau describes the people-first culture of the organization — within a safe, healthy, and inclusive environment. And each associate plays an essential role in bringing *The Creed* and Values to life through these programs.

Low Turnover and Company Pride

At Golden State Foods, all associates have skin in the game when it comes to *The Creed* and Values. They're often reminded that they are the company's culture, and whether GSF continues to evolve positively and flourish is up to them. They're continually invited to think about the principles within this values system, what they mean to them in their roles at the company, and what they mean to those around them — their fellow associates, their customers, and even their friends and family outside of the company — and to strive to hold themselves and others accountable to these standards.

"We all have a hand in maintaining the integrity of *The Creed* and Values," explains Bill Sanderson. "In many cases, they're what brought associates here in the first place and what's keeping us special, setting us apart from other organizations. Sometimes during our careers, especially when times get tough as they do in every business, it's easy to think that the 'grass is greener' somewhere else. But when problems arise at our company, we challenge our associates to 'water our own grass' a little before throwing in the towel in search of greener pastures. Cultures like ours are few and far between, and sometimes associates don't realize how truly special it is here until they leave and go somewhere else."

Most Golden State Foods associates, however, seem to want to stick around on their own turf.

Historically (barring unusual periods such as wars, pandemics, etc.), employee turnover has trended lower than its industry average, so it's not unusual to see many associates throughout the company who have been there for 20, 30, or even 40 or more years.

Lee Gragnano, a long-time (50 years!) distribution associate offers a glimpse into why. "Originally, like most young people, GSF was just a job to start my career with," he explains. "But after working for a few years, in addition to providing a positive work environment, the people here made it what it was, like an extended family. This includes my peers and those who worked for me: drivers, warehousemen, and supervisors. From having breakfast with Bill Moore at 6 a.m. on a Saturday before inventory, to Jim Williams stopping in the warehouse to talk with my father [who also worked at the company] on a regular basis, to Mark Wetterau continuing to talk to me as a friend and a trusted colleague, I've made some great friendships at GSF throughout the years."

CHAPTER 7: GOING BEYOND COMPANY BORDERS

Gragnano says in addition to working with some exceptional people, the job itself — along with company growth — has also been fulfilling. "It may sound cliché, but I enjoy coming to work because of the people we hire. I still get that excitement when we grow as a company. The opportunity to meet new associates and help out wherever and whenever I can is a rewarding experience." He adds that *The Creed* and Values have inspired him to treat people well and to contribute to the company's success. "I base what I do every day on *The Creed* and Values — especially, 'Treat others like you want to be treated' and 'treating people with dignity.' I've always strived to do the best that I can and work together with all associates and business partners to put us in the position to be successful."

Lee's example is one of thousands of similar perspectives. (See list of GSF's corporate programs and initiatives under the "Shared Values" section earlier in this chapter.) According to the company's recent associate attitudinal surveys, on average 94 percent of associates believe they "strive to live *The Creed* and Values every day" in their role at the company; 91 percent say they "have good friends at work;" and 97 percent say they "feel that GSF is *their* company." And these trends continue to climb higher each year.

Steve Becker, former senior vice president of human resources at GSF for 17 years, says that these significant retention motivators are some of the key indicators of the depth of *The Creed* and Values within the company culture. He explains that when these survey questions were followed up with deeper discussions in associate focus groups, the stats were underscored with responses like...

"Yes, *The Creed* and Values are the foundation of our company;"
"That's who we are;"
"It's meaningful, it's impactful;" and
"It's not just words on the wall, it's the real deal, and it's important to me."

Becker emphasizes that *The Creed* makes a difference to associates, and this is manifest by lower turnover rates. "People want to stay with companies that are fair and equitable, that give back to their communities, that have a social responsibility component. They don't necessarily say they want to receive the most money or the most benefits for the fewest hours — they want to work for leaders and businesses that have a strong value system. So there are quite a few people who come to Golden State Foods and stay at the company because [of that value system]. No one is perfect, and we all make mistakes, but we do our best to abide by those values. I know for a fact that *The Creed* and Values impact our people. They tell us so, and we know it through the numbers and our retention factor."

Clearly, *The Creed* and Values are more than just programs or words on a wall," says Mark. "They are part of who we are as an organization; part of what we stand for; part of our culture. I love my dad's statement that '*The Creed by itself is merely words. But it's the people who really bring it to life.*' When you think about *The Creed* and our Values, it's really all about 'WE.' While we care about individuals, there is nothing in the words of *The Creed* about 'I.' We are a 'WE' organization through and through."

Photos (left to right):

1) GSF family of companies' logos

2) Golden State Foods' partners and leaders at an annual leadership conference in 2022

3) A sampling of GSF's valued customers: Starbucks, Chick-fil-A, Zaxby's, Chipotle, and McDonald's

4) The company's anniversary logo, designed for the 75th celebration in 2022

CHAPTER 8

Continuing the Legacy

"If we truly believe in The Creed and Values, we also have a responsibility to [safeguard] their legacy. As people leave the company, it's important that we make sure The Creed and Values don't just get lost; we need to ensure they get passed along to other generations as well."

—**Steve Becker** (1952–   )
Corporate Senior Vice President of Human Resources (2009–2017)
Corporate Vice President of Human Resources (2000–2009),
Golden State Foods

Keepers of *The Creed*: Making HR's Job Easier!

Seventeen-year GSF human resources lead, Steve Becker, was intrigued with *The Creed* when he was researching Golden State Foods as a potential hire in 2000. He was impressed with the boldness of belief. He appreciated that it was on the facility walls, desks, business cards, and company collateral. But like many potential employees, he questioned if it was genuine or just too good to be true. "I wondered if *The Creed* really permeated the organization, or if it was just words on a wall," he recalls, explaining that many organizations claim to have strong values, but few actually demonstrate them throughout their culture. He particularly wanted to understand the depth and practice of the belief in the dignity of all people. This had poignant ramifications for his specific role in HR.

"If they truly believe in the dignity of all people and treating people with respect — following the Golden Rule so to speak — and that permeates the organization, then that makes my job heading up HR so much easier," Steve shares of his thinking at the time. "Because if everybody believes in the dignity of all people, then they are almost guaranteed the right to be treated with dignity and respect in this company."

Steve began to be convinced during the interview process, when, as many candidates observe, each of the senior leaders with whom he met (including the CEO) referenced *The Creed* and Values in some way. "I found that very impressive, that they all understood, could almost recite, and were comfortable with *The Creed* and the Values and that they embraced them. That gave me a very strong indication that they were real, and they were wrapped around the entire organization."

Once he joined the company, Becker led HR in a more expanded role than it was prior to his service, partnering more deeply with each of the business groups. It was in this capacity where he witnessed many other examples of *The Creed* in action, often seeing it used as a filter in business decisions, including disciplinary action. If the potential decision on how to treat an associate, customer, or supplier couldn't pass *The Creed* test, it was tabled, changed, or abandoned. "It was very impressive," he says, "that an organization really embraced those values, and they were embedded into business decision-making. I thought, 'This is very, very powerful. This is way beyond words on a wall.'"

Leading HR for many years, Steve and his department were often referred to as the "keepers of *The Creed* and Values," which he says was an honorable mantle to shoulder. "That meant quite a bit to me because it [said] that leadership felt the HR department was responsible for ensuring *The Creed* and Values were adhered to throughout the entire organization, beyond the corporate office and out into the field, into all the businesses. HR is out there supporting the people within the organization, and it's our responsibility to ensure fair and equitable treatment," he explains. "So we (HR) should use *The Creed* and Values as our filter in making decisions, which comes back to the phrase in the Values, 'giving the customer a fair deal.' I always felt that meant fairness to all. It goes beyond the customer because so often in a corporate support staff role, our managers, leaders, and associates are our [internal] customers, so the rule of fairness applies to everything we do."

While HR has been given the formal title of the "Keepers of *The Creed*," Becker emphasizes that the responsibility to uphold *The Creed* and Values goes much deeper than just HR or management. "I've felt that our associates have a responsibility, too. We all live *The Creed* and Values, and we're all accountable for abiding by them and ensuring that they're [upheld] in the field. It's not management's sole charge to make the rules and enforce the rules. Yes, they have a duty to make sure associates are treating others with dignity and respect, but associates have an obligation to hold us as leaders accountable as well. "So, if you see behavior inconsistent with these values in your bosses, your leaders in your facility, you are charged with calling it out," Becker continues. "Don't go quiet and just accept that perhaps there's a double standard. Obviously, you hold yourself accountable, but hold leaders accountable, too."

Human Resources' Role: Policing vs. Value Adds

Becker goes on to explain that when *The Creed* and Values are adhered to, they have a profound impact on a company, especially from an HR standpoint: Human Resources' function changes from a disciplinary role to a more innovative one.

"If a company does not treat its associates or employees fairly and equitably, then HR has a 'police role,' as I call it, where it is always trying to maintain control," Becker explains. "They have to come in after the fact, fix problems, and correct bad behavior. We have to lay down the law directly or [through] a supervisor. So if treating people with dignity and respect at all times is embedded into the organization, then the nature of that police role is reduced dramatically. There's always some of that because some people get out of bounds. But if you can minimize [such behavior] through a creed or your foundational value system," he continues, "then it makes the role of HR so much easier. You can spend less time on what I would refer to as 'non-profit, non-productive activities' such as threatening suspension and termination, and more time on 'productive, value-added activities,' like building out learning development systems or figuring out ways to enhance recognition programs, so you can better appreciate your people." (See the list of corporate programs and initiatives offered at GSF under the "Shared Values" section in Chapter 7).

Twenty-five-year associate, Wayne Morgan, who has led the company's Protein Group for nearly two decades, agrees with Becker's perspectives. He says that often, simple reminders can go a long way in motivating people to do the right thing. "Usually, that's all it takes," he says, of associates encouraging each other to think about their behavior or decisions and whether they're consistent with *The Creed* and Values. "It's not something to club someone over the head with. It's something to prick their heart or mind with, or just poke their conscience with, so they do a self-reflection and determine that maybe they need to take inventory of themselves."

Morgan notes that the constant awareness of *The Creed* within the company's culture has helped him create win-win situations with others. And it's helped him temper his own highly competitive spirit, a common character trait of most GSF associates. "I believe I've chosen to operate by a higher standard than just the normal 'do what it takes to get by,'" he explains, of his innate desire to get ahead and to "win." "You can call it winning, but it's not really about winning, it's about getting your own way. So I think *The Creed* and Values help put some guideposts or guardrails around how hard to drive towards 'winning.' It's really not about whether I get my way or not, but rather the bigger picture of how well I treat people. Yes, I have my personal faith and my personal beliefs to fall back on as well, but from a business standpoint, I think *The Creed* provides [perspective], and some excellent parameters to work by."

Continuing the Legacy

As succession continues throughout the company, Steve Becker underscores how all associates also play a part in continuing the legacy of *The Creed* and Values beyond their careers at the company. "If we truly believe in *The Creed* and Values, we also have a responsibility to [safeguard] their legacy," he says, explaining how managers need to make sure their teams have a clear understanding of them and that successors in all positions experience the same. "As people leave the company, it's important that we make sure *The Creed* and Values don't just get lost; we need to ensure they get passed along to other generations as well."

With Steve's retirement in 2017, he passed the baton to Ed Rodriguez, GSF's corporate senior vice president and chief HR officer. Ed believes that *The Creed* and Values are still alive and well at the company, perhaps more prominently and influentially than ever. "I think it shows the level of care we take with our associates," explains Rodriguez. "It's just a very different experience here at GSF than it has been with me in 25-plus years of doing this at different companies. *The Creed* and Values are our organization's 'true north,' and we always refer to them as a filter for our deeds and actions — how we interact with our associates, how we treat them during the good times and the tough times. You can tell right away this is a company that encourages individuals who are part of the organization to be fully vested in the purpose, beyond just the customers and the business, but in terms of our connection to communities and to helping kids in need and being fulfilled beyond financial and career motives. And I think we take a lot more care in all of our actions that impact our associates and their families than other companies where I've worked." The difference for Rodriguez, he explains, is the deeper level of authenticity that he's observed at the company. "In other places, organizations are trying to bottle or capture the essence of their culture and label it with a process that aims to articulate what that culture and company represents. Here, it's more organic."

Ed goes on to say that an authentic connection that exists among associates, including the leadership, and even their families is part of what makes Golden State Foods so different. "I felt more connected to GSF in three years than I did with other companies I'd been with for longer periods of time," he notes. "I think my family feels more connected to Golden State Foods as well. My younger kids feel a sense of joy and pride being a part of GSF. Some of the activities we provide for them to be involved in the experience, whether it's our summer picnic, 'bring your family to work' day, or other activities, have left positive impressions on them. And the level of intimacy — the feeling that you're fully vested — goes beyond a business relationship. A lot of that has to do with Mark and his leadership. A lot of it has to do with *The Creed* and Values. And a lot of it has to do with the type of people we attract. Whether we agree or disagree with them, we know we're all in this to help build a company and the community."

Today, Rodriguez and his global HR team are busily focused on bringing in people who reinforce and embrace *The Creed* and Values and that sense of belonging. As part of that process, *The Creed* and Values continue to be a prominent part of screening and onboarding, performance management, and disciplining, when needed. Senior executives also conduct regular presentations to their groups about *The Creed* and Values at all locations, underscoring the priority of these foundational ideals.

CHAPTER 8: CONTINUING THE LEGACY

Additionally, when GSF celebrated its 75th anniversary in 2022, among its many celebratory events and activities, the company instituted a multimedia "Our Legacy Journey" experience for all associates to go through and learn first-hand about the organization's history, culture, and legacy of values from the past into the future.

"This has been a game-changer for so many of our newer associates to better understand and appreciate who we are as an organization historically and culturally, beyond their scope of work and length of service," says Ed, "and perhaps more importantly, where we're headed together in the future."

Ed explains how sharing this rich legacy as a foundation throughout the company pays off, especially when things heat up. "The reality [of our business] is that it's fast-paced. It's highly competitive, and mistakes happen. Sometimes, things don't go our way. And I think during the heat of the battle, everyone can get emotional — we can jump to a conclusion, or we make a snap decision. In all those situations, having *The Creed* and Values as a filter for our actions helps us to step back and analyze the decision-making process through them. This again always helps us find the inner compass we need to make the right choices."

The Creed and Values: Foundational to GSF's 5 Pillars for Success

Golden State Foods' objectives in working within the tenets of a strong values system, such as *The Creed* proclaims, are represented in what the company calls the "5 Pillars," which its leadership team established to help enable the company's success.

These pillars are the foundation upon which the company's multi-year strategic plans and annual plans are established. Each business leader throughout the organization aligns their group goals to these plans and reports their progress on them each quarter to ensure the company's success.

The 5 Pillars

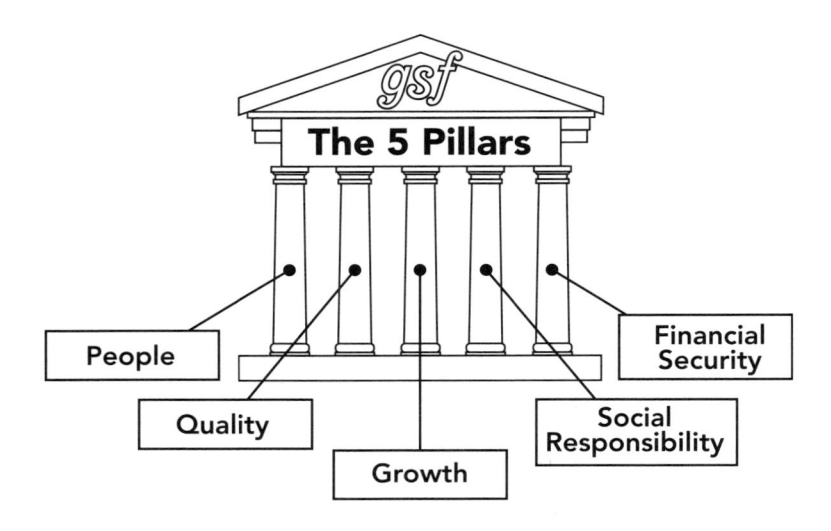

- People
- Quality
- Growth
- Social Responsibility
- Financial Security

Taking such steps to be sure the values of *The Creed* are interwoven within the very fibers of the company's structure — in addition to encouraging those values be lived and exemplified by its people — assures that every action and every decision will align along time-proven principles known to secure success.

Former Starbucks Chairman and CEO Howard Schultz affirmed this in his book, *Pour Your Heart Into It: How Starbucks Built a Company One Cup at a Time*, when he wrote: "Whatever your culture, your values, your guiding principles, you have to take steps to inculcate them in the organization early in its life so that they can guide every decision, every hire, every strategic objective you set."

The 5 Pillars, in line with *The Creed* and Values, help Golden State Foods achieve that very ideal, even down to daily tactics, while still allowing associates the latitude to make regular decisions according to their conscience.

CHAPTER 8: CONTINUING THE LEGACY

GSF's Progress Since Instituting *The Creed*

Since instituting *The Creed* at Golden State Foods just over two decades ago, GSF and its family of companies have experienced exponential success:

- GSF has grown from a $1.4 billion enterprise to more than $7 billion in annual sales in 2018, prior to spinning off some of its assets to reinvest into other areas of the business for future growth.

- The company has diversified its businesses, as well as its customer base, from virtually one customer to more than 125,000 restaurants and stores around the world, through more than 200 iconic brands.

- With approximately 15 facilities in 1998, operations have now grown to more than 50 around the world.

- Two thousand hard-working associates at the end of the 20th century have surged today to more than 6,000 worldwide, with approximately 170 partners who own stock in the company. (As of this writing, GSF is one of the largest S Corporations in the United States.)

- Golden State Foods has been listed among *Forbes'* largest private companies in America since the list's inception in 1985. In 2022, it was listed as number 101.

"It's astonishing to have that kind of growth," observes GSF board member, Sharon Davis. "We've had growth during bad years, and we've had growth during substantial years. Not that we don't have our setbacks, because every company has setbacks. But Mark Wetterau and his team grew this company in an environment that is very tough. It's not a high-margin business. It's a business wherein you have to be very smart. Very large companies have attempted to do what we've done and have not succeeded. In fact, in some cases, we have replaced large companies as suppliers that couldn't do it as well — companies that were double or triple our size and still could not deliver what we deliver. I think it says a lot about Golden State Foods, which is really based in *The Creed* — they're interwoven."

"They are what make the difference," says Mark Wetterau, of GSF's Creed and Values. "They are what set us apart from our competition — what propels us *from good to great*, as Jim Collins would say. They set a tone for our company, help us establish specific business standards and practices, and keep us customer-centric. As we've diversified our business more and more each year, many key customers have joined with GSF *because* of *The Creed* and Values. They help us work better as teams; and I believe that [they] continue to elevate us as human beings overall."

Establishing a creed early on — first at Wetterau Inc., then at Quality Beverage, later at Golden State Foods, and subsequently at various other companies — has certainly instilled enduring guiding principles that will live on decade after decade. It has given all of these organizations tremendous staying power through the belief, passion, and commitment of its generations of associates, and will continue to do so throughout time.

The Creed's underlying philosophy began in 1869 with George Wetterau's early values of honesty and integrity and has indeed endured the test of time for more than 150 years, through good times and bad. Whether through unprecedented growth; challenges of an attempted takeover; the rocky merger at Wetterau Inc.; acquisitions or union strikes at Quality Beverage; diversification or global expansion at Golden State Foods, *The Creed* has enabled these organizations to not only survive, but thrive in the face of adversity. It has galvanized cultures and lifted all stakeholders. Countless examples, testimonials, studies, and bottom lines underscore that *The Creed*, indeed, has been a positive gamechanger at the Wetterau companies.

CHAPTER 8: CONTINUING THE LEGACY

Incorporating *The Creed* into Other GSF Companies

Over the years, as Golden State Foods has grown and expanded throughout the world, it has started, partnered with, and acquired a number of different regional, national, and international companies. These include Centralized Leasing Corp. (CLC), Central Freight Management (CFM), Strategic Sourcing Alliance (SSA), Quality Custom Distribution (QCD), KanPak (U.S. and China), Groenz, Snap Fresh Foods, *GSF Fresh!* (including a joint venture with Taylor Fresh Foods), Q Performance, and others. Not surprisingly, *The Creed* has been a fundamental staple in each.

"As we continue to grow and expand throughout the world, *The Creed* becomes even more vital," says Mark Wetterau, of aligning amidst the company's business and geographic diversification. "It's critical for leaders and associates alike to clearly understand our beliefs and values and the fundamental role they play every day in each of these businesses because they are carrying out the day-to-day tasks and representing our company to the customers and communities in the various regions and environments. Our stakeholders need to experience the same high-quality values and service from us wherever they are in the world, whether it's China, Egypt, Australia, the U.S. or elsewhere," Mark continues. "And we've seen how *The Creed* and Values have had such a positive impact in each of these regions and in every type of business we operate, whether it's manufacturing liquids or meat, growing fresh produce, processing aseptic products, or distributing to our many customers in the various regions throughout the world."

While the impact of *The Creed* has indeed been felt by associates across the globe within the GSF family of companies, the process of incorporating *The Creed* varied, depending on whether the company was a start-up, a joint venture partnership, or a straight acquisition. For instance, Quality Custom Distribution, a U.S.-based distribution company, emerged in 2006 from GSF Distribution, which had serviced one dedicated customer for decades. As such, *The Creed* was a fundamental part of the company from the start. But as QCD continued to grow and expand throughout the country, it acquired other distribution companies and centers, which more often than not, expressed enthusiasm for becoming a part of the company's culture and creed.

For example, when QCD acquired a number of DPI (Distribution Logistics, Inc.) locations in the Northeast and Midwest in 2020, the Boston team was quick to engage in the organization's signature community outreach efforts to support those in need during the COVID-19 pandemic. "Since joining QCD, I have noticed many good things being done within the company across the country to help out the community," says Mark Donahue, former general manager of QCD Boston, just a few months after his facility was acquired. "Boston now feels a part of the GSF family, and we are doing our part in the community. It really does make you feel good when you help the local community that you work in."

Similarly, Centralized Leasing Corp., GSF's truck and equipment leasing company, and Central Freight Management, the organization's freight management business, began in 1999 and 2000 respectively, with *The Creed* and Values as their foundation, as were Strategic Sourcing Alliance (SSA) and *GSF Fresh!*. So it was a natural transition to adopt *The Creed* and Values into these organizations, as well.

Conversely, KanPak, an international aseptic dairy producer, New Zealand-based liquid products supplier Groenz, and Snap Fresh Foods, a New Zealand-based produce-grower and provider (which later merged with *GSF Fresh!*), were all joint venture acquisitions from other owners that eventually became 100 percent GSF-owned. But initially, the leadership of these companies was kept in place for several years until an agreed-upon transition time took place. As such, they needed time to fully understand and accept GSF's Creed and Values before instituting them into their companies.

"Every circumstance is unique," explains Mark Wetterau, when acquiring or partnering with another company. "But it's important to respect the values and priorities of companies you're bringing on board, and to not force your culture on them. Be patient and let them take time to choose to embrace your culture, rather than compelling them to accept it. By the same token,

CHAPTER 8: CONTINUING THE LEGACY

learn from their culture and what their business can bring to yours. While it should eventually evolve into one company culture, try to make it a 'win-win' along the way."

This approach was encouraged as GSF acquired KanPak, Groenz, and Snap. Like others, leadership at both KanPak and Groenz were somewhat suspect about *The Creed* and Values initially, but eventually embraced them. For instance, former Groenz managing director and retired board member, Fred Groen, is an agnostic who was unclear about the role a belief in God would play at Groenz. "It took me a while to get past the 'religion' part, but I fully respect other people who do believe," he explains.

Infusing *The Creed* into Groenz

As Fred and others within the Groenz business began to see the benefits, the cohesiveness, and the productivity *The Creed* encouraged, they embraced it as an organization. "It's really all about growing, building, and making money the right way and for the long-term, not just focusing on the short-term," he says now, as a full supporter of *The Creed*.

Since the Groenz acquisition in 2014, the company has grown more than 45 percent, employment has increased, and customer satisfaction is positive. Former Groenz Managing Director Taylor Harbison (who has now transitioned to another family company) said while he was in the role, that even though *The Creed* was relatively new at Groenz, it helped provide a positive ideal and clear direction to the team. "I focused a lot on the first paragraph and said, 'Look, we've got to treat everybody like we want to be treated and concentrate on something beyond just ourselves.' Absorbing that and understanding *The Creed* and the way we care for the people within the organization and the communities we're in [was a high priority]." He explained that he, and other leaders at Groenz, spent a lot of energy ensuring that they recognized and engaged associates. "We made sure we were communicating more effectively with them, listening to them, and giving them opportunities to raise [issues]. That meant spending more time with every associate and trying to be open and flexible as to what people needed to be happier at the company."

Though Taylor has since passed on Groenz leadership to four-year GSF and Groenz associate, Felipe Demartini, managing director of GSF Australia and New Zealand, he emphasized that *The Creed* also served as a driver at

Groenz to reach out to the community and serve where possible in charity work and being a good corporate citizen. "Groenz is not solely focused on how to make Groenz a better place. It's about how everyone at the company can make all of the places around them better and the people operating the company better. As Groenz becomes a more successful organization, the more it's going to be able to help the people within it, and the community that's surrounding it and the other communities within which it does business."

KanPak's Transition to a Creed-based Organization

At KanPak, the leadership followed GSF's lead and instituted the Values first then brought in *The Creed*. "While all of the Values are important, we really focused on 'treating others the way that you want to be treated,'" explains Larry McGill, former chairman of KanPak U.S. This meant providing associates more reasonable work hours, brighter career paths, and listening more to their input. Leadership held town hall meetings to discuss the meaning of the Values and sought to exemplify them every day through management behavior. "It wasn't just 'you'll do this, and you'll do that,' says Larry. "We made suggestions, but also invited associate recommendations and opinions when making decisions."

For instance, when the company transitioned to the new ownership, it didn't just automatically switch out the associates' health insurance benefits. Management discussed the existing and new options and incorporated the best of both plans. Likewise, they enhanced their succession-planning program, and gave the associates a clearer pathway to their future career growth.

Once the Values were in place at KanPak, leadership introduced *The Creed* during one of their town hall meetings. "We had a discussion about why it was important, and that it was really the pathway to move KanPak into more fully becoming a GSF company," says McGill, explaining that the associates had already seen the added value GSF's positive culture had brought them. "And it was just so favorably received, it was unbelievable."

Larry adds that while the associates were enthusiastic about *The Creed*, they were somewhat concerned that the company wasn't yet up to the high standards its principles purport. "We explained that even though we might not be there just yet, *The Creed* was an ideal we were striving for, and we would continue to work towards every day at this company."

CHAPTER 8: CONTINUING THE LEGACY

Since then, Larry has passed on KanPak's leadership to six-year GSF and KanPak associate, Chad Buechel, who's now serving as president of KanPak U.S. Both agree that KanPak has made great strides over the past few years because of *The Creed* and Values. "The biggest impact of implementing *The Creed* and Values into KanPak is that they allowed us to have a direction for career-minded people, making us the employer of choice in our areas where we have facilities," says Larry. "It's also contributed to us moving from an autocratic culture to a more team-oriented environment. Associates are freer to voice their opinions without being demeaned. We allow decision-making and recommendations to come from all levels of the company, which has not only made us a better organization, but also a better corporate citizen. This, along with the GSF Foundation, has had a huge impact on the personality of our company and how it's reflected in our communities."

Larry adds that associates carry themselves with more company pride and that turnover has decreased substantially since these values have been instituted and practiced at all levels of KanPak. "I'm so very proud of what the team has done in changing and allowing *The Creed* and Values to be the centerpiece of the company."

PART II

The Anatomy and Power of a Company *Creed*

SECTION 1

The *Creed* Deconstructed[*]

*While The Wetterau Creed, QB Creed, GSF Creed, and others are very similar in nature, the most recent version of The Creed — the GSF Creed — will be referenced for purposes of deconstructing, analyzing, and explaining each line of The Creed. For a comparative review of each company's creed, please refer to Chapters 2 and 4 (pages 41 and 95 respectively).

CHAPTER 9

We Believe in God and the Dignity of All People

"The belief in God that The Creed *talks about isn't so much a religious statement as it is a statement of commitment to the belief in a higher power that gives us direction and some reason to live in a proper way. It doesn't mean that you have to believe exactly what I believe, but this is what we collectively believe."*

–Wayne Morgan (1966–)
Corporate Vice President and President, Protein Products
and Operations Support Services (2019–present)
Corporate Vice President and President, Protein Products Group (2007–2019),
Golden State Foods

"We believe in God and the dignity of all people."

A belief in God? In business?! These words are probably the most controversial of *The Creed*, especially in this day and age. The idea of even mentioning God in the public sphere is not only politically incorrect but highly offensive to some. So the notion of showcasing it front and center as the headliner of a company creed — the spring from which the rest of the proclamation flows and thus, the foundation on which the company and its success rests — is at minimum highly unusual in the business world and at the other end of the spectrum, quite radical.

But the rebels at the Wetterau companies, who proudly proclaim *The Creed* and strive to abide by its principles, don't care. They boldly embrace and unapologetically assert, front and center, their belief in God. And these aren't just Christians making such declarations, as its originator,

Ted Wetterau was. Despite that Ted was a devout Presbyterian, the power of *The Creed* extends beyond a belief in Jesus Christ. It's so universal that the company's Muslims in Egypt resonate with it; Buddhists in Asia embrace it; and Hindus in Australia call it their own.

"The most valuable thing we have at GSF is our Creed and Values," says Saeed Mahmoud, managing director at GSF's Cairo, Egypt manufacturing and distribution center, who's also a devout Muslim. In fact, hundreds of Muslims cheerfully and diligently work at the thriving facility that has been serving the Middle East since the 1990s. "It's a place we advise many of our friends, family, and acquaintances to work for," says Saeed.

"It was a major positive," recalls GSF board member, Dick Gochnauer, about how the associates in Egypt embraced *The Creed*. "When you think about it, it shouldn't be a surprise because they're a very faithful people. Some are Christian but most aren't, and they certainly believe in God. So it's turned out to have the same positive impact [as it has in the U.S.]."

"There have been many religious organizations — Christian-based corporations and Christian-based private companies — that have reached out wanting me to become a part of them," shares Mark Wetterau, who understands why he would be approached due to the faith-based nature of *The Creed*. "I would explain to them that 'yes, I am truly a believer. I'm a strong Presbyterian. I believe in my faith, but that's not what we're trying to drive here.'"

Instilling faith in God while remaining open to diversity of religious thought is perhaps a unique organizational balance to achieve. Next Solutions CEO Doug Wilson, a prominent thought leader in building purpose-driven companies, explains the downside of incorporating too narrow of a belief focus, including Christianity. "I've been part of some groups where if you were not a certain religious stripe, it was hard to get ahead in that company, and people picked up on that. It was a subtle pressure, and it's not healthy," Wilson says. "It creates a closed system that can lead to a lack of diversity and a fear of speaking out with a different point of view. And that's the last thing you want to create inside of a company that requires pragmatic decision-making, looking at the facts, and ensuring you're not letting certain biases blind you to ways of seeing the world differently. But I've never sensed that being a part of the culture at [any of the Wetterau-owned companies], because I've seen the diversity of people and programs there." Doug says he was impressed with the language in *The Creed* that "honored God" and also "showed respect and dignity" for the value of all individuals, despite their religious point of view.

> *"The 'belief in God' in* The Creed *does not dictate how a company associate should believe. It simply declares that associates acknowledge something greater than themselves. This ability to believe in something beyond oneself better enables people to believe in a goal, in a team, and in a greater force that can drive an organization to success."*
>
> DOUG WILSON

Associates at GSF, Quality Beverage, and other Wetterau companies acknowledge that in the way they approach their work within their own beliefs. "It's so difficult to talk about honoring God and at the same time be very open to diversity and making sure you're not shutting down people or shutting out those who have different views of who God is or even if there is a god in that sense," continues Doug. "If you don't allow for that, you're not going to get the diversity you need in the modern world."

"I believe in God, and I know a lot of people do. But I also know that means different things to different people," explains GSF corporate vice president and president of protein products and operations support services, Wayne Morgan, who says many people in society today often use those statements to divide. "If you read it within the context of what it means to you, it can mean something positive to everyone. So, it really isn't so much a religious statement as it is a statement of commitment to the belief in a higher power that gives us direction and some reason to live in a proper way."

Morgan goes on to say that *The Creed's* statement about belief in God lays out a general, broad picture about what the company believes as a group. "It doesn't mean that you have to believe exactly what I believe, but what it's saying is this is what we collectively believe," he explains.

"*The Creed*, I feel, is a difference maker," Mark Wetterau says. "It certainly attracts believers. It attracts folks who can buy into the strategy of what we're trying to accomplish as an organization. I feel these individuals are strong leaders and better equipped to face challenging and even controversial situations with each other and with our customers. And since they are strong believers in God, I think they also recognize the fact that we're not going to be perfect all the time, but that moving forward towards an ideal together — including overcoming mistakes — is what brings unity and progress."

Former first lady of California and GSF advisory board member, Sharon Davis, agrees. "When you're a person of faith, you have to intentionally pray and be connected, because we're all human and we fall short. But I think having *The Creed* there — front and center — helps everyone understand that we're human. I think it sets an example of the high standards we want to achieve."

Regardless of one's specific beliefs, a person can still exercise their faith and appreciate one's dependency on a higher power and the strength of a team. "What *The Creed* does is it allows people of faith to reinforce that faith without having to dictate whose faith it is or that [something prescriptive] must be followed," says Dick Gochnauer. "It's clearly saying, 'We do believe in a god, okay?' [You don't have to be a Christian to appreciate this belief.] If you're a Hindu [or a Muslim, or a Buddhist], you can respect what that statement says and what it means and value it. It speaks volumes about how dependable you [as an associate] might be or how reliable you are in following through on what you say. It calls out that this is a company looking for folks who are interested in a higher purpose spiritually and not from a religious perspective [necessarily]. I think it reflects — regardless of religion — employees who have within them a sense of purpose and a sense of meaning."

CHAPTER 9: WE BELIEVE IN GOD

"Ninety-nine percent of people here believe in some higher being out there," says Conrad Wetterau, of the employees at Quality Beverage. "They may not believe the same way, but they believe there is somebody more powerful than us out there to whom they can look and who helps lead their lives, to steer them in some way. Everybody has a different interpretation, so we're not telling people to believe in a specific god, but we're saying that 'we *believe* ... we believe in God and the dignity of all people.'" Tom Haggai explained it this way: "By recognizing God and believing in Him, that means in return there's a good chance He believes in us, too."

Regardless of whom they worship, most people at the Wetterau family of companies say they are comfortable respecting others' beliefs while adhering to their own. "We can all live in peace as long as we understand that somebody else may believe something different," adds Merwyn Sher, a former Wetterau Inc. retailer, referring to people from multiple religions co-existing with tolerance in the workplace. "I think that's what America was founded on, [the fact that you can] believe in something different [from what I believe], but we can still get along."

The people at the Wetterau companies have found that if their associates can believe in God, however they choose to define that, then they'll be able to believe in and align with other relevant matters like the principles within *The Creed* and subsequently, the goals and objectives of the company. In fact, GSF encourages diversity of thought and background, which management believes is critical to its success. This is true not only in the area of faith and religion, but also in age, gender, race, geographic and cultural backgrounds, and professional areas of expertise. This is illustrated especially at Golden State Foods, where there is 76 percent company diversity in the U.S. Its associates say that this multiformity strengthens them as an organization and helps them continually improve.

GSF's Corporate Executive Vice President and Chief Administrative Officer John Page says, "Diversity really means including all so you get the best ideas. And without different people, you couldn't come up with different ideas. You'd be doing the same thing over and over again." Page, who previously served as corporate senior vice president and chief CSR and legal officer for the company continues: "But GSF makes a concerted effort to ensure that all associates are represented at the company and have a voice — whether it's formally through our associate surveys and focus groups or through our open-door policy at all levels — because we all matter, and we all deserve to be heard. This fosters a rich tapestry of ideas and opinions, which strengthens us as a company and actually helps move us forward with more unity."

Doubting the Doubters

Not surprisingly, the "belief in God" line has been challenged repeatedly by both well-meaning business leaders and cynics alike:

"How can you mix business and religious belief?"

"Why would you include specific language about God into a business statement?"

"Isn't that taking company values a bit too far?"

The people at the Wetterau companies don't think so. They feel so strongly about the importance of belief that even when this ideal has been challenged time and again, they've been unwilling to alter it.

"I've had many discussions with a number of CEOs and respected business colleagues who question how a belief in God fits into business today," says Mark. "I usually share our philosophy of belief and explain that our creed is really a *filter* of sorts within our company. Those of us who resonate with *The Creed* typically fit well into our culture and are enthusiastic about our goals."

CHAPTER 9: WE BELIEVE IN GOD

Most associates at each of the Wetterau companies agree, and actually appreciate keeping God in the conversations. "It starts at the top, and the management follows it," explained 11-year distribution manager for GSF, Ed Sowa, before his passing after a tough battle with cancer. "They walk the walk, not just talk the talk. Mark is proud to talk about God in his meetings. Yeah, we hear some cynicism from some of the guys like, 'Why is he talking about God? Is he a preacher?' But I have no problem talking about Him. I believe in God and a hereafter. Always have. Maybe it's not in vogue for everybody to believe in God anymore, but I especially need Him right now. I'm taking everybody's prayers. But the biggest thing is that [the leadership] live it. [They're] not afraid to talk about God. And you don't see many CEOs do that."

CHAPTER 10

Treat People as You Want to Be Treated

"What has impressed me about Golden State Foods is that The Creed and company Values are truly a part of its fabric. All GSF associates [seem to] live and breathe them. Whether you drive a truck at the distribution center, run a production line, or sit in the 'C-suite,' the culture is the heartbeat of the organization. As a customer, I see it come to life through consistent behaviors of all associates. In good times and even more so in tough times or with difficult situations, the values of the organization always shine through."

–Marion Gross (1960–)
Executive Vice President and Global Chief Supply Chain Officer (2022–present)
Various roles on purchasing and corporate management teams (1993–2022),
McDonald's

"We believe that people should be treated as we would like to be treated, and this applies to all of our associates, their families, our customers and suppliers and to all others with whom we do business."

At all the Wetterau companies, associates believe in treating others with respect — the way they would like to be treated, each and every day. Aligning with the company values that have been in place for many decades in all the companies Wetterau has been involved with, the Golden Rule is definitely at play. And this means everyone with whom company associates come in contact: customers at all levels, suppliers, fellow associates, and friends and families.

"We all deserve to be treated with respect and dignity," says Mark Wetterau of the people who work with him at GSF. "We're all equal as human beings, regardless of our role here. Of course, we have a hierarchy at our company for reporting purposes and for helping us stay focused as an organization. But at the same time, regardless of our position, we're all human, and we're all equal."

Most associates take this perspective seriously, which causes some daily self-reflection. Forty-two-year IT associate for GSF, Bill Runyan, now retired, says thoughtfully, "As I think about *The Creed* and our company Values, I have to ask myself, 'Am I treating others the way that I like to be treated?'"

Equal treatment is something associates continually monitor, as working relationships develop and evolve, and as tasks pile up, deadlines increase, and stress rises.

> "I often say, 'Put yourself in their shoes. We're talking about someone's livelihood and career, and you need to be very thoughtful about that: Are we treating others the way we would like to be treated? Would you feel comfortable that the decision was just, fair, and right? You may not like it, but is it fair and right? And if you were in their position, would you be able to honestly answer that question?' When we fall back on The Creed *and our first Value, we have sometimes modified our decisions based on that value — that's a very important thing."*
>
> STEVE BECKER

And this applies to all company constituents.

"The part I have always loved [about *The Creed*] is 'We believe that people should be treated as we would like to be treated,'" says former Wetterau associate, Cathy Heimburger Courtright, of her days with Wetterau Inc., "and this applies to the employees, families, and suppliers. I think it's true, especially when there are people going through hard times. In the 1980s, when the bigger stores were coming in, some retailers hung on as long as they could but others didn't survive because there were some doors

CHAPTER 10: TREAT PEOPLE AS YOU WANT TO BE TREATED

that had to shut. And I thought Wetterau handled [those situations] with a lot of grace as they tried to help those retailers so they didn't lose everything, keeping them going for as long as they could, they really did."

Cathy adds that part of the spirit of *The Creed's* admonition to treat people with respect is acting graciously and tactfully, even in challenging situations. "*The Creed* gives you that grace when faced with difficult decisions," she explains, referring to these opportunities as "velvet acts," a signature Wetterau quality. "It's really getting people through a hard situation, whether you're having to break a relationship and that person has to move on, or if somebody loses their job [through downsizing or other circumstances], there are so many situations that can be done gracefully."

Even board members feel the responsibility to exemplify *The Creed* in their personal, everyday lives. "When you associate with a company that has that strong of a creed, you really do have to look at how you spend your life, how you conduct yourself, and what you commit to that company," explains Sharon Davis. "Even though as board members we're not employees, I do feel like I represent the organization, that I'm part of the company family. When I come in contact with someone who knows I'm part of this company I want them to feel I reflect [well] what is in *The Creed*."

Treating others with dignity and respect doesn't just apply to one-on-one human relationships and interactions with others, it naturally lends itself to one of the GSF Values: *Maintaining the highest standards,* which means making the best product — the highest quality product — whatever one's role is in the business for making that happen. Associates across the Wetterau family of businesses strive constantly to help their organizations be gold standard companies. And with that comes maintaining top-notch conduct each and every day. This applies not only in product development and distribution but in how associates handle themselves, communicate with others, dress, maintain their facilities and their tractor-trailers (which are rolling billboards to the world), and every other daily practice at their various companies.

"Everything we do should strive for the highest standards," Mark admonishes company associates. As someone known for pointing out specs of dirt on the most pristine of trucks during inspections, he holds himself to those standards as well. "We can't be perfect all the time, but we can always strive for excellence. This is a *key contributor to building brand trust* with our customers."

So, has *The Creed* helped the Wetterau companies build that brand trust? A number of key customers seem to think so. Golden State Foods' relationships with McDonald's, Chick-fil-A, and Zaxby's are powerful illustrations of this.

GSF and McDonald's: A 70-year Relationship and Still Going Strong

In McDonald's case, the decades-long partnership tells the sweetheart story about the two companies' relationship of trust. Since the early days of Bill Moore building relationships in the 1950s with the McDonald brothers and later that decade, doing business on a handshake with Ray Kroc, Golden State Foods and McDonald's have been growing strong together for more than seven decades. GSF has helped McDonald's grow internationally; improve its logistics by rolling out one-stop-shopping; launch hundreds of new products and innovations throughout the system; and support various crises and challenges along the way. It has assisted the quick-serve icon to innovate year after year, decade after decade, and in turn McDonald's has continued to support Golden State in its business as GSF continues to grow and best serve its customers.

"What has impressed me about Golden State Foods is that *The Creed* and company Values are truly a part of its fabric," says Marion Gross, McDonald's executive vice president and global chief supply chain officer, who's served in leadership roles within the organization for decades. "All GSF associates [seem to] live and breathe them. Whether you drive a truck at the distribution center, run a production line, or sit in the 'C-suite,' the

CHAPTER 10: TREAT PEOPLE AS YOU WANT TO BE TREATED

culture is the heartbeat of the organization," she says. "As a customer, I see it come to life through consistent behaviors of all associates. In good times and even more so in tough times or with difficult situations, the values of the organization always shine through."

Former McDonald's global supply chain leader and current GSF board member, Jose Armario, agrees. "A company's values define the culture and heartbeat of an organization. The Golden State Foods Creed is the very pulse of GSF and one of the many reasons for its success. Writing down a company's purpose and values is no easy matter, but it is even more difficult to live and demonstrate those values on a daily basis," he continues. "Having worked shoulder to shoulder with Mark [Wetterau] and his team, I've always been impressed with the genuine care they have for their entire organization. This type of example gets duplicated all the way down the organization and becomes the expectation for each and every team member. This is an amazing way to lead by example and create a strong, vibrant, and purpose-driven culture."

McDonald's appreciation for GSF's values-driven performance extends throughout the organization, particularly through many of its owner/operators. "I consider Golden State Foods to be one of my 'best-kept secrets,'" says Bob Nabil, second-generation owner/operator of multiple McDonald's restaurants in Southern California. "I've had the advantage of learning this business at a young age from my father, who prepared me so well for today. He was one of the McDonald's pioneers, who paved the way for so many of us. So we know how to serve our customers and provide quality, service, cleanliness, and value as only McDonald's can. But for all our knowledge of the business, GSF might be one of our best-kept secrets. One of our most critical links to providing the ultimate McDonald's experience for our customers is the delivery of our products. And GSF, a long-time member of the 'three-legged stool' (McDonald's corporate, restaurant owners, and suppliers) is one of our most dependable partners in this effort, [a company] that clearly understands the importance of strong values in business."

"The role that *The Creed* and Values play in our success is really everything," adds 19-year GSF associate, Eric Treon, who serves as group vice president, global McDonald's business unit. "It's truly what runs and drives our business on a day-to-day basis. And it's truly what we want our customers and all of our stakeholders to understand about us that makes us different from the competition."

The Golden State Foods and Chick-fil-A Partnership: Common Values, Shared Success

Indeed, a number of customers have partnered with GSF over the years because of its strong value system, its exceptional customer service, and its quest for excellence. But one customer in particular uniquely resonated with the company's long-held values, as it sought to bring on a new distributor.

Like the Wetterau companies, Chick-fil-A (CFA) has been family-owned and operated for many decades, spanning several generations of the Cathy family leadership. It has succeeded over the years in part due to its own high ethical value system, which stemmed from the Cathy family's Christian beliefs. So, when Chick-fil-A was introduced to GSF, there was a natural connection.

"The Golden State Foods Creed and Values represent how and why [GSF] is in business," says Dan Cathy, chairman of CFA. "At Chick-fil-A, we also have a corporate purpose that represents the foundation of our business. When my dad and our founder, S. Truett Cathy, first opened his Dwarf Grill restaurant in 1946, he knew we should be about more than just selling food. We should be a part of our customers' lives and the communities in which we serve. We are grateful that our partnership with GSF plays a role in honoring our corporate purpose every day."

In the mid-2000s, Chick-fil-A was seeking another distributor to augment its fast-growing supply chain needs in the U.S. Veteran GSF distribution executive, Scott Thomas, now retired, received a call from Tim Yancy, Chick-fil-A's director of logistics at the time, who was interested

CHAPTER 10: TREAT PEOPLE AS YOU WANT TO BE TREATED

in GSF as a potential distributor. The two companies continued their relationship for the next four years, as Chick-fil-A observed GSF and its subsidiary, Quality Custom Distribution (QCD), to see if it really put words into action when it came to company values. As it turned out, GSF/QCD associates' integrity in living the values was one of the primary reasons Chick-fil-A opted to partner with them. Yancy noted Chick-fil-A's impressions after that critical investigative period: "We've been following you guys for some time, and we've heard about what you stand for. We stand for the same things. We've watched you, frankly to see if you live by your values, and it appears that you do, just as we believe we live by our values as well."

More than 15 years later, the relationship between Chick-fil-A and GSF/QCD is still growing strong. "I think the customers truly see how passionate we are about servicing them and about delivering the highest levels of quality each and every day," explains Ryan Hammer, corporate senior vice president and president of QCD. "They see how quickly we respond to their needs. Or when they ask us to think outside the box and get creative, we come with solutions that really address what they're looking for, both short-term and long-term. They view us as partners. Customers like Chick-fil-A truly see the culture of the organization and how it mirrors up with their culture," Hammer continues. "To me, that's been really one of the big successes for Quality Custom Distribution and its growth because we've partnered with customers where our values are very consistent, and it's really productive. It's helped us in terms of the overall partnership to better understand what they're looking to get accomplished in servicing their customers."

"What makes us unique and different is the relationships and the trust our customers have in GSF," adds 27-year associate, Gregg Tarlton, senior regional director, QCD Eastern U.S. "We have such similar values, and we believe in the same things, including taking care of people. Our customers' success is our success, and we achieve that by working together towards common goals. And at the end of the day, success usually does come out of that."

Over the past decade and a half, GSF/QCD and Chick-fil-A have expanded their partnership beyond regional distribution services to a national scale distributor. GSF also supplies dairy products (soft-serve ice cream and shakes) and liquid products (condiments such as mayonnaise and honey) throughout the U.S. Beyond food manufacturing and distribution services, GSF, QCD, and KanPak also serve as an overall innovation partner with Chick-fil-A to help transform new ideas into business value. This includes areas like restaurant concepting; new products and processes that reduce complexity; back-of-restaurant time, effort, and/or cost; and maintaining or improving the quality of the customer, supplier, operator, and team member experiences.

"Golden State Foods and Chick-fil-A have shared a commitment to quality food and service for more than 75 years," adds Dan Cathy. "Our pasts are united in a shared desire to serve our customers by glorifying God and having a positive influence on all who come in contact with us."

GSF and Zaxby's: Two Decades of Valuez-driven Partnership

"Golden State Foods is a rare gem in an industry of Greed over Creed," says Zach McLeroy, co-founder, chairman, and former CEO of Zaxby's Franchising, LLC, a GSF partner since 1999. "I believe their success begins with the right foundation. Their creed, 'We believe in God and the dignity of all people,' is a testament to the strongest foundation we can possess. When you start with God, you have a solid [base] to expand from."

When GSF began diversifying its liquid products business in the late 1990s, Zaxby's was one of its first non-McDonald's customers during that era. A relatively new chain, Zaxby's carved a market niche with its freshly seasoned chicken and zesty, zingy, zensational sauces (many now formulated and produced by GSF) and zany restaurant personality, or in Zaxby's terms, "saucenality." As the emerging chain grew throughout the

CHAPTER 10: TREAT PEOPLE AS YOU WANT TO BE TREATED

Southeast and beyond, it needed a supplier that could help support its increasing volume and innovations. Fortunately, Zaxby's and GSF quickly connected, and they attribute that natural alliance and camaraderie to the power of common values based on mutual respect and a shared vision. Today, GSF produces dozens of core items for Zaxby's, including signature sauces, salad dressings, and condiments.

"GSF truly embodies the meaning of partnership and is sincerely vested in the success of the business they support, McLeroy continues. "From day one, GSF has been dedicated to our partnership. They believe that our success is their success. They always offer support and resources to help our business grow and prosper. I am so proud to be associated with the GSF organization. I believe their Creed and Values personify the way they do business and the way they live their lives."

"I think as a customer you're looking for performance from your supplier," says Mark Wetterau, who seeks to interface directly with each one when possible. "And as we work with every brand, every leader, every team, we look for trust and performance from each other, and if we make a commitment to do something, we want to do it. What *The Creed* helps us believe is that we are giving our best all the time and that we always have our customers top of mind and they believe that we are always working in their best interest. Yes, stuff happens. You're only as good as your last case produced and your last delivery, which are never perfect. But there's a calmness, I think, that's instilled in them too, that the quality of folks at our company they deal with through customer service or the drivers or the general managers will always be there."

Former GSF Corporate Senior Vice President and Chairman, KanPak U.S. and Q Performance Larry McGill concurs: "The way we go to market and approach our business is as a trusted advisor," he explains, having worked closely with Zaxby's, Chick-fil-A, McDonald's, and many other GSF brands. "We bring unprecedented quality, new products, and innovative services to our customers. We become that true thought partner as a resource for them. We are there to help and service them by making sure there is no break in supply, so they can make sure their customers are taken care of. They know they can count on the products and services we offer them day in and day out, which makes us a real partner to them and what I think is the key to our mutual success."

Customer Achievements and Vendor Recognitions

Underscoring its strong customer relationships and service, Golden State Foods (along with other organizations in the Wetterau family of companies) has earned multiple awards and recognition from a variety of its customers over the years:

- Supplier of the Year for Yum! Brands, Zaxby's, Popeyes, McDonald's, Wendy's and Famous Dave's
- Best New Supplier of the Year for Jack in the Box
- Quality excellence and innovation awards from McDonald's, Subway, Wendy's, Jack in the Box, Yum! Brands, and KFC
- Outstanding system performance awards from Chick-fil-A and Starbucks
- Various leadership and teamwork awards from McDonald's
- Additionally, Golden State Foods leads in performance survey scores for a number of customers (including Chick-fil-A and McDonald's) in various categories, maintaining its high level of service year after year. (Please see *Appendix F* for GSF's complete list.)

Mark explains that while most companies can eventually earn the trust of their customers (with or without the awards), *The Creed* helps GSF get there faster. "I think it gives us the edge to get into places quicker and help folks get comfortable with us faster. Like anything else, it's your reputation

CHAPTER 10: TREAT PEOPLE AS YOU WANT TO BE TREATED

that's critical here. If you haven't lived by *The Creed* — or whatever culture you've tried to instill and whatever words you're putting on the wall — it will hurt you. What we're finding is that our creed has continued to help us enhance our customer relationships because we do have that belief in the philosophy of what we stand for as an organization, and our customers see that. So, our mutual trust continues to increase."

With customers and vendors alike.

Fourteen-year associate, Stephen Wetterau, corporate senior vice president of strategy, innovation, and technology, says he experienced this first-hand when he worked with Centralized Leasing Corp. (CLC), GSF's equipment and truck leasing company. "So many of our vendors with CLC appreciate what we do as an organization — how we conduct business, our impact from the Foundation, and the influence of *The Creed*," he says. "And a lot of times we even get preferential treatment because we do what we say we're going to do, we treat each other respectfully, we don't necessarily demand anything, but when we do, since we have that business relationship that's built on *The Creed* and Values, we get things done more quickly. For example, if we need to move tractors and trailers around (always a very difficult thing to do) or need new trailers, they must be booked a year to 18 months in advance. But through the great relationships we've built on the procurement side we get responses like, 'No problem GSF, we've got you covered.' And off we go. Those relationships stem from *The Creed*, on that strong foundation around it and the Values, which ultimately impact our organization as well as theirs."

"You can't believe how many times I give out my business card to different vendors and if they don't turn it over, I'll tell them to read the back of the card [which includes *The Creed*]," explains 24-year GSF associate, Bill Pocilujko, managing director of CLC and former 18-year Wetterau Inc. associate. "I'm proud of it, and I want them to understand who and what we are." But for Pocilujko, the words of *The Creed* are just the beginning when it comes to his vendors. He takes them to dinner and recognizes them. He brings them together every year for a vendor appreciation event, where he recognizes various achievements, including Vendor of the Year. "I ask a lot of them all year. I expect them to deliver a product when I ask for it, so this gives me a chance to say, 'Thanks guys!'"

Most vendors say that GSF is the only company that goes out of its way to make such gestures of appreciation. But then, for GSF associates, it's all about treating others the way that they would like to be treated — including vendors and suppliers. "I'm very proud to do it," adds Pocilujko. "I think we owe it to our vendors and suppliers, who work very hard for us. We want them there for the long haul, so I think they deserve to be treated right."

CHAPTER 11

Successful Independent Business Is the Backbone of Nations

"The Creed really did help make the retailers successful. It wasn't one thing [they did], it was a collection of all the operations Wetterau was there to help us with. I appreciated it then, but I probably appreciate it a lot more today as I look back. Everybody in the company lived by that creed. And we tried to live by it, too."

—**Merwyn Sher** (1940–   )
Multi-grocery store owner (1980s–2000s)

"We believe that successful independent business is the backbone of nations, that our success is dependent upon the success of our customers, and that only by working together can the ultimate success of all partners be assured."

Call it pro-capitalism, entrepreneurialism, or just plain good business. However it's defined, the Wetterau companies seem to understand the needs of those engaged in free enterprise and how to help them flourish. Whether it's the independent grocery store retailers during the Wetterau Inc. days, the owner/operators of the quick service restaurant industry, the managers of retail convenience stores, or the distributors of the beverage industry, Wetterau organizations strive to maintain a unique respect and relationship with these small-yet-powerful business owners.

Early leaders of the Wetterau companies felt strongly about the organization's dedication to the independent retailer and credited its success to that devotion. As Wetterau Inc. was approaching a billion dollars in sales during the 1970s, Chairman and CEO Ted Wetterau, wrote: "We have been, we are, and we will continue to be dedicated to a central principle — the principle of concentrating our food distribution efforts exclusively to our own independent retailers. These merchants have demonstrated superior profit performance over the years because their capital is on the line and because they take great pride in being leaders in their communities. We believe that our past success is based largely on adherence to this policy, and we believe our future progress is assured in continuing to serve only IGA (Red and White) and other stores included in our overall system."

In 1976, Wetterau was highlighted in the *St. Louis Post-Dispatch* as helping hundreds of independent business people "build small fortunes." Of course, when those operations succeeded, so did Wetterau. So they stuck together. Even in the 1980s, when they had a lucrative opportunity to team up with a major big box retailer on a regional and national scale, Wetterau stood by the independent business owner. Underscoring the company's support of these merchants, Ted said, "We don't think it would be prudent for us to provide equal service to the competitors of our own independent retail merchants."

As such, all innovation was aimed at improving the support offered to these self-supporting store owners, to give them an edge in the day-to-day struggle of grocery retailing. Bob Crutsinger, who became the first non-family Wetterau Inc. president and chief operating officer in 1979 and himself a one-time IGA retailer, stressed the company's commitment to and admiration for independent merchants: "Our retailers are the backbone of the American free enterprise system," he stated at that time. "They play a vital role in the communities in which they live and work and have their investment. They are not simply supermarket managers passing through town on the way to another job. They do not answer to a boss in New York or Cincinnati or to Wetterau in St. Louis. They answer only to themselves and their customers. And they are rated for their performance each week at the cash register."

CHAPTER 11: SUCCESSFUL INDEPENDENT BUSINESS

Having a creed that in no uncertain terms declared Wetterau's loyalty to independent business owners only served to further cement relationships and to ensure the continued achievement of both Wetterau and these smaller, yet very valuable business partners. "Dad taught us that 'the success of the retailer is in direct proportion to how successful we are going to be,'" says Conrad of Ted Wetterau's regard for the grit and determination of independent merchants. "So, if we as a distributor or as a supplier can help that retailer be successful, it will only help us be successful. And that's really one of the core tenets of *The Creed*."

"What *The Creed* says about the success of the independent retailer being tied to our success was just absolutely so important," explains Mike Waitukaitis of the Wetterau Inc. era, "and in our case was so apparent because on the wholesale side we dealt primarily with retail grocery stores more than the big chains. These were smaller operators who owned anywhere from one to maybe 30 stores. They came out of World War II and got into the grocery business, and learning how to deal with them symbiotically was so vital because their future and our future were so linked together." Mike adds that *The Creed* galvanized the company's commitment to a collaborative relationship with the small business owner. "It nailed spot-on what we believed about the power of these retailers and how we treated them at Wetterau Inc. I don't think there's any question about that."

> *"From a business standpoint, a creed is much more powerful than just earnings per share. I really do believe a creed is a manifestation that the ownership and leadership of a company have decided to make the people they work with — the customers they serve, everyone [in their sphere of influence] — a focus of mutual respect and mutual success. That's very rare because most businesses will say their customers are important, but they are actually driven for financial reasons."*
>
> — ANDY BLASSIE

"*The Creed* really did help make the retailers successful," says Merwyn Sher of his experience as a multi-store owner during the Wetterau Inc. days. "It wasn't one thing [they did], it was a collection of all the operations Wetterau was there to help us with. I appreciated it then, but I probably appreciate it a lot more today as I look back. Everybody in the company lived by that creed. And we tried to live by it, too."

What Merwyn said to his team just before they opened the doors at the grand opening of a special store they had built from the ground up illustrates how he and his associates tried to exemplify *The Creed*: "When we open this store, this is our house. And all of the customers that are coming into our house are our guests. And I want to treat our customers like they are coming into our house. You have to make people want to shop. What differentiates us from any other business or any other person? Being honest. Be a person of high integrity, and do what you can to help somebody. When you do the right things, good things happen."

Recalling his relationship with the Wetteraus, Merwyn explains that he felt comfortable doing business with them because of the way he felt while associating with them: "It's just an inner feeling you have of comfort and confidence — like going to war with somebody … you know you can do this because you know they have your back. And if we need some help, we are going to get it. And Wetterau did [provide it], as opposed to someone who says they have your back, but you're still looking over your shoulder. [The Wetteraus] were true partners. In the grocery store business I dealt with a lot of people, but I can look back and say they were one of the few who were truly my partner."

The precept of acknowledging and honoring free enterprise that is illuminated so clearly in *The Creed* has endured decade after decade. As Mark Wetterau and his team lead Golden State Foods to support thousands of independent restaurants and convenience stores around the world every day, and as Conrad and his team lead Quality Beverage to distribute to thousands of retail stores in the Northeastern U.S., it's clear that supporting independent businesses is as relevant and important today as it was a century and a half ago when George Wetterau first started the tradition — maybe even more so.

"When you look at the success of our businesses, I've said many times that it's a direct reflection of the success of our customers," says Mark. "At GSF, we deal with hundreds of thousands of customers around the world, and we make sure we do everything we can to drive success within that operation all the way down to the smallest detail. Truly, we believe that this type of partnership we have with these customers is the primary reason for our success at Golden State Foods and all the Wetterau companies I've been able to be a part of over the years. *The Creed* has permeated the Wetterau companies and has proven itself out through time," Mark continues. "It's shown decade after decade that it works in multiple companies. This includes the GSF Values, which preceded *The Creed* here, as well as the launch of the GSF Foundation, which has brought the company to new heights. It's helped elevate the importance of what we stand for as an organization. And today, we're stronger than ever."

"The role that our Creed and Values play in our success is really everything," adds GSF's Eric Treon, group vice president, global McDonald's business unit. "It's truly what runs and drives our business on a day-to-day basis. And it's truly what we want our customers and all of our stakeholders to understand about us that makes us different from the competition."

This values-driven approach that's permeated the Wetterau companies through time does indeed seem to be timeless. And it's certainly enabled not only the success of these companies, but also those it partners with.

Seeking the success of all partners is a mindset. It's an attitude of service, of looking out for the team and not just for one's own self-interest. As Ted Wetterau would say, "We're all in this together," describing the company's interdependent partnerships between the employees, suppliers, and independent retailers in a speech given in 1975. "We at Wetterau also realize that our partnership extends to the employees who make our endeavors possible, whose inventiveness sparks our progress. We also know our partnership extends to the many suppliers who have geared in with us for many years. Our partnership is founded on the basis of dignity, trust, integrity, and respect, and it also involves a certain sense of freedom. As independent retailers, you have the freedom to do as you wish. On our side of the partnership, we want to merit your loyalty, your affiliation, and your continued friendship. Together, in this magnificent land of freedoms, with God's help, we can accomplish our ultimate goal."

"Winning together is something relatively unique, especially nowadays," explained Ted's grandson and former GSF associate, Taylor Harbison, during his tenure at the company. "You see a lot of companies that are just very out for themselves. They'll drive margins up and do things they believe are solely focused on just their success in particular, and they'll do whatever they have to do to make sure their shareholders are happy. If that means gouging other companies to get what they need, then they do that. And that statement in our Creed expresses the opposite of that. It's saying, 'Hey, we're all going to grow — we need to all grow together. We need to make sure we're taking care of the people who are taking care of us.' I've just always found that to be really unique. And it becomes more and more unique as every day passes in the business environment we're operating in."

Part of this "mutual success" mindset is captured in one of GSF's Values which states, "Give the customer a fair deal." While this could in part mean offering a fair price, according to GSF leadership, it's not about price alone — it's about offering tremendous overall value to customers. "There are capabilities we try to mix and match that bring an overall value proposition to each customer," says Hugues Labrecque, who serves as vice president of sales at GSF. "Part of this is that our associates really get to know our customers. They get to know their brands and how they operate, including how they reach out to their customers. It becomes an integrated part of who we are to make sure our customers are successful."

CHAPTER 11: SUCCESSFUL INDEPENDENT BUSINESS

"When you think about companies that haven't been successful, you ask yourself, 'What were they focused on?'" adds Harbison. "You don't hear, 'Oh, they were so focused on making sure their customers were happy.' You would never come across that. You'd find they'd spent all this money on putting a new product line in so they could go sell more stuff, and it didn't work out. Or they leveraged up too much. Or they brought in the wrong people. But it's never been because they were too focused on satisfying their customers that they weren't able to be successful. So, seeking the success of all we're involved with is definitely a very cool part of *The Creed*."

Indeed, *The Creed* seeks the success of all partners locally, regionally, nationally, and globally — whatever their goals and objectives are. "What we seek to do in our international business is build a strong relationship based on trust in order to help our customers grow, succeed, and achieve their dreams," says 24-year GSF associate Brian Dick, president and chief executive officer and board member. "This means they require trusted suppliers to help them with their expansion, with core products and new innovation in their menu items, and with consistent, reliable, assured supply to deliver those products throughout the world. We, therefore, continue to expand geographically to support their success, whether it's in Asia Pacific, the Middle East, the U.S., or in various other global regions. The key ingredient is always trust."

The Creed and Values definitely encourage associates to put extra effort into customer relationships. "I like what Chick-fil-A's Chairman Dan Cathy said about the secret of their organization's success: *'going the extra mile,'*" adds Mark. "'The *first* mile is about doing it right; the *extra* mile is about going above and beyond.'"

In fact, going beyond quality customer service, GSF often takes on some of the financial risk for their customers to help them achieve their goals. Golden State Foods' former Corporate Senior Vice President and Chief Financial Officer Joe Heffington, now retired, considers this gesture a demonstration of the company's ideals. "*The Creed* and Values drive Golden State Foods. They are embedded in our company to support our customers and the mutual benefit of all stakeholders. And since GSF is a private company, we're not driven for the next quarter's results. We're driven for the long-term, best results for the organization and for our customers as well. What that means is we can take a higher-cost approach for them sometimes. We can do that for a customer knowing that we're going to get to our end goal and our customer's end goal, so that both achieve mutual success."

This gesture of going the extra mile is not unique to only a few at Golden State. Associates at all levels of the company take great pleasure in providing the best possible service to their customers at every turn, whatever their role is in the company. GSF Associate Survey trends have indicated for nearly the last two decades an average of 95 percent of associates pride themselves in the customers they serve. They understand and support the success of their independent businesses and truly want to help their customers achieve their dreams. Because at the end of the day, as *The Creed* declares, *"our success is dependent upon our customers' success."*

CHAPTER 12

Pledging Best Efforts to Ensure Mutual Success

"Our people and their commitment to daily excellence is a key component to our success."

–**John Page** (1965–)
Corporate Executive Vice President
and Chief Administrative Officer (2023–present)
Corporate Senior Vice President and Chief Corporate
Social Responsibility and Legal Officer (2012–2023),
Golden State Foods

"We, therefore, dedicate ourselves to work for our mutual success and pledge our best efforts always toward the attainment of our common goals."

McDonald's icon, Ray Kroc, often said: *"None of us is as good as all of us,"* referring to the power of the "three-legged stool" (McDonald's corporate, restaurant owner/operators, and suppliers) working effectively together. Such a perspective fundamentally invokes the value of each individual and the value of a team. It assumes that no matter how capable, intelligent, experienced, or likable one individual may be, that person is still not as effective as a willing team — even one that is flawed in some respects — working well together as one. As *The Creed* punctuates, it's all about *mutual* success, which can only be attained by working collectively as a united body.

"I think our successes have come because we have chosen to try to work together towards a common goal," says Wayne Morgan of his decades of service at GSF as a corporate vice president and president, protein products and operations support, adding that the collective winning spirit can be even more powerful when tempered by adherence to the precepts of *The Creed*.

"We have, for the most part, chosen to subscribe to *The Creed* and Values, we have chosen to try to treat people with dignity and respect and in the cases where people get out of line [in that regard], that gets called out and some people aren't with us anymore. ... I do believe that people working toward a common theme, having a common goal, and having a common set of guidelines allows us all to work [effectively] toward the same thing. [*The Creed* reminds us that] it's not a 'win at all costs,' it's a 'win together' mentality."

That mindset of working towards mutual success is not only an integral part of GSF, but is also germane in the other organizations within the Wetterau family of companies and is a natural result of *The Creed* being interwoven into the fabric of each organization. This has certainly been the case for Quality Beverage over the last 30 years. "You get so much more accomplished [by having a creed]," says Steve Doherty, who serves as marketing vice president for QB. "And it can work everywhere...from supplier to wholesaler or wholesaler to retailer. It can work retailer to customer. It can work employee to employee."

"It's the Golden Rule: treat people the way you want to be treated. That alone to me is *The Creed*," says Tom Nicholson, who served as general manager at QB for 28 years. "I just think that you get a lot more done by working with your people and being fair and honest with them. I think that's why you see associates around all the time [even beyond work hours]. ..." He stressed how important this was to Quality Beverage retailers: "I think they took *The Creed* to heart when they [found] that [we] really did want to work with them [and that] made them want to work with us."

For former GSF senior executive, Bill Sanderson, working together towards the attainment of common goals means listening to the opinions, perspectives, and concerns of all parties. "Everyone's opinions are valued, we want to hear different thoughts and perspectives," he explains. "At the end of the day, we have to align on a common direction, a common plan, a common objective, and when we do that, we seem to do it so eloquently because typically there aren't hurt feelings. And we do gain alignment, because when all is said and done, everyone knows we've been thoughtful. We've considered all perspectives and all stakeholders. Sometimes you may be 100 percent aligned in a meeting or you may not have been at all, but you can respect the process, what we're trying to accomplish, along with the reason we're doing it."

Mark Wetterau certainly agrees. When it comes to aligning on a given decision made in a meeting or throughout the organization worldwide, he credits *The Creed* for bringing people together. "*The Creed* has helped us stay aligned and focused throughout our company, particularly as we've grown in the number of facilities and associates and as we've diversified our business throughout the world," he says.

Indeed, many GSF associates say that *The Creed* and Values encourage them to find a way to "deliver the difference," literally. GSF advisory board member, Sharon Davis says that ability to deliver is all about commitment: "If you work for a company with a creed [such as ours], and you really believe it, I think you can always find a way to deliver on your commitments because you've made a promise, a vow, a pledge to others. Anybody who's got any amount of background in any religion understands commitment. When you make a promise, it's solemn. You've made your own personal [guarantee] and you have to come through. [People need to know: 'you have our word on it.'] The idea of caving into the approach too many people are taking in the business world — 'Well, it didn't work out and we're sorry' — is not acceptable."

"Our people and their commitment to daily excellence is a key component to our success," explains John Page, regarding the dedication of each associate and their pride in knowing how their role contributes to the company's success.

The Creed: Coming Full Circle

Associate John Pecoraro Dedicates Nearly 40 Years to Three Wetterau Companies

Top-performing KanPak sales manager, John Pecoraro, now retired, is one of the few employees who has worked for several Wetterau companies (including Shop 'n Save, KanPak, and Quality Beverage) over the course of his nearly four-decade career, so he has a very unique perspective on the impact *The Creed* has had in a variety of settings. Pecoraro says that *The Creed* is just as influential today at KanPak and at GSF as it was more than 35 years ago, when he started as a grocery manager at Shop 'n Save in Gorham, Maine. Working alongside his wife, Cathy, who was also employed at Shop 'n Save as a bakery manager, John worked his way up to assistant store manager and from there had the opportunity to become a buyer for Milliken-Tomlinson, a grocery wholesaler in Maine that had been acquired by Wetterau Inc. in the 1980s.

During those early years at various Wetterau-owned companies, John says *The Creed* reminded him of the military's Code of Conduct, and he saw it play out in the way management regarded the employees. "Everybody was treated so well there," he recalls. "I never heard of anybody being yelled at. I never saw anybody being dished on about anything. And if people had [special health] needs, [the company's response was always], 'Take whatever time you need. We'll take care of things around here.'"

He tells of a husband and wife team whose IGA store burned down, and Wetterau Inc. graciously helped them out financially. "I saw those types of things on a daily basis," Pecoraro says, fondly recalling many company

Photo (above): John Pecoraro, 35-year associate at three Wetterau companies — Shop 'n Save, Quality Beverage, and KanPak U.S.

CHAPTER 12: PLEDGING BEST EFFORTS

picnics, holiday parties, and dinners. But most of all, he was impressed by the equity exhibited throughout the company. "Everybody was treated the same. Nobody was dealt with any differently, from the president to the guy sweeping the warehouse floor."

Several decades later, John joined KanPak and was reunited with Mark Wetterau during one of the company's Creed and Values town hall meetings in 2017. Pecoraro recounts having the thought, "Wow, my career's come 360 degrees!" He knew that he was in for a positive experience at KanPak because of the Wetteraus and *The Creed*: "I knew that we would definitely get the structure we needed [at KanPak]." Having come full circle within the Wetterau family of companies he was confident in the synergistic company culture it would create at KanPak, just as it had in all the other Creed-based operations he had worked for in the past.

Pecoraro was inspired by the enthusiastic leadership of Larry McGill, KanPak's former chairman, who encouraged associate camaraderie and created new opportunities at the company. John attended a presentation about the GSF Foundation led by McGill and noticed how responsive the associates were to the many opportunities to unite in helping others because of the way McGill galvanized them with his Creed-based leadership.

"They practice what they preach," John says of the KanPak leadership. "The management takes *The Creed* and Values very seriously." Even customers have acknowledged it, he says. "One of my first customers when I worked in sales told me, 'JP, these people don't just preach it. They really do it!' And we've had that conversation quite a few times since."

Pecoraro explains that he felt a high level of confidence and optimism in KanPak's future because he had such positive experiences with the Wetterau companies in the past. "I really put my heart literally into Wetterau, I really did," he says, of his long career at Wetterau Inc. "Then when it broke up, it really kind of hurt me, you know? But I was still young, 30 at the time. It gave me a great background, and I carried *The Creed* and those values with me everywhere I went." Whether or not all the companies he worked for had those types of values, John says he tied *The Creed* into the company goals and objectives. "In my management experience, when I've had teams under me, I always used *The Creed* and Values. That's how I treated my people, and how I expected them to treat other people."

Those ideals that John learned by working for the Wetterau family of companies have flowed into the way he treats his family as well. "You know, it just sticks with you and sticks with you in family life, too. It's just the way I live my life on a daily basis, and the way I trained and taught my children," he says, emphasizing things like honesty and integrity. Both of John's sons have become "exceptional professional people" he says proudly and are now instilling the same values into their children. Seeing this has been very rewarding for him.

"I love KanPak because we're a family," Pecoraro explains. "We really are. And I think that again reflects back on *The Creed* and Values. Of course, it's a business; let's make no mistake — we're here to make money — we're here to service customers. But one of the reasons I came here in the first place is because it is also a family."

John adds that he appreciates the example Mark Wetterau sets personally for the organization, particularly through the time he takes to meet with associates around the world and encourages them to carry out *The Creed* and Values in their areas of responsibility. "Never mind the fact that he goes out and literally presents this to everybody personally," Pecoraro says with a bit of awe. "It's not just a piece of paper that's handed out, which I've seen at other companies, or a big plaque on the wall. I've seen all that through my career. Here [*The Creed*] is authentic. And to see that it's evolved throughout all the Wetterau companies and is still the foundation for everything is really amazing." He notes that he's worked for companies where their so-called values weren't real, and in fact day-to-day operations were quite opposite of what they claimed to be. There were times he couldn't sleep at night worrying about "what's going to hit tomorrow" or what unethical practices were going on. But at all the Wetterau companies the moral bar has always been set high.

As he looks back on his career, most of it at a Wetterau company in one form or another, John reminisces in a spirit of appreciation. "I love working for Wetterau. It's been great. It's where I trained and where I cut my teeth in the industry. And to see how [*The Creed*] has evolved throughout all the Wetterau companies and is still the foundation for everything [today] is really amazing. This is where I've seen the evolution of *The Creed* helping shape us into what we are as a company today with KanPak and Golden State Foods."

SECTION 2

Can A *Creed* Help Your Organization Succeed?

Photos (left to right):

1) QCD St. Louis Warehouse Management Systems (WMS) associates show solid "teamwork" in 2016! From left: Scott Harriett, Walter Wallen, Tyler Merriman, Tim Mathias, Jason Jacobs, Jesse Wisch, Mike MacAtee, Khanh Nguyen, and Himesh Patel.

2) GSF Foundation volunteer and 29-year associate, Lourdes Cerpa-Smith, receives heartfelt gratitude from a young elementary school girl during a "Back(pack) to School" event in the mid-2000s.

3) Representatives from GSF's Liquid Products North America, National Account Sales, Product Development and Operations at City of Industry and Conyers teams accept the company's prestigious 2016 Innovation Award. Top row: Dan Wenker, Jonathon Yawson, Mike Wilson, Mark Wetterau, Joe Soran; second row: Jared Dunn, David Hutchinson, Miguel Salas, Jorge Hasbun, Dan Sharf; bottom row: Wendy Bauman, Natalie Roesler, Nancy Hulse, Skip Munn, and Marta Londono.

4) QCD Fontana warehousemen, Raymond Rodriguez (left) and David Gonzales (right), show a positive attitude during their shift in 2023.

CHAPTER 13

The Need for a Creed — Benefits of Instituting a Company Conscience into Your Culture

"When you lead with a creed or a strong purpose statement, you're really saying: 'This is the kind of company that you should be able to trust.'"

–**Dick Gochnauer** (1949–   )
Board Member (1994–present)
Vice Chairman and President, International (2000–2002)
President (1994–2000),
Golden State Foods

As the previous chapters have indicated, a company creed can serve an organization, its associates, its customers, and all of its constituents well. It can enable the company to attract, maintain, and align better employees.

It can increase associate morale, dedication, and longevity by giving them a sense of greater purpose beyond day-to-day tasks. It can serve as a regular reminder of ethics and higher principles, especially when employees are at a crossroads during tough decision-making times. It can help unify associates as a team and reconcile relationships when people have disagreements or get off-track. It can aid in establishing or strengthening a company's culture through a solid, values-based foundation. It can give top leadership a sense of security by clarifying elements of the organization's culture that affect all decisions throughout the company. In short, it can give an organization a leading edge in the marketplace and help it be more productive overall.

Higher Quality Employees

Naturally, a creed that encourages a positive environment for all its stakeholders, including its internal associates, will attract higher caliber, higher-performing employees. Often these individuals are seeking a deeper connection with their employer and with their career experience and can potentially represent the company and its values more effectively.

"If a company really wants to embody a creed — not just use it as a symbol but truly embody it in everything they do, then I think they would see how it would benefit them [in terms of appealing to the best talent]," explains GSF board member, Sharon Davis. "A creed sets you up to attract a different kind of candidate to fill a position, one who knows and understands what a creed is, and wants to embrace it. [Such a] candidate might have a stronger sense of loyalty and commitment and lets you feel good about how they will represent you. I think that's what every CEO would want — knowing that every single person who's out there every day representing the company is doing it in a way that reflects well on the organization. And the only way you can ensure that is to make certain they share your [company's] belief system."

CHAPTER 13: THE NEED FOR A CREED

Collective Aspiration: Creed as a Promise

Not only does a creed have the potential to attract higher quality employees, but once they're a part of an organization, a creed has an amazing power to align them in various capacities within a company along a common path, with clear direction, so they can work together more fluidly. "A creed is different from a vision or mission statement because it's almost like a set of operating principles," says Bill Sanderson, former corporate executive vice president and chief administration officer at GSF. "There's a great deal of value in it. Unlike a vision statement, a creed is what we *aspire* to — how we strive to operate. By having a creed we're saying, 'This is the way we want to work together. This is what we believe. This is the way we're going to treat each other. This is what we're going to do for the customer. If you see us fall short, let us know because that's really important to us. We want to be held accountable.'"

Brian Dick, GSF president and chief executive officer and board member, explains that *The Creed* and Values are at the center of everything GSF does: "So in China, or Australia, or the Midwest of the United States — anywhere in the world, I've never seen any company with people who play with such heart. What I like to say is that our Creed and Values are our company's promise, and it's all of our jobs to keep that promise."

Stephen M. R. Covey, co-founder and CEO of CoveyLink Worldwide and former president and CEO of Covey Leadership Center, agrees. In fact, he explains how that kind of "promise" can actually build hope and trust into an organization. Covey, along with the Covey organization, partnered with Golden State Foods for several years through FranklinCovey's Speed of Trust program, wherein he engaged personally with an array of associates at all levels. "What impressed me about GSF is that their Creed and their Values are real. They're not just words or platitudes," says Covey. "They're not just a mission statement. This is who they are, their way of doing business, their way of operating, of leading in the organization and the world. . . ."

He further explains his experience with seeing *The Creed* in action at Golden State Foods:

> "As much as any organization I've been with I could see, sense, feel and have conversations and interactions where I knew The Creed was real. It was the law of the land. It was [GSF's] constitution. I felt a congruence, an alignment, a sincere desire to live and model a creed at the top and at every level."
>
> STEPHEN M.R. COVEY

"It doesn't mean everyone there is perfect, as none of us are. It's an ongoing journey, a process of striving," Covey continues. "But [trying to live their creed] sincerely felt authentic — not just in words, but in actions and in deeds — they're trying to walk the talk and model this creed. And from that, there's integrity and credibility and power that emerges. So in that sense, *The Creed* is a promise. And making a promise builds hope. Keeping the promise builds trust. And in a low-trust world, building both hope and trust [is deeply valuable]. Then, when you keep [that promise], when you live it, when you apply it, when you implement it, that increases the trust."

Productivity through Trust

"When you lead with a creed or a strong purpose statement, you're really saying, 'This is the kind of company you should be able to trust,'" explains Dick Gochnauer, GSF board member, backing up Stephen Covey's observations about the particular brand of trust companies project to the public when they incorporate a creed. "And if you can trust the company, then maybe you can work at a partnership level with them, and that's a whole different level than a transactional level."

Harvard professor, Rebecca Henderson has been leading a significant research effort on the difference companies that lead with values are making. One of her findings is that when they're able to live out those values, a fundamental shift within the organization's culture begins to occur, which is a shift towards greater trust — trust with employees, trust with customers, and trust with other stakeholders.

Doug Wilson, Next Solutions CEO and co-founder of the CEO Leadership Alliance – Orange County, [California] explains how this trust conveys an atmosphere of principled conduct that everyone (both internally and externally) can get behind, and which in turn increases productivity: "[Having company values and living by them gives] the sense that you're always going to make the decision to do the right thing. And I [as a stakeholder] can with agency, put myself all the way behind what you're doing and have confidence in it. And that begins to make a real difference [in an organization's productivity] because as the trust grows, the transaction costs go down. And the cost of non-engaged employees starts to go down. [And I'm not referring to the costs of high] turnover, though turnover can go down. I'm talking about the costs to a company of workers who don't care enough about their job or the business to give everything they've got. The worst thing we can have today in our companies is employees who are not fully engaged with their minds and their hearts. That's where productivity is lost. So, if you can make that shift towards greater trust through believing and living a set of strong values, as a creed encourages, that begins to make a real difference."

Wilson and other experts say organizations that live out their stated values are two-and-a-half times more productive than those that don't. They say that when an organization lives out the "multi-stakeholder model of values" (i.e., values encompass not just a focus on customers but a focus on employees, suppliers, shareholders, and community — a focus on the whole system and not just one of those groups), then that's when those values and that company make a difference and when the organization's worth really begins to escalate.

Stephen Covey asserts that this type of multi-stakeholder model of values can build strong organizational trust, which in turn increases the productivity gap even more. He characterizes trust as "a performance multiplier," and says that it is "the highest form of human motivation [because] it brings out the very best in people."

This is certainly apparent in the array of studies Covey points to, suggesting there's at least a three-times performance multiplier with high-trust organizations, compared to low-trust companies, which is "quite substantial," he says. For example:

- Human capital consulting firm, Watson Wyatt, found in a 2002 study that high-trust organizations returned to shareholders nearly three times more than low-trust organizations — which represented a 286 percent total return.

- A similar study in 2005 conducted by the Great Place to Work Institute and Russell Investment Group showed that over a 13-year period, the contrast in performance with high-trust businesses versus the market was at 288 percent, nearly identical to the Watson Wyatt study — about three times.

- Boston-based organizational coaching firm, Interaction Associates, studied the revenue between high- and low-trust organizations over a two-year period and found that high-trust companies increased revenue two-and-a-half times over their counterparts — nearly three times.

Interestingly, this same three-times "multiplier effect" in performance and productivity found in high-trust business entities also holds true in schools. Studies conducted by Professor Tony Bryk of Stanford University indicated that high-trust schools have a three-and-a-half times greater probability of increasing test scores than do low-trust schools.

"So a high-trust culture is a performance multiplier that gets manifested in a whole variety of ways," confirms Covey, "and low trust is a diminisher — a 'destructive tax' and it can literally get you at almost every turn," which, he says, equates to apathetic or unengaged employees, dissonance among associates and/or customers, lack of alignment, decreased creativity and productivity, loss of business, decreased brand value, etc. "High trust multiplies and makes you better at everything else you're trying to do, including productivity, innovation, creativity, and pure economics of shareholder value, among many other things," Covey emphasizes.

Innovation

An environment of trust, respect, support, and even diversity fosters the freedom to create. And Stephan Covey explains that in some areas of the workplace, like innovation, the productivity multiplier is even higher than three times. "Innovation flourishes when there are differences that collide in an environment of trust," he shares, "because the trust enables the differences to become strengths — to be seen as uniting versus divisive. And that's where innovation comes from — these differences coming together in an environment of trust. When people don't trust each other, they're often suspicious about differences, they won't come together, and they won't take risks. If you're not willing to take a risk, you won't learn, and you won't innovate. However, in Silicon Valley, [where many are willing to take risks], they're calling this 'fail fast, but fail forward, and fail often.' As long as you're learning and getting better. But for people to be willing to fail, there's got to be trust," Covey explains.

Stephen adds that a study in 2016 from LRN Corporation, a New York City consultancy firm, shows that in a high-trust culture, people are 32 times more likely to take responsible risk and 11 times more likely to innovate. In a low-trust culture, they won't take that risk, and they won't innovate.

Want More Trust?
Start by Looking in the Mirror

Trust expert, Stephen M. R. Covey, author of *The Speed of Trust* and *Trust & Inspire*, has advised top leaders and organizations across the globe on building and maintaining trust for decades. Whether it's with individuals, customers, or companies he says that one thing's constant: creating trust with others always starts with oneself.

"Often companies want to focus on building more trust in the marketplace with customers. And that's all a good thing. But the trust in the marketplace comes about and is sustained because you first build trust in the workplace," Covey says. "And you build that trust when each person looks in the mirror and starts with themselves and asks, 'Can I trust myself? Do I give to my team a teammate they can trust?' So it's really self-reflective: 'Is it smart to trust me? Should others trust me?' Then you naturally move to building relationships of trust and teams of trust."

Covey explains that too often, when it comes to trust, people look at others and think those people need to change their behavior first. "They'll say, 'Yeah, when they change [I'll think about changing] … they need this bad.' Many times I'll teach about *The Speed of Trust* and people will say, 'This is really good stuff, Stephen, but it's just too bad that the people who really need to hear this aren't here today — our board of directors, our partners, our customers, this group, this team, or this department — they're not here, and they really need this!' Most people tend to go 'outside in.' But trust is built from the 'inside out.'"

This suspicious "outside in" attitude often shows up in Covey's trust surveys, where members of a team assess themselves on a scale of 0-100 in terms of their credibility and trustworthiness. "When we do trust surveys that

CHAPTER 13: THE NEED FOR A CREED

measure the 4 Cores of Credibility [integrity, intent, capabilities, results] or a dimension of The Speed of Trust [program] among people who are part of a team, they assess themselves on that team and then assess their teammates. When they measure themselves, they typically rate themselves between 85 and 95 percent [trustworthy]. But when they rate their teammates, these people come in at 50 to 55 percent. So there's a 30-to-40-point gap. In fact, I just saw an 80-point gap [on a group of surveys]! People had rated themselves at 90 and everyone else at 10. So if you think that the problem is 'out there,' meaning everybody else, that very thinking is the problem. And so often when it comes to cultures people think, 'Everyone else needs to change — that department, that team, management, the board — they need to change.' People tend to look outside."

But Covey makes it clear that trust is built by taking a look at oneself first, as noted earlier "and then ripple out from there to your relationships with your teams and then between teams and within departments and then within the organization, and then you can move out to customers," he explains, which creates workplace trust, and with that in place it's easier to build marketplace trust.

"It's really not sustainable to tell people on your team who you don't trust to go build trust with customers. That's incongruent. So internal trust precedes external trust. Workplace trust precedes marketplace trust. The key to building workplace trust, building the [company] culture, is starting with each person where they assess themselves and focus on increasing their [own] credibility and trustworthiness, their behavior, being aligned with their values, so you do what you say that you value. So there's very little gap between what you say and what you do. That's integrity. That's alignment. That's trust," Covey continues, emphasizing that it's vital that company leadership and personnel know what they stand for "in order to have integrity. And that's why having a creed and having a mission and having values are important because that declares your intent of 'Here's who we are; here's what we're about.' Therefore, you can then be true to that and be aligned with that, and be constant with that, which builds [further] trust. So it all fits together."

Deeper Purpose

Once mutual trust is established at all levels, organizations are freer to grow beyond the bottom line and become more "purpose-driven" or "Plus 1," as Mark Wetterau terms it. This means enhancing employees' quality of their experience in the workplace and positively influencing the community and society at large for the greater good. A creed or a purpose statement can help focus an organization on its true, broader objectives beyond the bottom line and help others around them live richer, more meaningful lives.

A Case for Purpose: "Plus 1" Companies and the Search for Meaning

In *Harvard Business Review's* "The Business Case for Purpose," researchers concluded that purpose-driven companies are more likely to succeed because of the increased energy, commitment, creativity, and morale that they foster.

Such businesses have a "new leading edge," writes Valerie Keller, global lead for the EY Beacon Institute, which partnered with *Harvard Business Review* in a special study among 474 global executives about the impact of purpose on the success of their organizations. "Those companies able to harness the power of purpose to drive performance and profitability enjoy a distinct competitive advantage."

In 2012, GSF's Dick Gochnauer and Next Solutions' CEO Doug Wilson helped establish a new cutting-edge organization called the Center for Higher Ambition Leadership that helps companies become more purposeful

Photo (above): Members of the Conyers, Georgia team gather for a strategic meeting in 2021. Left to right (clockwise): Jason Slipsager (center top), Mike Wilson, Justin Smith, Allison Brumfield, and Patrick Doyle.

CHAPTER 13: THE NEED FOR A CREED

and more purpose-driven. He says that recent research has revealed that not only is a healthy culture a prerequisite for successful companies these days, but employees are demanding deeper, more purposeful organizations to work for, if they want to attract top workforces. "In the evolution of business thinking, one of the early findings in the '70s and '80s was all around strategy," says Gochnauer. "For you to be successful and differentiate your company from others, you had to have a really good, strong, robust strategy that pointed you in the right direction. If you had that, everything else would be good. But what they have found years later is that if you don't also have a good supporting structure — a culture — then your strategy will fail. And that's when Peter Drucker's maxim, 'Culture eats strategy for lunch' [became popular]. A lot of research was done around culture. And around 10 to 15 years ago or so, a high-performing culture became recognized as something that was not a 'nice-to-have,' it was a requirement if you were going to compete in today's world. So, [companies began asking], 'Okay, how do I get one of those?' Easy to ask … not so easy to do," says Gochnauer.

Larry Senn, founder and chairman of Senn Delaney, a global culture-shaping firm, and others who work with corporations are finding, notes Gochnauer, that "being purpose-driven is now [as significant] as *culture* was 15 years ago. There's more research coming out and more being written about it," says Dick "and companies are learning about it, but we're still in the early stages of it. The research that Harvard is doing says purpose is becoming the 'secret sauce.' And the more research validates this, the more companies get on this bandwagon."

"People have a very deep need to feel like they make a difference, and purpose helps them do that," explains Senn, who defines purpose as a "noble cause, a reason for existing and how you're serving humanity," and culture as "how people behave and work together."

Deemed the "Father of Corporate Culture" by *CEO* magazine, Senn conducted trail-blazing research on the concept of corporate culture during the 1960s as a University of Southern California doctoral student and has more than a half century of research under his belt. He explains that "it's not that purpose will *diminish* culture, but it's a *multiplier* of culture because purpose pulls people forward in a positive way. It creates people's 'discretionary effort.'" He adds that purpose creates a deeper ownership of an organization, not just by its employees, but by vendors, suppliers, and other stakeholders as well.

"It's almost become protocol for people to have values statements in their companies," adds Doug Wilson, who is also an executive fellow at the Center for Higher Ambition Leadership. "You see that in almost every company. The question is, 'How robust is that values statement? And how does it relate to an overall purpose the company has created?' That purpose statement is linked to the values and how those values will be measured. While a company doesn't necessarily need a purpose statement, it's helpful. However, you do need your values in place and be able to talk about what those are. That's absolutely critical. Most companies have a value set, like Golden State Foods, but the difference is," he continues, "how well that organization is able to talk about those values and measure them and be passionate about living them out. And are those values ultimately customer-centric, as well as employee-centric? And do they integrate these together with the customers, employees, suppliers, and the community? If those values are not integrated into a whole and lived out, and people understand the trade-offs, decisions are not made productively. [Living, breathing values such as in the GSF Creed] are 'where the rubber meets the road,' if you will, and help you see clearly what decisions you're willing to make [that will be in harmony with those values and that creed]. That's where having a creed makes all the difference."

Company Purpose: A Matter of the Heart (and Head and Hands)

When it comes to how a company's purpose relates to a creed, Dick Gochnauer says actions speak louder than words. Semantics don't hold as much weight as an organization's authentic behavior, he posits. "What matters is that you bring in the heart. [Your deeds should say], 'We're more than just about making money. We're really about making a better world.' And how you craft a creed and tie the pieces together and what name you give it (creed, purpose statement, etc.) is probably less important than doing it," he concludes.

Covey agrees: "A creed itself does matter," he says, "but what matters more is what's behind that creed — the meaningfulness and purpose behind

CHAPTER 13: THE NEED FOR A CREED

it, the alignment and connection, the integrity behind it — that's where the power is. The words are important, make no mistake — the words do matter. But what's behind the words and the modeling of them is even more important. And GSF does that so well."

"To me, *The Creed* is part of laying the groundwork for becoming or being a purposeful company, which means in GSF's case, we care about all of its stakeholders," Gochnauer continues, indicating that *The Creed* is very similar to a purpose statement that reinforces a company's values statement. "You have a sense of morality and values that are very deep, and because of that you bring your heart to business, as well as your head and hands. That's where the caring comes. *The Creed*, I think, says indirectly, 'Yes, it's about caring about others.' But that's second — first God, and then second, how you view your fellow man. So what we are currently finding in research is companies that have this higher standard — that take the highest road in values and ethics and caring, that bring in the heart — have a kind of 'secret sauce' to use a McDonald's term, in creating a high-performance culture." Gochnauer goes on to explain that companies that lead with the heart bring energy to their culture, which is a differentiator enabling them to outperform other businesses at the top that are outperforming everyone else. "Between the top and the bottom performers, it's generally about a two to two-and-a-half times delta," he says, "so it's a very significant thing. Bottom performers understand the need for continuous improvement and establishing a high-performance culture, but what these lower-performing companies typically miss is the power of a higher purpose, the culture that says, 'We care about the world.'"

Gochnauer notes that companies striving to find meaning tend to reach out by being environmentally responsible and addressing sustainability and human rights issues. And they tend to help others, emphasizing that there are many ways to do that. He points to Golden State Foods as an example of making this difference through its globally aware businesses and charitable organization. "There are lots of avenues for giving back that become the heart of an organization," he says, citing the GSF Foundation and the quality of the company's food products as illustration of this caring. "And as you unlock that heart, you get this tremendous amount of energy, creativity, loyalty, and engagement, all these positive attributes that high performers want to have. And if you have a creed that says, 'We believe in God and the dignity of all people,' and you really believe that then you can't just sit back and pollute the environment, for example or [disregard] poverty-stricken kids and all their needs. You have to say, 'No, I've got a bigger purpose.' A company creed helps reinforce [that mentality]."

In addition to the extensive efforts of the GSF Foundation, detailed on page 160, one of Golden State Foods' five foundational pillars is corporate social responsibility (CSR) (in addition to people, quality, growth and financial security) detailed on page 179. Golden State's CSR efforts are keenly focused on engaging a diverse workforce; treating all of its employees equally and ethically; maintaining sustainable, transparent food production operations; as well as being a good steward over the natural environments within which it operates, for current and future generations.

"We believe in going beyond expected business practices to embrace our responsibility to people and the planet," explains Mark Wetterau. "Fundamentally, this is who we strive to be as a company."

"Sustainability means different things to different people," adds Wayne Morgan, who currently heads up GSF's global sustainability efforts. "At Golden State Foods, we want to be leaders in our communities and do the right thing for the people around us and for our customers and help fulfill the needs they have. We want to be leaders in making the products in the best way, the most responsible way we can by reducing waste, and water and energy use." Wayne explains that at each one of GSF's facilities, associates carefully measure different traits and characteristics that help them be as sustainable as possible. This includes monitoring various metrics to aid the company in making informed decisions on how they can continually improve their processes and provide the most sustainable products to their customers.

Beyond GSF, Wayne recently served as president of the U.S. Roundtable for Sustainable Beef, a group Golden State Foods has supported since its inception and helped launch in 2015. "We have been not just participants but leaders in this group to help develop indicators and metrics that will guide the beef industry forward in the efforts of sustainability and continuous improvement."

Millennial Meaning and Gen Z Zen

Research and observations of Millennials and Gen Zers have been indicating for some time now that they are looking for jobs that have meaning. "Millennials are saying, 'Hey, I don't have to go work for a non-profit or NGO [to find meaning in my work],'" explains Gochnauer. "'Maybe I can find companies like Golden State Foods and others who actually live this way, and where I might find a way in which I can personally live out my purpose at work, or I can make a difference and feel good about what I'm doing, not just because I'm earning a paycheck or hanging out with the people there, and not just because it's a friendly, positive culture.' But rather, 'I think they're doing good stuff. I think I'm making an impact. I think the company's making an impact on the world.' So we're seeing [the culture of companies like GSF] resonate more and more with the younger workforce as higher percentages [of them] seek careers [where they can make a difference]. They're always so excited to find they can have their cake and eat it too at places like GSF — 'I can work for a corporation and also make a difference in the world.'"

This is evident at Golden State Foods, where former Groenz Managing Director Taylor Harbison, a Millennial who served in various manufacturing roles around the GSF world, explains how *The Creed* helps attract and maintain quality associates who are more purpose-driven, who want to be a part of something more than just a job. He says that it also helps them assimilate into the company more quickly and to feel a stronger sense of community. "When you have the right person and they're aligned with what *The Creed* says and with the Values of the company, it aligns them with the business a lot faster."

Harbison recalls feeling "isolated" earlier in his career at other companies that lacked a sense of team play and deep connection. He says *The Creed* helps create a sense of family at GSF in a uniquely powerful way. "It does that for everybody new at Groenz or anybody who's brought into any of the Wetterau family of companies. Those new recruits are very caring, and they're mission-driven. They're not just thinking, 'Okay, you've hired me to improve the ketchup department at this production facility, so that's what I'm going to do.' Everyone I've seen come in who's embraced *The Creed* has been about something more than just the job they were hired to do. And I think that's extremely unique. … People get attached to what *The Creed* is delivering. They'll say, 'Hey, we're here to do something more than just make sauce!' And I think that's pretty powerful."

A creed-based work environment can be particularly important for Gen Zers, many of whom had to jump into their careers during the COVID pandemic. Cigna International Health's 2023 survey of almost 12,000 workers worldwide reported that 91 percent of 18- to 24-year-olds say they are stressed in the workplace. London-based Eliza Filby, a generational researcher who advises companies on managing and recruiting people in their 20s, says young workers are struggling with interpersonal relationships. "There are still a lot of question marks around … having to go into an office, socialize, and be managed. [This] feels very alien to a lot of young people," due to the isolation and social distancing that was being practiced during the pandemic. All this has caused Gen Z to be the most disengaged group at work according to 2022 Gallup research, leading to ambivalence and withdrawal in their professional lives.

Organizations that provide a deeper purpose for employees, such as a creed-based environment allows, are better equipped to help young associates deal with the fallout of the pandemic and the issues facing them today in

CHAPTER 13: THE NEED FOR A CREED

the workplace. Stephen Covey notes that companies that trust Millennials and Gen Zers in their roles have a significantly better chance of not only attracting them to their companies but retaining them over time. He cites a multi-generational study from the Great Place to Work Institute that shows high-trust organizations have 22 times greater probability of keeping specifically Millennials in their workforce than low-trust cultures. "[Younger workers] want to be part of something meaningful like *The Creed*, but they also want to be trusted. And when they're trusted, they'll stay. When they're not, they'll leave. People are asking all the time, 'How do we keep our Millennials and Gen Zers? They seem to just want to move on.' My answer is, 'Go trust! Have purpose and meaning.' And when there's a high-trust culture, there's a 22 times improvement when it comes to retaining younger associates."

GSF and *The Creed*: Next Gen Perspectives

"*The Creed* has been instilled in me since I was born," explains 38-year-old Stephen Wetterau, 14-year associate and son of GSF's third chairman, Mark Wetterau. He recalls seeing *The Creed* on his father's and grandfather's business cards and hearing conversations that included the principles held within *The Creed*. But it wasn't until later in his teenage years that he grew to appreciate the difference a creed could make in business.

Photos (left to right):
Stephen Wetterau, GSF Corporate Senior Vice President of Strategy, Innovation and Technology
Taylor Harbison, former Managing Director of Groenz

During high school, Stephen worked a summer crew job at a local McDonald's, cooking fries, taking orders, and mopping floors. He saw first-hand the solid relationship between Golden State Foods and one of its key customers, as GSF would produce the food and deliver it to the stores, then Stephen would serve it in the restaurant. He would later have jobs in both food manufacturing and distribution at GSF, working his way up in a variety of leadership roles, most recently serving as a vice president of logistics at Quality Custom Distribution, a GSF company. "I saw how those relationships were built," explains Stephen, looking back on his decade of company tenure in all aspects of the supplier/customer partnership. "And I saw how *The Creed* flows through all of our associates in manufacturing and distribution and then really impacts the consumer. And it certainly impacted my life, because the long-term growth at GSF is really attributed to what *The Creed* is — *The Creed* and Values, but specifically *The Creed*. It gives us a unique edge."

Currently serving as corporate senior vice president of strategy, innovation and technology for Golden State Foods, Stephen explains that this uncommon advantage is manifested in more productive employees; a smoother operating organization; occasional preferential treatment from vendors because of their trusted relationships; and more efficient business growth. On several occasions, GSF has been the beneficiary of customer loyalty when they've faced facility right-sizing due to customer optimization. Instead of laying off associates due to shifting business for instance, other customers have come in to fill the gaps. "If we didn't have *The Creed* and Values," explains Stephen of those tenuous times, "who knows where we would be today?"

"The more time I've spent within GSF the better I've understood going 'all in' on *The Creed*," says Taylor Harbison, former GSF associate, who worked for 10 years at the company. Harbison, at age 31, served in various aspects of liquid products manufacturing throughout the world, and recently led one of GSF's subsidiaries, the New Zealand-based food manufacturer Groenz, as its managing director. "The more time you spend here, the more committed to *The Creed* you become," he said before leaving to serve in another family company.

A nephew of Mark Wetterau, Taylor recalls as a teenage boy, Mark talking about *The Creed* and showing him a framed version hanging on the wall in his home. "He took me over to it and walked me through it and kind of explained

CHAPTER 13: THE NEED FOR A CREED

it and what it meant and how he was using it at GSF," he recounts. "That was the first time I remember someone actually reading *The Creed* to me." But he first saw it in action years earlier, through his grandfather Ted (better known as "Papa" to the grandkids). Taylor recalls Ted's dedicated charity efforts for organizations like "Old Newsboys Day," which raised funds for underprivileged youth in the St. Louis area by personally selling newspapers. "He was always on the same corner where we would drive by on our way to school, so my mom would stop and buy the newspaper from him. Here you have this guy in his 60s, standing out there still selling newspapers! So that was a highlight. But once I started to understand *The Creed* a little bit more, I began to think back on the ways Papa would act in his day-to-day life and what his commitments were and where his priorities and focuses were, and *The Creed* is a mirror of everything he did. You can read that little statement [*The Creed*], and that's a look into his heart. And if you look at Mark and Conrad, it's very much the same [with them]. Everything they've done through their engagement in the church and in their communities and how they've run their businesses, I think has been a reflection of *The Creed*."

Continuing the Leadership Legacy

Today, both Stephen and Taylor feel the responsibility to continue the Wetterau leadership legacy by perpetuating and exemplifying *The Creed* in action at Golden State Foods and its family of companies and even beyond. "I think it's a different level of responsibility you carry with you," says Taylor. "But it's extremely important. Once you remove it, you become just another multi-billion-dollar private company. When you've got a creed like we have that was originally generated from a family, everybody working within the company can feel like they're part of that family, and you get a different level of commitment from them. *The Creed* is something unique to GSF. I think if you remove it, you remove the heart of this business and the core of its real success."

Taylor is particularly optimistic about *The Creed* enduring, despite evolving worldviews and business trends. "The world changes, but I think there will still be tons of people who will align with *The Creed*. And as long as the business operates to those standards, you're going to attract those people. And those people will bring on [like-minded] people. So *The Creed* has to continue if GSF wants to stay as a unique employer and contributor to its communities and associates and customers. There will always be people who will seek those values, and if you stick with *The Creed* and treat everybody with respect as it encourages, then I don't see how it could go away."

"*The Creed* will always be a part of Golden State Foods and any business the Wetterau organization touches," adds Stephen. "It's always important to honor the past, but in looking to the future understanding that the core of *The Creed* will not change [is the key to its longevity]. You can always change the words and whatnot (though I don't even see that happening), but the core values of *The Creed* are what attracts individuals looking for the culture we have here at GSF. And there will always be people who want a purpose-driven organization that's rooted in deep values, where they can call home for their career. It's like a magnet. That's why so many people have joined this company and don't leave because they truly believe in it, and that they can impact what we're doing as an organization."

Gentle Governance

In addition to allowing for a greater sense of purpose, attracting cream-of-the-crop employees, and creating an atmosphere of trust that leads to increased productivity, a creed can also help a company's leadership maintain a sense of governance and control, but in a gentler way.

"Often the need to create a creed comes from a leader who is trying to put his or her arms around a huge piece of business they've created," explained Dick Federer, in a 2009 interview regarding the pressures that many business heads face to maintain order, consistency, and effectiveness throughout their company.

"Such leaders may be thinking, 'We have dozens of divisions, they're all over the U.S. or the world, and we can't control them, we can't hire enough controllers to control them; we [could really use] a built-in creed so that our employees will internalize it and govern themselves," Federer continued.

"Psychologically, the CEO of the firm feels a lot better when a creed or purpose statement is in place. [The leadership team] now has reigns to pull back

CHAPTER 13: THE NEED FOR A CREED

on, should they have to. They feel that employees are closer to them than they were without a creed. Churches, schools, and those kinds of organizations love creeds too, because they're a form of control that doesn't look like control," said Federer. "You don't need to come down hard on everyone with 'Thou shalt not steal,' for example. A creed allows you to say those words in a softer way: 'We believe in the dignity of all people,' for instance, is saying the same thing but in a gentler manner. Human dignity means that you don't dishonor your fellow man by stealing his goods [or perpetrating other harmful acts upon him]."

Enduring Values

A creed is also something that can live in perpetuity, beyond any one leader or era. "A creed has a wonderful way of blending the past, present, and future, particularly if it's an older company," said Tom Haggai, Wetterau family friend and IGA board member, who described *The Creed* as "a monitor" and "a stabilizing force" for employees. "I love the quote that says, 'You can't live in the past, but the past lives in you.'" He went on to explain that this is what a creed allows because it keeps the original dream, vision, and values from past leaders very relevant and fresh within the current organization. A creed may be the one thing that rides out every twist and turn along a company's history, especially one that has been in business a long time. Because in the case of the Wetterau companies' creeds, "it starts off acknowledging an eternal God," he continued. "So don't be afraid to state your values, state what you believe in a creed, [even if it includes God]. You'll find the vast majority of employees will perk up and have a different respect and appreciation for you because of it."

Anchor during Storms

Certainly, as previously illustrated, a creed can serve as an anchor during challenging times. Whether it's an economic downturn, a global pandemic, natural disaster, company transitions, intense competition, or even growth, a creed can help pull an organization's constituents together in a way that permeates the company more deeply than a mission or vision statement. As demonstrated in Chapter 3, with the attempted takeover of Wetterau Inc. and its subsequent merger gone bad, the Wetterau Creed kept the dreams of the Wetterau family and the company's associates alive until things could stabilize. In addition, the impact of the 2008 recession on Quality Beverage, Golden State Foods, and the other Wetterau companies, along with the exponential growth of these organizations that followed was tempered by *The Creed*. More recently, during the 2020-2022 COVID-19 pandemic, *The Creed* enabled all the Wetterau companies to continue to thrive — albeit with a few adjustments — and propel them forward post-pandemic. So whether it's helping organizations prioritize well or turn their attention to what matters most, a creed helps companies stay focused on people — what truly makes them run — so "the success of all can be achieved."

Healthy, Winning Cultures

Finally, a creed can substantially contribute to building or strengthening an organization's overall culture by establishing a clear, solid values-based foundation upon which all other aspects of the company are built. In fact, Mark Wetterau claims that it can "supercharge" your culture. Research shows that organizations with strong cultures are more likely to enjoy sustained success over time, including happy employees, loyal customers, and satisfied stakeholders overall.

"Nearly everything about your organization — including your strategy, products, and systems — can be replicated except one thing: the effectiveness of your people," says Robert Whitman, chairman of FranklinCovey. "Culture is the ultimate competitive advantage."

Photo:

GSF associates at the City of Industry, California Manufacturing plant share company and customer pride!

CHAPTER 14

Top 20 Tips for Implementing a Company Creed

"Keep looking for what your noble cause is, what your reason for existence is, what your highest order of service is. But it's hard to do that purely intellectually. [Determining that noble cause] is a matter of the heart and not of the head. So we find that we need to use more reflective, right-brained processes in order to achieve that."

–**Larry Senn** (1935–   )
Founder and Chairman, Senn Delaney (1978–present)
Partner, Heidrick Consulting (2013–present)

Tip 1: "Know thyself" first.

Before you put pen to paper, experts recommend taking a good look in the mirror, figuratively speaking, and stand there for a long, long time. It's critical to understand who you are as an entity, what you're about, and what you aspire to be, so your creed can be as unique as your organization. Here are a few probing questions that may help you uncover your distinct identity:

- Why do we exist?
- How did we come to be?
- What role do we play in society?
- Does it matter that we exist in the world? If so, why? How is the world better off because we're here?
- What are we trying to accomplish?
- What do we believe (about the world, business, service, how people should relate to one another, and so forth)?
- What do we value?
- How are we going to act?
- What are our guiding principles?
- How do we want to be perceived? Are we perceived the way we want to be perceived?
- How do we want to affect the people around us? Are we affecting those around us like we want to?
- How do we want people to experience us?

Gaining clarity on these types of questions may take time. Getting answers may require investing in some deep thought and careful conversation not only with your team but with all your stakeholders. Understanding how others perceive you is critical. This will help create clarity around who you are and your role in the world, which will help create the foundation upon which to formulate your creed.

CHAPTER 14: TOP 20 TIPS FOR IMPLEMENTING A COMPANY CREED

"It's something that you approach not necessarily from a business perspective, but from how you would like your life to function, and how you would incorporate that life into your business," suggests Sharon Davis, GSF board member, author, and former First Lady of California. "It's almost as if the business is a person [and you need to decide] what you would want that person to be. A creed outlines all the characteristics you'd want it to have. It's very unique, and I think companies could benefit just by going through the exercise, even if they never published it, because it would make them look at the way they do business and how they approach their enterprise."

Tip 2: Listen to your heart — and head.

As you work through your organization's purpose, listen to your heart at least as much as your head. Some of the best inspiration comes that way. Ask yourself some of the questions listed in Tip 1, either individually or as a group, and then just listen quietly to the ideas that come to mind. Then, share them with others and note those that really inspire you.

"Keep looking for what your noble cause is, what your reason for existence is, what your highest order of service is," advises Larry Senn, founder and chairman of Senn Delaney, a leading culture-shaping firm. "But it's hard to do that purely intellectually. [Determining that noble cause] is a matter of the heart and not of the head. So we find that we need to use more reflective, right-brained processes in order to achieve that."

Tip 3: Build a solid foundation.

Once you know who you are, it's important that strong company fundamentals are in place before instituting a creed. For instance, you should have a clear vision of where you want to go; a solid mission statement that each employee understands and knows his or her role within that mission; a good strategy in place to achieve that mission; and certainly, the right structure to support that strategy. You'll want to have a team that can align with your basic objectives and direction, and then a creed can enhance direction even more.

"If your fundamentals are rocky, you'll spend too much time adjusting," explains Mark Wetterau. "A creed is not about saving a company. It can help stabilize an organization through added clarity and understanding of what its boundaries are and help develop trust. It's about taking it to the next level, enhancing it into a 'Plus-1' organization. But the fundamentals must be in place first."

Tip 4: Don't implement a creed until you're ready to embody it.

If not, you could pay a price.

"If you're not prepared to live a creed in everything you do then you shouldn't have one," says Nabil El-Hage, GSF board member and founder and chairman of the AAE (Academy of Executive Education) International. "You shouldn't do it lightly. You shouldn't just hire a public relations firm and say, 'Come up with something that resonates.' Because really, if you don't believe it, if you're not prepared to live it through everything you do, you shouldn't have a creed. It really has to be something that connects with your culture and represents who you are, what you stand for, how you want to be perceived, how you want people to experience you.

"One of the most difficult things to understand in business is how people experience you," El-Hage continues. "And what makes you a great leader is when you make people feel good about themselves, even when you're giving them negative feedback. And if you're not able to do that, and you're not prepared to do that, you shouldn't pretend. A creed that is pretend is harmful, it's dangerous. So you have to be ready for it. [Truly believing and living a creed] is a sign of maturity, it's a sign of strength. Frankly, it's a sign of courage because once it's there a creed shouldn't change very often. It's not to say that everything is going to last a lifetime — I'm not saying you can't amend a creed — but it really should be something very lasting, very powerful. In short, a creed is really for anybody who's ready for it."

Tip 5: God is in the details.

Well, even though you're not God, you might possibly be the head of your organization. So when you think you're ready for a creed, be sure to get involved in the details of creating it. Resist delegating it to such a degree that you're not intimately acquainted with it and comfortable with every word. Be honest upfront. If there's something in it that bothers you or makes you feel uncomfortable, keep working through it until you're satisfied with it. Because you're the top dog who will have to articulate it, explain it, defend it, bring meaning to it, and add color to it with specifics. You're the person who must do all this in front of your executive teams, your internal associates, customers, suppliers, the media, and even the public. So make sure that not only are you deeply familiar with every line and every word, but that you can passionately express and defend each part of it.

Bob Crutsinger, former president and CEO of Wetterau Inc., notes that in the process of creating a creed, it can be helpful to know where you are in the belief cycle in terms of how strongly you can stand behind it. "Where are you in that cycle? How much do you believe in it yourself? And are you going to live that?" he asks. "Then find where you are trying to go with a creed. You have to be pretty clear in your mind about that and how you want to get to that objective. Do you want to do it in a very honest, God-fearing way? Or do you want to just go out there and knock 'em dead, without any care as to how many lifeless bodies you leave behind? It's important to know where you stand."

Tip 6: Get personal.

Make sure you can *personally* identify with the ethics that you're putting forth in your statement. You'll be allocating much of your time educating your people and associates about what your creed is, why it's important, and how it permeates your culture and makes a difference in your organization. So if you're not willing to live it yourself as the boss, it's probably not the best idea to publish it.

"It's not complicated, I don't think," says Conrad Wetterau. "Developing a creed is really simply deciding as a CEO or business owner what you stand for as a person, your personal beliefs, and philosophy. Everybody has a certain idea of how they want people to live their lives within the framework of the company that they run, so it's important to get clear with yourself about what those values are."

Tip 7: Engage your management team and make it "home grown."

Whether it's your fellow management team or folks from the ranks, don't go it alone. Alignment among your associates is critical — not just with the final version of *the creed*, but all along the development process. If they don't buy into it, don't force it. Just keep working together until you come to a consensus. A creed is a philosophy the entire organization should stand for, so make sure associates are on board.

"Get input from your people," says Marlene Gebhard, former eight-year president of Shop 'n Save. "Especially if you're a new business and don't have something pretty well-established; find several key people from leadership and the ranks and say, 'I want to stand for something. Let's sit down and talk about what we want to stand for. And let's put it together, and then let's discuss how we can incorporate it into the organization, how that becomes our foundation.' When you get input from every level, then ownership takes over. That becomes part of who they are then because they say, 'We were part of the team [that helped create *The Creed*]' and 'I was on that committee' and then their fellow associates might ask, 'What part did you do?' And you kind of spread that around, and you get more people involved. Then it doesn't become something that came down from the top. Instead, it's something that is a part of the entire organization. Make a creed 'home grown.'"

CHAPTER 14: TOP 20 TIPS FOR IMPLEMENTING A COMPANY CREED

Tip 8: Keep it simple, smarty.

When writing a creed, elegant simplicity is better than elaborate wordiness. This is not the time to show off your erudite mastery of language. Sure, you want it to be meaningful, but don't get so caught up in fancy words that *seem* impressive that you lose your reader before they can actually *be* impressed by your message. Remember, you want your employees and others to remember your creed and even share it, so don't make it too tough on them.

"It's got to be simple enough for everyone to understand," says John Marin, 33-year distribution manager at GSF Phoenix, who's now retired. He prides himself on being able to recite by memory the company's Creed and Values. "If your creed is too lengthy or complicated, no one will be able to (or want to) recall it, let alone live by it. Keep it simple so they can really remember it and internalize it."

Tip 9: Don't set rules or regulations. (Don't do "do's and don'ts.")

Rather than instituting a checklist of do's and don'ts within a creed (which could never be long enough for every situation), encourage broader, universal principles, and let your associates govern themselves.

"If you just have a statement of do's or don'ts, you will educate your people to go up to that line and stop," explained Dick Federer, Ted Wetteraus' childhood friend who worked with him on creative pursuits at Wetterau Inc. "[This should not be the case] with a company creed or code of ethics. A code of ethics is giving you much broader powers, and you can float across that line or float back, depending on the agencies of the situations. That's the key. Your area of expertise exceeds the do's and don'ts because all of life cannot be reduced to those. All professions — whether it's medicine, law, or accounting — have an unspoken code of conduct, the violation of which will ruin you in your profession (despite the fact that you won't necessarily be subject to criminal prosecution by the law). So a creed is an internal, unspoken code of conduct — something you can believe in and internalize — and it becomes a part of you to the point that if you violate your creed, you will turn yourself in. The boys at Westpoint, they all have creeds. And if they do something wrong, like try to sneak a girl in the dorms or something, they turn themselves in. And if they don't, that's a separate 'sin' for them right there. That's the way a creed should be internalized."

Federer continues: "You don't want to turn your organization into a Gestapo, where everybody is looking at everybody else across the line, 'so I can report you.' So you need to use good judgment. And that was the reason why managers [at Wetterau Inc.] were given special training to educate them not to be nitpickers, because that's not what a creed is supposed to ignite in an organization."

Conrad adds to Federer's observations about a creed not becoming a police action: "It goes beyond what an employee handbook is, which is all the rules and regulations. Frankly, I think if you put a good enough creed together, you can throw out the handbook because a creed really will encompass what the employee handbook is saying."

"It's like *The Creed* is sitting on the shoulders of all of our associates throughout the world," explains Mark. "Because we, as a leadership team, can't be everywhere at all times. But *The Creed* can. It can be a part of each one of our associates 24/7 to guide and direct them. If they have a conflict about what to do, they can read *The Creed*, read the Values, which nearly always provide some added guidance to their situation."

Tip 10: Consult with other companies.

You don't need to reinvent the wheel or start from scratch. While your creed should be unique to you, the process by which you arrive at it doesn't have to be. So leverage the experience and learnings of other organizations that have gone through the process and benefit from their wisdom.

"Go witness it firsthand and borrow from the many years of experience other companies have had with their own creed and values or whatever they call it," advises Steve Becker, retired GSF senior HR leader, who helped incorporate the GSF Creed into the company. "You don't need to build something like this from scratch. Look at a few other organizations and determine whether or not there's power in such a thing as a creed and values statement. So many of us at Golden State Foods believe in the power of *The Creed* and Values, how important they can be to guide our behavior and to stand for something. And there are other companies that have derivatives of that, something different, something similar. So no one should try to reinvent the wheel. Just look at perhaps two to three other businesses that have something like what we have, and decide what's right for you, because it is something you have to truly and deeply believe in and that will align [well] with your vision and mission statements."

Following are some specific suggestions for consulting with others on a creed:

- Invite an outside advisor, consultant, or even a clergy member to partner with you on the development of your creed.

- Visit companies that already have a creed, values statement, or purpose statement. See how it's being played out. Ask them how they came up with their creed or values statement and what role it's playing in their cultural fabric and in their success. Ask for examples of how that's happening and then help draw the line between operating with a creed and being able to say to the stakeholders that it's going to pay off for them, too.

- Check out organizations like Center for Higher Ambition Leadership or Senn Delaney (part of Heidrick Consulting) that help with high-level leadership advisement and activities. Such consulting firms help companies develop high-performance cultures and become more purposeful. This will allow you to learn what other businesses are doing in these areas.

- Look into universities like Harvard, Stanford, University of Michigan, Northwestern University, and University of Southern California that may have programs or a research focus in these areas. As indicated earlier, purpose-driven organizations and company cultures are becoming a growing area of scholarship in both business schools and positive psychology departments, and there may be opportunities for business-educational partnerships in this area.

Tip 11: Everyone should have skin in the game.

Just like a company brand identity, a creed is not something that lives solely at the top. Associates throughout the organization are those who bring it to life. So employees should not only be aware of your creed (and hopefully you're hiring good people who resonate and align with it), but they should be an active part of holding each other accountable to continually nurture the integrity of a creed and ensure its legacy beyond themselves.

"We have an obligation to hold each other accountable," explains Bill Sanderson, former corporate executive vice president and chief administrative officer at Golden State Foods. "We all have a hand in maintaining the integrity of *The Creed* and Values. In many cases, they're what brought associates here in the first place and what's keeping us special, setting us apart from other organizations."

"We also have a responsibility, if we truly believe in *The Creed* and Values, to ensure its legacy," says Steve Becker, who spent 17 years leading GSF Human Resources before retiring. "That would mean in my case for instance, I have to absolutely make sure the new head of HR gets it, and he understands it, and we (as leaders or managers in the company) are also the 'keepers of *The Creed* and Values,' and our teams don't just talk about it, but they really live it. We all need to pass on that message to maintain the legacy of *The Creed* and Values so as people leave the company like me, that degree of awareness, and sensitivity, and level of importance that our roles play, don't just get lost. We need to make sure *The Creed* and Values get

CHAPTER 14: TOP 20 TIPS FOR IMPLEMENTING A COMPANY CREED

passed along to the next 'generation' and don't just fade into non-existence when dynamic executives retire or pass away. It's more significant than that. It should continue with the company itself."

Tip 12: Communicate your creed and display it with pride.

Start communicating before you roll it out. Talk about the principles of your creed with your people and let them know something special is in the works that will enhance the company. Remind them that many associates at all levels have been engaged in its development and how it will benefit all involved (see Tip 7). Share how a creed has helped other companies in the past and how it will help enrich your organization in a very unique way.

When rolling out a creed, it's important to communicate it both verbally and in writing, however your associates best receive information. If it's something new to the company, it's important for employees to learn about it directly from the top leader — in person, if possible, even if that means multiple meetings at various locations. Since your creed underpins everything in your organization, it's critical to explain its value, why it's important, and emphasize the meaning and responsibility it carries to every associate. Each should understand it and see it on a regular basis, so a creed doesn't just get written down and then put away.

Posting it prominently in company facilities or on websites can underscore its importance and help keep it top of mind, as internal and external associates see it on a regular basis. Executives and management can lead out initially and reiterate its priority with regular, ongoing communication in pre-shift or staff meetings, executive speeches, town halls, or one-on-one discussions. Talking about a creed often and sharing testimonials among all associates empowers others throughout the ranks to do likewise.

"It starts out by putting that philosophy and those beliefs into writing," says Conrad. "Then publicize and implement it by making it a part of your regular communication with the company, whether it's written or verbal. Then over time, if you set the example and live it along with your management team, then the writing on the wall becomes less important and the philosophy becomes inbred in the company going forward."

"Many people are moral, but they don't know it, so a creed sort of helps them realize it," explained Dick Federer, who noted that when people see it displayed and talked about frequently, they begin to take notice of the various ways they resonate with the values proclaimed in a creed. "A creed says, 'Hey, here's what we are,' and associates will begin to think, 'Oh yeah, I do that, too. I'm working for a company that believes this, and I can live with that.' Of course, nobody is putting their hand on the Bible and swearing [to uphold its principles], it isn't that kind of commitment, but associates will begin to internalize a creed the more they see the company and its leadership aligning to it."

Tip 13: It's a dynamic process — keep the power going.

Remember, rolling out a creed is not "one and done." Introducing it initially is one thing, but keeping it alive is another — especially as associates turn over, whether it's new hires, retirements, attrition, etc.

"If you make a commitment to a creed, once you begin the process, it's a never-ending endeavor," explains Mark. "You've got to constantly not only keep it front and center and talk about it, but you've got to live it and demonstrate it throughout the whole organization. It needs to flow not only from the CEO, but to all the leadership all the way down to mid-management to the supervisors to the folks on the floor. They need to be a part of living it, so they can feel like it's their own. And it's really that ownership piece they've got to take in."

Commenting on the tendency to minimize the prominence of the written creed around the company as time goes on, Mark underscores the

CHAPTER 14: TOP 20 TIPS FOR IMPLEMENTING A COMPANY CREED

importance of keeping it front and center: "If you think your associates have internalized your creed to such an extent that you can take the words off the wall, off the business cards, or other places, the company may continue to move forward effectively for maybe a year or so, but with turnover within the organization, it's important to constantly work at it and remind each other what a creed is and what it stands for and the strength that it brings the organization. So if those words aren't front and center before you, a creed becomes secondary, and it can lose its power. A creed needs to stay primary. It's critical, like a marriage that you work at hard every day. And if you don't keep it top of mind, the fruits and the rewards of what it can bring to an organization will be lessened.

"It can also negatively impact an organization and your customers' perception of you," Mark continues, "because if you're not working at it, your customers will see it; your people will see it. And suddenly the boundaries become broader, and then you get people shooting way outside those boundaries that are there to help guide your organization. And that's where those breaches will create a significant issue and could actually take your company in the wrong direction real fast."

Tip 14: Speak a common language.

Ever feel like you're in a foreign country and you haven't even left the office? Maybe that's because we assume everyone around us knows and speaks our "beliefs" language. It's important to remember your associates may or may not be fluent in that dialect. One way to help is to establish a common language, when it comes to your creed.

"The more you make it known that 'this is our approach, our methodology, and these are the behaviors we find consistent with our [philosophy],'" explains Stephen M. R. Covey, "the more people will have a common language, a common framework, and a common process, then they can get on the same page and understand how [your ideals] apply to them. Too often, people are just disparate. They're scattered. They're approaching things separately and without an accepted language, framework, or process. So the more you can give them these tools, the more you can build a norm around it of how this creed plays out in the company. And when you get enough people doing this — a critical mass — that's when you'll change a culture."

Tip 15: Commit to it and live it!

A creed is meaningless unless you and your associates live it. Not just here and there, but on a continual, ongoing basis at all levels throughout the organization. If there's not universal buy-in to begin with and little-to-no effort toward that ideal, then a creed will do your company more harm than good. You could be viewed as hypocritical and not trustworthy, which could negatively affect your brand and even business.

"Don't put anything in writing that you don't mean," says Tom Nicholson, 28-year general manager at Quality Beverage, now retired. "If you're just going to write words down, don't even bother. Come up with what you really want to establish as your creed, get it in writing, and then live it day-to-day because the worst thing you can do is put down the words and then never live by them."

"The most dangerous thing is to have what I would call a 'hypocritical stand,' which is to put out a great creed and not believe it and not be prepared to live it," concurs GSF board member, Nabil El-Hage. "A creed is a little bit like a fiduciary duty, which does not sleep. The obligation is 24/7. Once you decide what you really stand for, you then need to ask yourself, 'Are we willing to uphold these ideals through thick and thin? Are we willing to stick by our creed, or are we going to compromise it to satisfy different criteria?' If you put out a creed that you're willing to bend the first time you hit a crisis, then it's not a creed, it's just a hypocritical statement, and you'll lose credibility because hypocrisy eventually [gets exposed] and destroys trust."

Tip 16: Leverage collective power.

Besides personally conducting yourself in line with your creed, organizations can further demonstrate collective commitment to a creed in the following ways:

- Incorporate its principles in performance reviews, leadership expectations, and the way you drive those expectations. Talk about it in meetings at all levels. Encourage your leaders and managers to keep your creed in their group and individual dialogues with their teams. Make it a part of your everyday culture, so it connects with every associate and every aspect of the company. "Give all associates, all the way to the hourly workers, an opportunity to speak and talk about your creed," adds Mark. "Let them give examples of how it's working in their lives — so it really begins to become engrained within each associate throughout the entire organization."

- Share and reward successes. Recognize associates who exemplify your creed with special awards and do it in front of others. Programs like the Wetterau Inc. and Quality Beverage "Spirit of the Creed" award or Golden State Foods' "Golden Spirit Award" not only encourage positive creed-like behavior, but they spotlight the positive benefits resulting from a creed in action and encourage all associates to be on the lookout for fellow do-gooders to nominate.

- As a natural extension of your creed, consider incorporating an employee-run foundation or charitable organization, where associates at all levels have the opportunity to lead within the organization among their fellow associates and out in the community as they serve others. As at Golden State Foods, this type of non-profit organization can break down barriers in terms of rank, and it can also be a powerful way for employees to learn, grow, and serve together as they help others in the community. This kind of service enhances their own lives and gives the important purpose and meaning to the company that organizations need to succeed in today's business world.

Tip 17: Don't seek perfection. Continually strive for excellence.

Perfection sounds so perfect, doesn't it? Well, maybe on paper, but it's not very realistic among fallible human beings over the long-term. People generally understand that human nature cannot be without error. So don't set yourself up for failure by expecting perfection from everyone all the time. Instead, continually strive for excellence towards your ideal, as Stephen M. R. Covey advises:

"Before we merged with Franklin to create FranklinCovey, we [at Covey Leadership Center] added this phrase into our mission statement: 'In carrying out this mission, we *continually strive* to practice what we teach.' And the key is 'continually strive.' Otherwise, you're setting yourself up [to an impossible standard]. When we teach these 7 Habits and these Trust Principles, we're setting ourselves up to a high standard! So if we would have just said, 'In carrying out this mission, we perfectly practice what we preach,' people could take pot shots at us and say, 'You say this? You're not doing this well!' But the key was, 'we continually strive' [to do these things]. … Because none of us fully arrive. The *striving* in this journey, however, is what makes it so valuable and worthwhile."

Tip 18: Re-examine how your people are living your company philosophy every few years.

While the fundamental philosophy of a healthy organization should endure over time, it can be a productive exercise to examine how its associates are living out its corporate philosophy, and evaluate those findings every few years. This doesn't necessarily mean your creed would change at that time, but it's a good exercise to determine how company associates feel about a creed and the role it's playing in the organization. Perhaps like strategic planning, leaders could solicit feedback from their business units and come prepared to discuss it with executives. Or the organization could send out a periodic,

CHAPTER 14: TOP 20 TIPS FOR IMPLEMENTING A COMPANY CREED

company-wide survey to all associates to solicit anonymous input, attitudes, and perspectives about your creed. The survey could include questions such as:

- How committed are you to your company creed?

- How do you see your supervisors and co-workers living (or not living) your creed?

- How could you see your creed better incorporated or encouraged within the company?

Regular surveys and focus groups can be useful tools in better assessing and understanding associate perspectives regarding company philosophy and how it's carried out over time.

"I think it would be very helpful for business leaders and leadership teams to talk to their direct reports," explains Steve Becker, using GSF as an example. "Talk to associates on the floor or in focus group meetings. We have asked such questions as: 'What do you think about *The Creed* and Values? Do you think it is still as meaningful today as it was when you joined? Why or why not?' Get input from all levels within the organization and bring that input to a strategic planning meeting, then discuss and debate it. Create a healthy dialogue to assess your creed and company values and continue to evaluate their impact. This can be very helpful to organizations."

If a creed is right, chances are it won't evolve much. The business may evolve, the strategy and even the culture may evolve, and how people live that creed may evolve over time, but if it's written thoughtfully and with careful focus to the organization, it probably won't change much.

Tip 19: Measure what you value.

It's one thing to walk the talk. It's another to measure your steps. It may seem tedious, but according to Doug Wilson, Next Solutions CEO and chairman emeritus of the CEO Leadership Alliance, an early adopter of the value of measuring values, we measure what we care about.

"If you're not measuring it, you probably don't really take it seriously," explains Doug. "If we take our weight seriously, we weigh ourselves. If we take money seriously, we look at our profit and loss statement. If we take what it means to treat people with respect seriously, or building collaborative teams, or caring about how well people think we're doing in our company, then we measure these things. We determine what questions would help us understand [these issues]. Now, does that make us feel vulnerable? Absolutely, but that's what you've got to do."

So measure your moves, and keep moving forward.

Tip 20: Sweeten your successes by sharing.

The fruit of any success is sweeter when it's shared. So share generously with other individuals, companies, organizations, and educational institutions how a creed has impacted your business and you as an individual. Becoming a part of the greater body of learning can only help enrich your organization and you as a person. Help advise other businesses that are seeking to incorporate a creed into their enterprise. Be a part of a case study. Support university research in the area of purpose-driven companies. There are many opportunities to share knowledge. You can't go wrong by giving back.

"Our responsibility as a Plus-1 or purpose-driven organization is not only that we instill solid values to create strong ethics within a company and a solid philosophy on how we treat each other," says Mark Wetterau, "but it is also keeping our folks very top of mind on what drives success within an organization. Then, hopefully as our value set evolves and grows, we also take those values out into our communities through charitable service and letting our actions speak for themselves. From there, you hope that those values are carried into stakeholders' families — that some of the good practices of what we represent and stand for [in the business world] are added to their beliefs and their philosophy in their personal life. Maybe in turn they have conversations around it that help their family be better and stronger among themselves, in the community, and within their workplaces. But it shouldn't stop there either," Mark continues. "It needs to carry on. We need to carry the messages to our fellow business leaders and perhaps charitable organizations and churches and events that include other leaders of entities and companies. It's important that we speak out and share the power of a creed and what it represents, what it stands for, and the difference it can make in the lives of the people within our organizations."

Looking Back: The Journey in Retrospect

If you're considering developing a creed for your organization, executive experts from the Wetterau companies agree that while it may take some time to create, implement, and see its fruits, it's definitely worth the effort.

"You don't really realize how powerful a creed can be until you really do it," says Conrad, reminiscing about his own philosophical journey. "As I think back about what *The Creed* has done for the businesses I've been involved with and for me, I'm even more energized about the power of a creed. So I do think it's a very inspirational thing. It's not an overnight thing. People may think you're probably a little kooky at first, but at the end of the day, if you lead by example and that creed really is who you are and how you want to live your life within that company, it will pay big dividends for the culture of your business."

"Sometimes you can only see the value and importance of a creed in retrospect," adds Mark, "once you look back and realize what it really did for you and your business. Remember that embracing it as an organization takes time. Be patient. Chances are, getting buy-in from all your associates and having them internalize it to the point that they're evangelizing a creed may take years, even decades. But as long as you put your money where your mouth is, it will start to grab hold. It's truly a 'sell' not a 'tell.' People will need to be converted."

Ultimately, Mark explains, a creed is really a snapshot of your culture: "It asks, 'Who do we want to be as human beings together as a company?' Once you can answer that, it will explain your culture better. You'll be in a position to be evaluated more easily. But be prepared to be exposed. A creed opens doors to your customers and suppliers. It gives them a tool to challenge you and hold you accountable because you're wearing your ideals on your sleeve," he continues.

"A creed won't automatically make you successful on its own. It's an assist to what you already stand for," Mark explains. "In the case of Golden State Foods and other Wetterau companies, *The Creed* has brought the right associates and customers to us and helped us establish the right guidelines for our organization. But we've had to execute effectively and consistently. A creed will *supercharge* your culture. It will assist with onboarding, help build morale, and support the discipline process, among other things, but it's a process to get to the point that it can influence all that. The journey will take time, but if traveled wisely, it will definitely be worth it. In fact, many people who have lived through it at the Wetterau companies have carried the spirit of *The Creed* — that conscience — into their own families and even created their own personal or family creed. *That*, to me, is the power of a creed."

CONCLUSION

More than 150 years after young George Wetterau ventured into the world of the food business and four generations (with multiple siblings and cousins) of Wetteraus later, it's incredible to see how the fruits of his ethically based labors have flourished today: billions of dollars of business flowing on five continents across the globe through the efforts of thousands of dedicated associates from all walks of life. Instituting a fundamental business standard of honesty, hard work, and caring for his partners, George may not have imagined the far-reaching effect of his simple ideals. Yet after generations of perpetuating these solid values — spoken or unspoken, written in some fashion or in the form of a creed — his legacy and the legacy of any ethical associate of any of the Wetterau companies lives on. And whether business is up or down, thriving or struggling, one thing's for sure: any associate or organization that consistently strives to live the Golden Rule at work or otherwise, has indeed, struck gold.

"At the end of the day, living by *The Creed* — that company conscience — allows us to go to sleep at night and feel good about what we've done," says Conrad Wetterau, of his dedication to *The Creed* personally and in leading his businesses. "The value of our creed is not necessarily on a piece of paper, but in the actions of the people within our company. It may have stemmed from a small piece of paper called the Wetterau Creed, but ultimately, it's essence can be found in the way our people live their lives within our companies, and I think it extends to their homes as well, through people like Ted Wetterau and the examples he set at the top that proliferated down and became real. Whatever my father originally wrote on that first piece of paper became an actual living thing within the organization. And I think that speaks for itself, doesn't it? *The Creed* has gone beyond words on the wall, and it's become a part of the people within the company. The spirit of *The Creed* has become who they are."

Both Mike Waitukaitis and Mark Wetterau certainly agree about the rich, far-reaching effects of *The Creed* — intended and unintended. What may have started on paper decades ago has seeped deep into the souls of many associates, customers, vendors, and even their families in so many cases. And what's remarkable is that the power of *The Creed* continues to inspire those associated with it year after year, company after company, regardless of which associates are employed.

"I believe *The Creed* has also had a substantial impact — even an unintended financial impact — on the Wetterau companies, particularly QB and GSF," adds Mike, who explains how it has truly shaped the Wetterau Associates' businesses for the better over the years. "It brought us together during the Wetterau Inc. days; enabled us to effectively establish Wetterau Associates; and then subsequently purchase a number of companies, including Quality Beverage and Golden State Foods. We know from the sellers that *The Creed* played a huge role in our ability to acquire these businesses, because we were not the highest bidder in either case. Without the power of *The Creed* and how it was represented by Ted, Mark, and Conrad, we may not have been able to acquire either of those organizations, because in both cases, the sellers had treated their people well and both wanted to leave their companies in the hands of someone who would do likewise. So *The Creed* distinguished us from the other bidders."

But that was just the beginning, according to Mike, of this timeless philosophy. He says that the best was still to come. "As associates became familiar with *The Creed* and saw Mark and Conrad walk the talk, they became a more cohesive and trusting group. Guided by *The Creed*, our associates' behavior did not go unnoticed by our customers. Some watched us for years to see if we were for real before awarding us with their business. We were, and they did. So *The Creed* got us through the door, got our associates working better together, and got our customers believing we do what we say. It truly did give us a unique competitive advantage, which is evident by the extraordinary double-digit growth of our stock over the past

CONCLUSION

two decades. Our financial success — not just for the Wetterau group but for many, many associates over the years across all our companies — is a direct result of the guidance of *The Creed* and the caretakers of it — a true multiplier effect."

"I feel so blessed and honored to have been able to work with Mike, Conrad, Ted, and the countless other associates mentioned and not mentioned throughout this book," shares Mark. "To be able to function within the framework of the ideals of *The Creed* has surely been — and will continue to be — a cherished experience for all of us. No question, the power of *The Creed* is real, and has served as a unique enabler of the Wetterau business success for decades, even generations. And I am truly grateful to my father and for those who have gone before me for passing down their wisdom, business ethics, and high morals in such a way to effectively guide us all into such a bright future."

What Mark, Mike and Conrad would like all of their associates and stakeholders to know is how deep their own beliefs are in *The Creed*, rivaled only by their faith and trust in it. "We believe in the power of *The Creed* and have seen the key role it's played in the success of our companies," they each share sincerely. "We believe in each of our associates and the power they have to make a difference in the critical role they play in our companies and in their lives, if they're willing to live these ideals. And we know if we continue to work effectively together as a team, adhering to these important principles each and every day, the next 150 years at all of our companies will be even greater than the first."

And *that's* something we can all believe in!

APPENDICES

APPENDIX A

SERVICE, AWARDS, AND RECOGNITION – TED C. WETTERAU JR.

Service

- Board chairman and chief executive officer of Wetterau Inc.
- Board chairman of the National-American Wholesale Grocers Association (NAWGA)
- Board chairman of Independent Grocers Alliance (IGA)
- Director of Food Marketing Institute (FMI), the country's largest retail association at the time of Ted's service
- Chairman of the board of the St. Louis Regional Commerce and Growth Association (RCGA)
- Director of the United Way of Greater St. Louis; chairman of the 1991 fundraising campaign, which raised $50 million
- Director of the Salvation Army; director of its "Tree of Lights" fundraising drive
- Ex-officio trustee of the Food Industry Crusade against Hunger and honorary chairman of its 1988 campaign
- Chairman of the 1989 St. Louis Civic Progress Arts and Education Council fund drive
- Director of Operation Food Search, Inc. (St. Louis)
- Chairman of Goodwill Industries' $3.5 million "Growing with Concern" capital fundraising campaign in 1986
- Chairman of the University of Missouri St. Louis Business School Advisory Board
- Board of trustees of Westminster College (Fulton, Missouri)
- Board of trustees of St. Louis University
- Board of trustees of Ranken Technical College (St. Louis)

- Board of governors of the Tom Haggai & Associates Foundation (Winston-Salem, North Carolina)
- Board member of the St. Louis Symphony Association
- Board member of the Municipal Theater Association and the Arts and Education Council of Greater St. Louis
- Director of the Mark Twain Institute (St. Louis)
- Director of the Mary Institute (St. Louis)
- Director of the Greater St. Louis Area Boy Scouts of America
- Director of Jobs for Missouri Graduates
- Chairman of Washington University (St. Louis)
- Chairman of Lindenwood University (St. Charles, Missouri)
- Chairman of Old Newsboys (St. Louis)
- Director of the St. Louis Zoo Commission
- Director of the Metropolitan Zoological Park and Museum District (St. Louis)
- Director of the National Chamber of Commerce (Washington, D.C.)
- Chairman of the Missouri Committee of Employer Support for the Guard and Reserve (MCESGR)
- Member of the President's Council of the St. Louis Conservatory and Schools for the Arts
- Director of the Automobile Club of Missouri
- Director of Barnes Jewish Hospital (St. Louis)
- Director of Enterprise Bank (Clayton, Missouri)
- Director of Boatmen's National Bank (St. Louis)
- Director of General American Life Insurance Co. (St. Louis)
- Director of Maritz, Inc. (Fenton, Missouri)
- Director of Security Equity Life Insurance Co. (St. Louis)
- Director of the St. Louis V.P. Fair Foundation
- Director of Knights of the Round Table of St. Louis

- Director of the Knights of the Cauliflower Ear of St. Louis
- Director of Godfrey Grocery Co. (Godfrey, Illinois)
- Civilian Aide to the Secretary of the Army
- Deacon and Elder of the Ladue Chapel Presbyterian Church (St. Louis)

Awards and Recognition

- American Heart Association 2007 Missourian Award (posthumous), acknowledging the most accomplished citizens of the state of Missouri
- IGA 1992 J. Frank Grimes Award for outstanding service to IGA, its highest recognition, exhibiting the passion and charisma of its founder, Frank Grimes
- Mental Health Association of Greater St. Louis 1992 Silver Bell Award for generosity to the community and exemplifying civic-minded business leadership
- St. Louis Regional Chamber and Growth Association (RCGA) 1990 "Right-Arm of St. Louis" Award for business and civic contributions in the St. Louis area
- *The Wall Street Journal* 1990 Bronze Award for CEO performance in enhancing overall enterprise value for stockholders
- National-American Wholesale Grocers Association (NAWGA) 1990 Herbert Hoover Award for significant contributions to the food industry and to society, one of the highest honors bestowed on an executive in the supermarket business at the time
- Boy Scouts of America 1990 "Silver Beaver" Award, the organization's highest honor
- Goodwill Industries 1989 "Philanthropist of the '80s" Award
- American Academy of Achievement 1974 "Golden Plate Award" for exceptional vision and accomplishment in Computerized Food Distribution
- *Progressive Grocer* 1966 "Man of the Month"
- *Argus* "Distinguished Public Service Award"
- Religious Heritage of America "Business and Professional Award"

APPENDIX B

SERVICE, AWARDS, AND RECOGNITION – CONRAD WETTERAU

Service

Board of Directors:

- Golden State Foods (Chairman)
- Argos Family Office, LLC (Founding Partner)
- Wetterau Inc.
- Wetterau Associates, LLC (Founding Partner)
- Beer Distributors of Massachusetts
- Anheuser-Busch National Advisory Panel
- Massachusetts Beer Wholesalers Association
- Dana-Farber Cancer Institute (Board of Trustees)
- Juvenile Diabetes Research Foundation (St. Louis Chapter); also former executive committee member, chapter president, and corporate committee chairman
- Juvenile Diabetes Research Foundation (New England Chapter) and chapter president
- St. Louis V.P. Fair Organization
- Taunton Development Corporation (Taunton, Massachusetts)

Other Organizations:

- Taunton Area Chamber of Commerce (Taunton, Massachusetts)
- Young Presidents Organization (YPO) (St. Louis Chapter, New England Chapter)
- World Presidents' Organization (WPO) (New England Chapter)

Awards and Recognition

- Easterseals of Massachusetts 2019 Team Hoyt Man of the Year Award
- Juvenile Diabetes Research Foundation 1992 Man of the Year (St. Louis Chapter) and 2001 (Northeast Chapter)
- Wetterau Inc. 1986 and 1988 Chairman's Challenge Awards

APPENDIX C

SERVICE, AWARDS, AND RECOGNITION – MARK WETTERAU

Service

Board of Directors:

- Golden State Foods (Chairman)
- GSF Foundation (Chairman)
- Quality Beverage (Chairman)
- Consolidated Beverage
- Shop 'n Save (Chairman)
- St. Louis V.P. Fair (Chairman)
- Second Harvest Food Bank of Orange County (Chairman)
- CEO Leadership Alliance – Orange County
- Wetterau Inc.
- Wetterau Associates, LLC (Founding Partner)
- Argos Family Office, LLC (Founding Partner)
- Easterseals of Massachusetts
- Boys and Girls Club of Boston
- Arthritis Foundation (St. Louis Chapter)
- St. Louis Council of the Boy Scouts of America

- St. Louis Children's Hospital
- St. Louis Regional Commerce and Growth Association
- Missouri College Fund
- Food Marketing Institute

Other Organizations:

- Young Presidents Origination (YPO) (Orange County Chapter)
- Deacon of the Ladue Chapel Presbyterian Church (St. Louis)

Awards and Recognitions:

- Best in Biz 2022 Silver Award – Executive of the Year
- Passkeys Foundation 2011 Ethical Edge "Leaders of Integrity" Award
- Concordia University 2010 "Faithfulness and Excellence" Award
- Wetterau Inc. 1990 Master Quest Award
- Wetterau Inc. 1989 and 1990 Chairman's Challenge Awards

APPENDIX D

WETTERAU INC. RECOGNITION AND AWARDS

- *St. Louis Globe-Democrat* 1972 "Missouri Growth Company of the Year"

- Free Enterprise Awards Association (circa 1962) "American Success Story" Award (accepted by Theodore C. Wetterau)

- Metropolitan Retail Food Dealers Association of Greater St. Louis 1962 Food Industry Award for contributions to the success and improvement of the grocer's status in the food industry in this area (accepted by Oliver G. Wetterau)

- Metropolitan Retail Food Dealers Association of Greater St. Louis 1961 Food Industry Award for contributions to the success and improvement of the grocer's status in the food industry in this area (accepted by Theodore C. Wetterau and Oliver G. Wetterau)

APPENDICES

APPENDIX E

QUALITY BEVERAGE RECOGNITION AND AWARDS

- Feast of the Blessed Sacrament 2019 Presenting Partners Award
- Boys and Girls Club of Metro South 2019 Community Partner of the Year Award
- Taunton Area Chamber of Commerce 2019 Economic Development Impact Award
- Easterseals of Massachusetts 2019 Team Hoyt Award
- Constellation Brands 2018 Gold Crown Award EBU
- Anheuser-Busch 2018 Ambassadors of Excellence Bronze Award
- Boys and Girls Club of Taunton 2011 Corporate Service to Youth Award
- Constellation Brands 2009 Top Wholesaler Achievement Award New England
- Anheuser-Busch 1996 New England Wholesaler Sales Team of the Year Award

APPENDIX F

GOLDEN STATE FOODS RECOGNITIONS AND AWARDS

Quality

- Pratt Industries 2023 Environmental Impact Award (GSF Liquid Products North America and KanPak U.S.) and 2014 and 2013 Sustainability Award (GSF Protein Products)
- Association for Dressings and Sauces 2021 Technical Achievement Award (Mariana Manole and Suzanne Mailman, GSF Liquid Products – U.S.)
- McDonald's 2021, 2020, 2019, 2018 and 2017 A Quality Award (*GSF Fresh!* China – Guangzhou)
- North American Meat Institute (NAMI) 2021, 2020, 2019 Worker Safety Recognition Award (GSF Protein Products – Opelika)

- Association for Dressings and Sauces 2020 Sauce of the Year Award for Zaxby's Caribbean Jerk Sauce (GSF Liquid Products – U.S.)

- McDonald's 2020 Encouraging Improvement Award (*GSF Fresh!* China)

- McDonald's 2020 Collaboration Award (*GSF Fresh!* China)

- Wendy's 2018 Supplier of the Year Award (City of Industry, Manufacturing)

- Whataburger 2018 Leap of Faith Award (GSF Liquid Products – U.S.)

- Popeyes 2018 and 2008 Supplier of the Year Award (GSF Liquid Products – U.S.)

- Illinois Sustainability Award from the Illinois Sustainable Technology Center (GSF McCook), 2018, 2017, 2016, 2015, 2014

- Countrywide Foodservice Distributors 2018 Shooting Star Award (Groenz Liquid Products, New Zealand)

- Wendy's 2018, 2016 Best Quality Compliance, Dressing and Sauces Overall Winner (City of Industry, Manufacturing)

- Wendy's 2017 Supplier of the Year Award (City of Industry, Manufacturing)

- Wendy's 2017 Outstanding Compliance, Dressing and Sauce Category (City of Industry, Manufacturing)

- McDonald's 2017 Supplier of the Year (GSF Liquid Products – Egypt/ Middle East)

- Jack in the Box 2015 Best New Supplier Award (GSF Liquid Products – U.S.)

- Subway 2014 and 2015 Excellence in Customer Service Award (Groenz Liquid Products, New Zealand)

- Hazard Analysis Critical Control Points (HACCP) 2014 Outstanding Multi-site Company (GSF Australia)

- Famous Dave's 2013 Supplier of the Year (Conyers)

- Whataburger 2013 Game Changer Award (GSF Liquid Products – U.S.)

- YUM! Brands 2011 Supplier of the Year Award (GSF Liquid Products – U.S.)

- McDonald's 2011 Quality Award, Formulated Products, Sandwich Sauce, Taiwan Supplier Symposium (City of Industry, Manufacturing)

- KFC 2011 STAR Supplier Quality Award (GSF Liquid Products – U.S.)

APPENDICES

- Zaxby's 2008 Supplier of the Year Award (GSF Liquid Products – U.S.)

- Zaxby's 2005 inaugural Supplier of the Year Award (GSF Liquid Products – U.S.)

- YUM! Brands (KFC) 2005 Menapakt Regional Quality Supply (GSF Liquid Products – Egypt)

- YUM! Brands 2005 Star Supplier of the Year Award (GSF Liquid Products – U.S.)

- YUM! Brands 2004 Menapakt Supplier of the Year (GSF Liquid Products – Egypt)

- YUM! Brands 2004 Star Supplier of the Year Award (GSF Liquid Products – Egypt)

- YUM! Brands 2004 Star Supplier Quality Award (GSF Liquid Products – U.S.)

- 31 Silliker Platinum/National Supplier Leadership Council Awards between 2003 and 2018 for outstanding commitment to food safety with four 100 percent perfect scores (GSF Distribution – U.S.)

- McDonald's Liquid Products Target Holder for various products more than 85 times between 2003 and 2021 (GSF Liquid Products – U.S.)

- YUM! Brands 2002 and 2001 Star Supplier of the Year Awards (GSF – Australia)

- McDonald's 2000 Beef Council Great Burger Cook-off Award (GSF Protein Products)

Service

- McDonald's "Elevating the Arches" 2023 Awards:
  - Efficient Digital Supply Chain recognition (Guilda Javaheri)
  - Food Safety and Quality recognition (Mariana Manole)
  - "As One" supplier collaboration recognition (GSF Liquid Products – U.S.)

- Starbucks FoodShare 2023 "Super Sustainer" Award (QCD Denver) and "Community Champion" Award (QCD Miami)

- National Safety Council 2022 Industry Leader Award (GSF – Opelika, Alabama)

- *Food Logistics* 2021 Top 3PL & Cold Storage Providers List (QCD)

- Tim Hortons Top 10 "Best Business Partner" 2020, 2019 (KanPak – China)

- Chick-fil-A Outstanding Service Award 2018, 2017, 2016 (all QCD)

- Chick-fil-A 2015 Outstanding Performance Award (KanPak – U.S.)

- 53 Starbucks Distribution Excellence Program Service Efficiency Scorecard (formerly Pike Place Awards) for quarterly excellence, most improved, and annual siren awards between all locations/facilities from 2015–2023

- Chick-fil-A Best-in-System Award for "On-Time Champion" 2014, 2012, 2011, 2010 (QCD – Orlando)

- Chick-fil-A 2013 Best-in-System Award for "On-time Champion" (QCD – Charlotte, North Carolina)

- McDonald's 2010 Best in Class Performance, PD/Commercialization Team (City of Industry, Manufacturing)

Innovation

- Boomi 2023 North America Customer Innovation Award – Integration Excellence (GSF Information Technology)

- Kansas Water Environment Association 2023 Class 6B Plant Award for Wastewater Treatment (KanPak U.S. Arkansas City)

- YUM! Brands 2022 STAR Innovation Award for KFC Buffalo Ranch (GSF Liquid Products – U.S.)

- Jack in the Box 2021 Supplier Innovation Award (GSF Liquid Products – U.S.)

- Association for Dressings and Sauces 2021 Packaging of the Year Award for CRYOVAC® brand FlexPrep® portion-dispensing pouches (GSF Liquid Products – U.S.)

- *Food Processing* 2021 R&D Teams of the Year Award, Large Company Category (Liquid Products North America)

- Best in Biz 2020 Gold Award – Most Innovative Company of the Year

- Greater Irvine Chamber of Commerce 2020 Celebrate Resilience Innovation Award

- *Orange County Business Journal* 2020 Innovator of the Year Award

- *Financial Times* 2019 Intelligent Business Award (Supply Chain Management) (GSF/IBM's Food Trust Initiative)

- Telly Bronze Award 2007 – Film/Video Non-Broadcast Productions – Corporate Video (GSF)

- State of Georgia 2004 Wastewater Facility of the Year Award (GSF – Conyers, Georgia)

- McDonald's 2001 Beef Innovation Award winner (GSF Protein Products)

- McDonald's 2001 Operators Purchasing Advisory Committee Partnering Award (GSF Distribution)

- McDonald's 2000 Partners in Innovation Award winner for 10-1 mold plate technology (GSF Protein Products)

Leadership

- National Safety Council 2022 Industry Leader Award (GSF Opelika)

- American Business Awards® 2022 Silver Stevie® Award, Company of the Year – Large Food & Beverage (GSF)

- McDonald's 2022 Global Diversity, Equity, and Inclusion Award (GSF)

- *Food Logistics* 2022 Rock Stars of the Supply Chain Award (Tim Bates/QCD, Mariana Manole/GSF, Guilda Javaheri/GSF)

- Kansas Governor's Award of Excellence 2021 – Manufacturing/Distribution Category (KanPak – Arkansas City, Kansas)

- *Heavy Duty Trucking* 2021 Top 30 Green Fleets (QCD)

- *Food Logistics* 2021 Rock Stars of the Supply Chain Award (Ryan Hammer QCD)

- McDonald's 2021 China Supplier Summit Outstanding Contribution Award (Michael Hu/*GSF Fresh!* – China)

- McDonald's 2019 Supplier Summit Leadership for Fresh Beef Initiative (GSF Protein Products)

- CleanTech OC and Sustainability Council of Orange County 2015 Van Vlahakis' Sustainability Excellence Award (GSF)

- *Orange County Business Journal* 2008 CFO of the Year Award (Mike Waitukaitus/GSF)

- McDonald's U.S. Supply Chain 2007 Supplier Summit Leadership Award for Liquid Products (GSF Liquid Products – U.S.)

- McDonald's U.S. Supply Chain 2007 and 2005 Supplier Summit Teamwork Award for Liquid Products (GSF Liquid Products – U.S.)

- McDonald's U.S. Supply Chain 2007 Supplier Summit Teamwork Award for Meat Products (GSF Protein Products)

- McDonald's U.S. Supply Chain 2004 "None of us are as good as all of us" Ray Kroc Teamwork Award for Liquid Products (GSF Liquid Products – U.S.)

- Association for Corporate Growth 2004 Founders Award for consistent leadership in corporate growth (GSF Corporate)

- McDonald's 2003 Beef Council Teamwork Award for Australian beef (GSF Protein Products)

- GSF listed among *Forbes* "Largest Private Companies in the United States" since the list's inception in 1985 (1985–2022)

- GSF listed among *Orange County Business Journal*'s top five "Largest Companies in Orange County" (1992–2021)

Values

- Best in Biz 2023 Gold Award – Environmental Program of the Year (QCD)

- *Orange County Business Journal* 2023 ESG Special Report

- *Orange County Business Journal* 2022 Companies that Care

- Best in Biz 2021 Gold Award – Most Socially Responsible Company of the Year

- Women World Awards 2020 "Company Response of the Year" Gold Winner

- Opelika Chamber of Commerce 2020 "Large Business of the Year" Award (GSF Opelika)

- McDonald's 2020 "Global Volunteer" Award (John Page/GSF Corporate)

- The All American Boys Chorus 2016 American Compassion Award (GSF Corporate)

- McDonald's 2010 "Best of Green and Sustainability" Award (GSF Corporate)

- National Philanthropy Day 2010 "Outstanding Large Corporation" Award (GSF Corporate)

- Ronald McDonald House Charities 2009 and 2005 "National Corporate Donor" Award (GSF Corporate)

- *Orange County Business Journal* 2009 "Best Places to Work in Orange County"

- *Orange County Business Journal* 2009–2016 "Fastest Growing Private Companies in Orange County"

END NOTES

INTRODUCTION

Peter Drucker, "Culture eats strategy for lunch* every time." Some sources cite Drucker as saying, "lunch*," but most refer to him as saying, "Culture eats strategy for breakfast." In addition, while the "breakfast/lunch" quote is largely attributed to Drucker, there are some sources that give credit to Giga Information Group, a technology consulting firm founded by Gideon I. Gartner (of the famed Gartner Group) when it was quoted as saying the "breakfast" line in the September 2000 issue of PIMA's North American *Papermaker* publication. There is also some speculation that the saying may have been in circulation before the 2000 Giga reference. By 2011, Drucker appears to be given the credit for saying this, as it began appearing in textbooks and in business publications such as *Forbes*, attributing him as the originator.

Nilofer Merchant, "Culture Trumps Strategy, Every Time," *Harvard Business Review*, (March 2011), https://hbr.org/2011/03/culture-trumps-strategy-every. "The best strategic idea means nothing in isolation. If the strategy conflicts with how a group of people already believe, behave, or make decisions it will fail. Conversely, a culturally robust team can turn a so-so strategy into a winner. The 'how' matters in how we get performance."

Eric Flamholtz, "Culture and the Bottom Line," *European Management Journal*, (2001), Volume 19, Number 3, pp. 268-275. "Your bottom line next year will largely be determined by your current strategies; your bottom line in the *following* years will be more influenced by your current culture."

Sue Dathe-Douglas and **Shawn D. Moon,** "Building a Winning Culture: A Top Priority for Leaders," https://www.franklincovey.com/wp-content/uploads/2020/10/downloads_culture-whitepapers_FC_WinCul_TopPri_WhitePaper.pdf, (2019), quoting Robert A. Whitman: "Nearly everything about your organization — including your strategy, products, and systems — can be replaced, except one thing: the effectiveness of your people. Culture is the ultimate competitive advantage."

George Bradt, "The Root Cause of Every Merger's Success or Failure: Culture," *Forbes*, (June 29, 2015). "When you merge cultures well, value is created. When you don't, value is destroyed. While some will suggest other factors — silly things like objectives and strategies and implementations — they are all derivative. The game is won or lost on the field of cultural integration. Get that wrong and nothing else matters."

Larry Senn, www.senndelaney.com, (2019). "Culture plays a role in [this] and can be systematically addressed to make that happen."

CHAPTER 1

Interstate Grocer, St. Louis, (1889). "He is ever alert to the interests of those with whom he comes in contact, and is possessed of shrewd buying qualifications and ample capital to enable him to forge rapidly forward in the commercial world."

Wetterau Incorporated: 120 Years of Progress, 1869–1989, Wetterau Inc., St. Louis, (1989). "[Wetterau Grocery Company is] one of the most modern wholesale grocery stores in the western country."

CHAPTER 2

Roy Malone, "Wetterau Believes in Keeping Its IGA Grocers Independent," *St. Louis Post-Dispatch*, (December 22, 1975). "… He was treading not only on a family name but a corporate philosophy the Wetterau folks say has been the key to four decades of uninterrupted profit increases and annual sales that have now reached $800,000,000."

Ted Schafers, "Wetterau: 'Growth Company of the Year,'" *St. Louis Globe Democrat*, (January 29-30, 1972). "Our goal is to help our supermarkets become one-stop-shopping centers in their market areas. This is part of our overall program to help our retailers become the most successful in their communities. As they succeed, so do we."

Roy Malone, "Wetterau Believes in Keeping Its IGA Grocers Independent," *St. Louis Post-Dispatch*, (December 22, 1976).

Damian Menzies, "Speak Up! How Building a Good Organisational Culture Can Help Manage Disruption," https://choiceaustralia.com.au/2020/04/fight-disruption-with-good-work-culture/, 2020. "What separates some businesses from others at times [of disruption] isn't their action plan, but their organisational culture. The way that businesses build a work environment without the presence of disruption hugely impacts how well they manage when things suddenly start going south. ... Companies who have a truly inclusive work culture [where] ... there is diversity of thought ... [and] a strong sense of belonging by all team members ... [who] feel comfortable speaking up in the 'good' times, can help you more successfully weather the difficult ones."

CHAPTER 3

"Wetterau Incorporated," *The Wall Street Transcript*, Volume CXI Number 4, (January 28, 1991). "I've got two sons in the business and in very good spots, so they will help perpetuate the company. I am very proud that they're extremely hardworking and bright, and are growing quickly and handling major business units of Wetterau."

Margie Manning, "Former Wetterau Execs Thrive in Beer, Burgers, Boats, Banking and Beyond," *St. Louis Business Journal*, (December 1, 2002).

CHAPTER 4

David Cottrell, *Monday Morning Leadership*, (Horseshoe Bay, Texas: Cornerstone Leadership Institute, 2002).

CHAPTER 6

Dun's Review, "The Millionaire Meatman," (July 1975). "A guy I met said, 'Geez, have you seen that hamburger stand in San Bernardino? Man, you got to go look at that thing.' So I blew out there and sure as hell, there were these long lines of people. I couldn't believe it. Of course, this story is practically a legend now, but you couldn't imagine then, back in 1953, what an operation the McDonald brothers had going."

Dick Gochnauer, "The majority of jobs in U.S., around two-thirds, are created by small businesses," referencing data reported by the Small Business Administration (SBA), 2011.

Ohio University, "Ethical Leadership Case Studies," onlinemasters.ohio.edu, (February 6, 2020). "Companies that exhibit ethical leadership practices generate goodwill with consumers, protect their assets, and increase value for shareholders, while unethical leaders can put the entire organization at risk for short-term or personal gains."

CHAPTER 7

A&E Television Networks, "Modern Marvels: Fast Food Tech," *History Channel,* (2007).

Golden State Foods, Awards and Recognitions through 2023. (See *Appendix F.*)

Golden State Foods, *Associate Surveys,* 2000-2021 Irvine, California.

WorldatWork, Promotional Guidelines Survey, September 2016, Scottsdale, Arizona, www.worldatwork.org

WorldatWork, Salary Budget Survey, 2017-2018, Scottsdale, Arizona, www.worldatwork.org

Qualtrics WorldNorms Database, 2016-2018, Provo, Utah, www.qualtrics.com.

CHAPTER 8

Howard Schultz, *Pour Your Heart Into It: How Starbucks Built a Company One Cup at a Time* (New York: Hyperion, 1997), p. 81. "Whatever your culture, your values, your guiding principles, you have to take steps to inculcate them in the organization early in its life so they can guide every decision, every hire, every strategic objective you set."

Forbes, "America's Largest Private Companies," Golden State Foods listed every year since the list's inception in 1985.

Jim Collins, *Good to Great,* (New York: HarperCollins, 2001).

CHAPTER 10

Golden State Foods, Awards and Recognitions through 2023. (See separate list in *Appendix F.*)

CHAPTER 12

Patricia Sowell Harris, *None of Us Is as Good as All of Us,* (Hoboken, New Jersey: John Wiley & Son, Inc., 2009), p. 18. "None of us is as good as all of us."

CHAPTER 13

Rebecca Henderson, *Reimagining Capitalism in a World on Fire,* (New York City: Hachette Book Group, 2020).

END NOTES

Andrew Mariotti, 2017 Human Capital Benchmarking Report, Society for Human Resources Management (SHRM), Alexandria, Virginia, December 2017.

WorkUSA Study, Watson Wyatt Worldwide, Arlington, Virginia, 2002.

Fortune's "100 Best Companies to Work for" Study, Great Place to Work Institute and Russell Investment Group, Oakland, California, March 15, 2005.

"Building Workplace Trust" Study, Interaction Associates, Boston, Massachusetts, 2014–2015.

Anthony S. Bryk, "Trust Improves Schools," Stanford Educational Leadership Conference, Stanford University, November 5, 2004.

Anthony S. Bryk and Barbara Schneider, *Trust in Schools: A Core Resource for Improvement*, (New York: Russell Sage Foundation Publications, 2002).

The How Report: A Global, Empirical Analysis of How Governance, Culture and Leadership Impact Performance, LRN Corporation, New York City, 2016.

Stephen M. R. Covey, *The Speed of Trust*, (New York: Simon and Schuster, 2006).

Valerie Keller, "The Business Case for Purpose," white paper for the EY Beacon Institute/*Harvard Business Review* (Harvard, Massachusetts: Harvard Business School Publishing, 2015).

Megan Carnegie, "Are Gen Z the Most Stressed Generation in the Workplace?" BBC.com (February 16, 2023) reporting on Cigna International Health's 2023 survey of almost 12,000 workers worldwide.

Eliza Filby, "Are Gen Z the Most Stressed Generation in the Workplace," Megan Carnegie, BBC.com (February 16, 2023). "There are still a lot of question marks around ... having to go into an office, socialize, and be managed. [This] feels very alien to a lot of young people,"

Megan Carnegie, "Are Gen Z the Most Stressed Generation in the Workplace?" *BBC.com* (February 16, 2023) reporting on 2022 Gallup research on Gen Z ambivalence and withdrawal in their professional lives.

Sue Dathe-Douglas and **Shawn D. Moon,** "Building a Winning Culture: A Top Priority for Leaders," https://www.franklincovey.com/wp-content/uploads/2020/10/downloads_culture-whitepapers_FC_WinCul_TopPri_WhitePaper.pdf, (2019), quoting Robert Whitman.